MEDICAL
BREAKTHROUGHS
2004

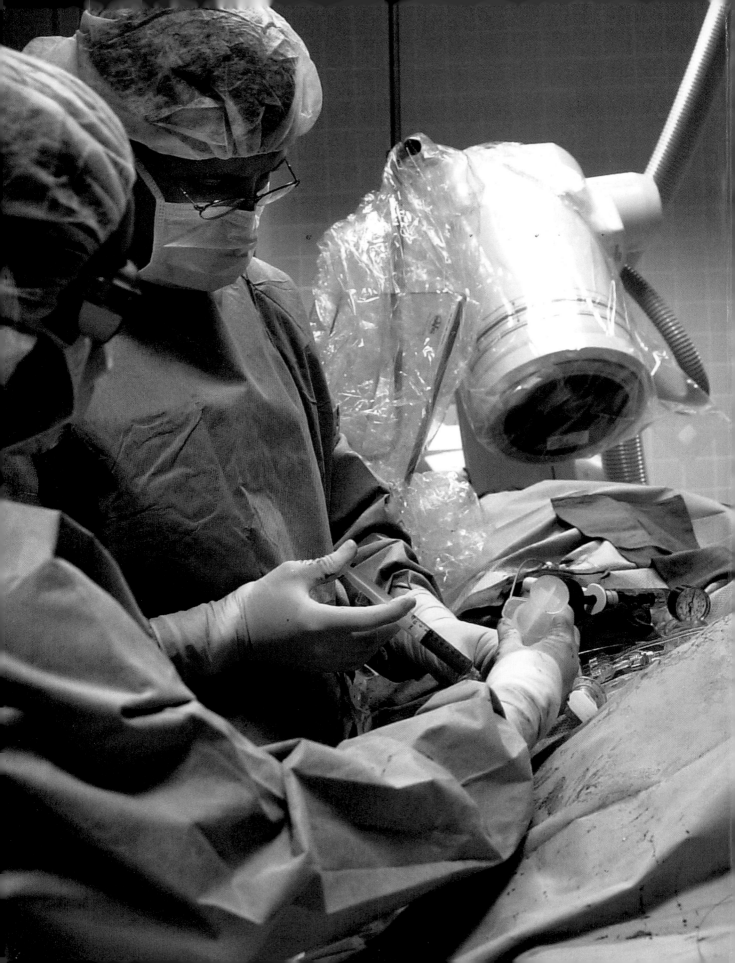

MEDICAL
BREAKTHROUGHS
2004

The Year's Most Important Health Developments

The Reader's Digest Association, Inc.

Pleasantville, New York • Montreal

MEDICAL BREAKTHROUGHS 2004

READER'S DIGEST PROJECT STAFF

Senior Editor
Marianne Wait

Senior Design Director
Elizabeth Tunnicliffe

Production
Katherine S. Frattarola

Production Technology Manager
Douglas A. Croll

Manufacturing Manager
John L. Cassidy

*Special thanks to
Chandni Jhunjhunwala and
Jennifer Samuels*

READER'S DIGEST HEALTH BOOKS

**Editor-in-Chief and
Publishing Director**
Neil Wertheimer

Managing Editor
Suzanne G. Beason

Art Director
Michele Laseau

Marketing Director
Dawn Nelson

Vice President and General Manager
Keira Krausz

READER'S DIGEST ASSOCIATION, INC.

**President, North America
Global Editor-in-Chief**
Eric W. Schrier

ISSN 1537-0674

Address any comments about *Medical Breakthroughs 2004* to:
Editor-in-Chief, Reader's Digest Health Books
Reader's Digest Road
Pleasantville, NY 10570-7000

To order additional copies of *Medical Breakthroughs 2004,*
call 1-800-846-2100

Visit us on our website at **rd.com**

NOTE TO OUR READERS
The information in this book should not be substituted for, or
used to alter, medical therapy without your doctor's advice.
For a specific health problem, consult your physician for guidance.

Any references in this book to any products or services do not
constitute or imply an endorsement or recommendation.

Printed in the United States of America

1 3 5 7 9 10 8 6 4 2

IE 0088A/IC-US

CONTRIBUTORS

Editor
Jeff Bredenberg

Writers
Alisa Bauman, Susan Freinkel, Kelly Garrett, Debra Gordon, Eric Metcalf, Rob Waters

Designers
Susan Bacchetti
Andrew Ploski

Copy Editor
Jane Sherman

Indexer
Ann Cassar

Picture Research
Carousel Research, Inc.
Laurie Platt Winfrey, Van Bucher, Mary Teresa Giancoli, Cristian Pena, Fay Torres-yap

MEDICAL ADVISORS

Charles Atkins, M.D.
Medical Director, Western Connecticut Mental Health Network; Assistant Professor, Yale University School of Medicine, New Haven, Connecticut

Jacob Bitran, M.D.
Professor of Medicine, Finch University of Health Sciences/The Chicago Medical School; Section Chief, Hematology/Oncology, Lutheran General Hospital, Park Ridge, Illinois

Lawrence C. Brody, Ph.D.
Senior Investigator, Head, Molecular Pathogenesis Section, National Human Genome Research Institute, National Institutes of Health, Bethesda, Maryland (contributions rendered as an individual, not in the name of the U.S. government)

Nicholas A. DiNubile, M.D.
Orthopaedic Consultant, Philadelphia 76ers Basketball and Pennsylvania Ballet; Clinical Assistant Professor, Department of Orthopaedic Surgery, Hospital of the University of Pennsylvania, Philadelphia

Marygrace Elson, M.D.
Associate Clinical Professor of Obstetrics and Gynecology, University of Iowa Hospital and Clinics, Iowa City

Bradley W. Fenton, M.D.
General Internist, Clinical Associate Professor, Thomas Jefferson University Hospital, Philadelphia

Donald R. Henderson, M.D.
Assistant Clinical Professor of Medicine and Gastroenterology, UCLA School of Medicine, Los Angeles

Joel A. Kahn, M.D.
President, WorldCare Global Health Plan Ltd., Boston

Barry Make, M.D.
Director, Emphysema Center, National Jewish Medical and Research Center, Denver; Professor of Medicine, University of Colorado School of Medicine, Denver

Randolph P. Martin, M.D.
Director, Emory Non-Invasive Lab, Emory University Hospital, Atlanta, Georgia; President of the American Society of Echocardiography (for 2003)

Antoni Ribas, M.D.
Assistant Professor of Medicine and Surgery, Assistant Director for Clinical Programs, UCLA Human Gene Medicine Program, Los Angeles

Jeffrey Schlom, Ph.D.
Chief, Laboratory of Tumor Immunology and Biology, Center for Cancer Research, National Cancer Institute, National Institutes of Health, Bethesda, Maryland

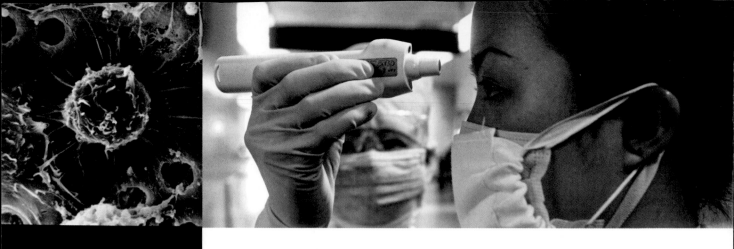

Contents

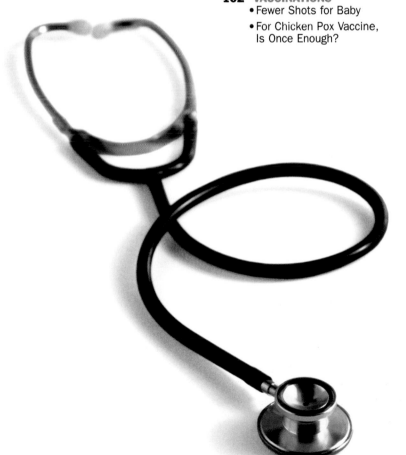

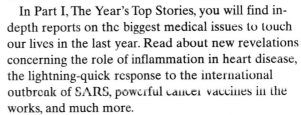

J ust a few decades ago, most people looked at their health as something of a crapshoot. If you came down with a chronic disease, those were the breaks—what could you do? People who exercised regularly, who were careful about what they ate, and who craved medical information were just plain weird. Remember the term *health nut?*

All of that has changed. The interest in medical information has mushroomed as health-conscious consumers take on more and more responsibility for managing their health. That's why we bring you this unique book. *Medical Breakthroughs 2004* is your must-read summary of the year's most important and most interesting medical advancements.

In Part I, The Year's Top Stories, you will find in-depth reports on the biggest medical issues to touch our lives in the last year. Read about new revelations concerning the role of inflammation in heart disease, the lightning-quick response to the international outbreak of SARS, powerful cancer vaccines in the works, and much more.

Part II is devoted to general health updates that affect you and your loved ones. Discover the device that appears to stop Alzheimer's disease in its tracks, the new alternative to Ritalin (it's not a stimulant), and surprising findings about high-protein diets.

Turn to Part III for news about specific medical concerns. Find out about the robotic heart surgery that's done through pencil-sized holes, the quicker and easier vasectomy (no snip—just a clip), and the teen who invented a glove that translates sign language into written words.

The science behind such innovations may be mind-boggling, but we've taken great pains to give you the details in plainspoken language. To ensure accuracy, we had every word reviewed by medical experts.

You will find this book valuable in making decisions about your own medical care or that of your loved ones. Remember, though, that many of the treatments you learn about here are experimental and not yet widely available. Yes, you may be able to participate in clinical trials that test the effectiveness of new treatments (consult the National Institutes of Health website at www.clinicaltrials.gov). But for the moment, it may be that tried-and-true, conventional treatments are the best course for you.

"It is of paramount importance that every individual advocate for their own health care needs," says one of our medical advisors, Barry Make, M.D., director of the Emphysema Center at the National Jewish Medical and Research Center in Denver, Colorado. "The only way to do this effectively is to stay informed. *Medical Breakthroughs 2004* is one of the best ways to keep informed and effectively manage your health care." ■

PART 1

THE YEAR'S
TOP STORIES

WE'VE HAD TO unlearn some fundamental lessons in the past year. The once rock-solid Food Guide Pyramid is facing a renovation, and the formerly humble RNA, once a poor cousin to DNA, promises the power to turn off troublesome genes. Health threats sprang from unexpected places, too—with inflammation identified as a major factor in heart disease, and the previously unknown SARS triggering an international scare. And medical scientists continued to astonish us with powerful cancer vaccines, new insights into the real causes of Alzheimer's disease, and an ever-expanding list of lifesaving uses for statins. On the following pages, you'll find an in-depth look at these and other top health stories.

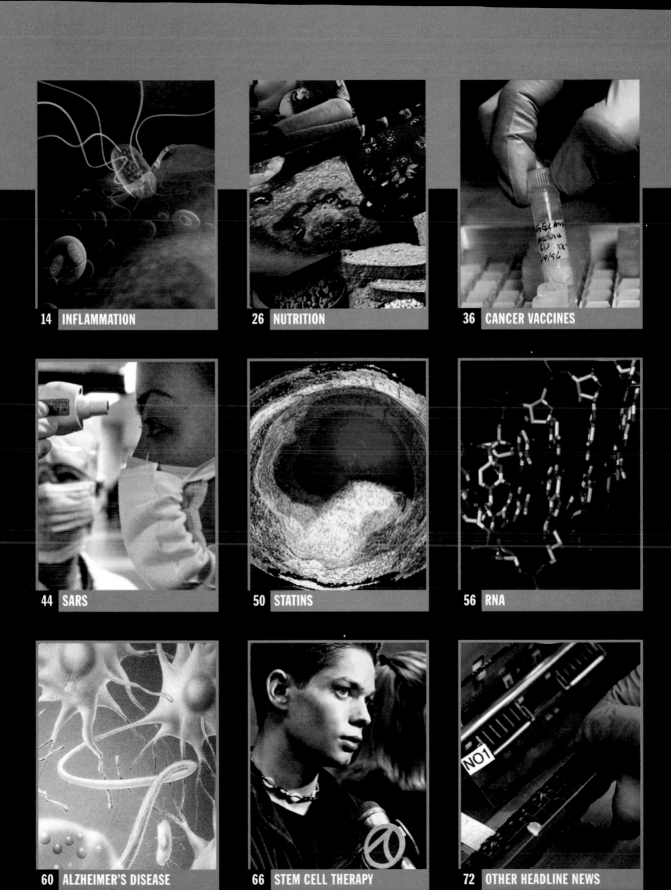

CRP SPELLS HEART ATTACK RISK

Several years ago, Paul Ridker, M.D., then a young Harvard doctor, went to a scientific meeting of cardiologists with a novel finding in hand. He'd done a study of middle-aged men that showed that the guys most at risk for heart disease weren't the ones beset by the well-known villains, high cholesterol

1 Inflammation occurs when white blood cells invade the artery wall in response to an "attack" by LDL cholesterol particles. It's these immune cells, together with the LDL, that form fatty streaks that turn into plaque.

and elevated blood pressure. Instead, the men most likely to have heart attacks were those with increased blood levels of a less familiar substance called C-reactive protein (CRP), which is released by the body in response to inflammation. No one showed up to hear his findings.

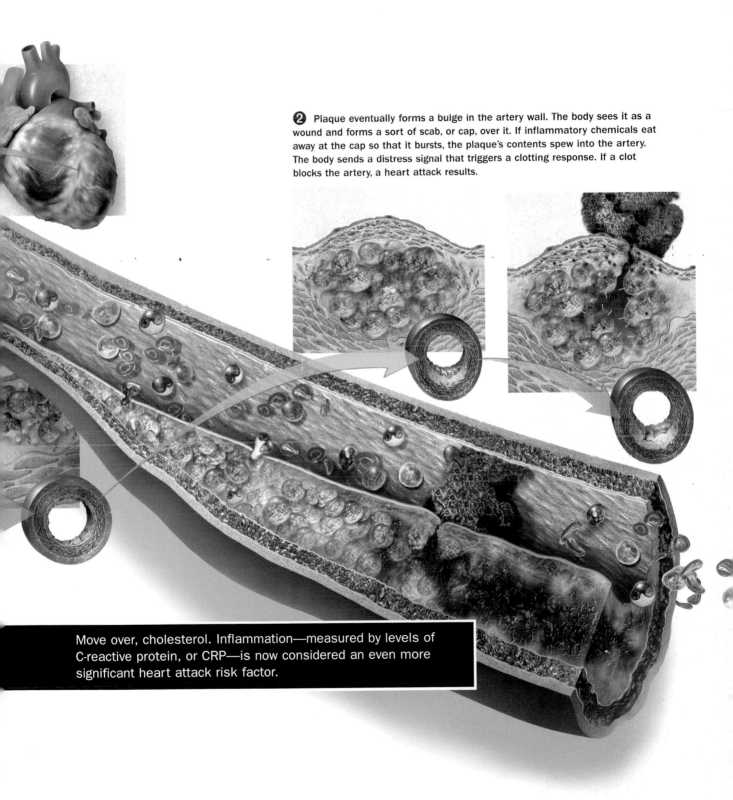

2 Plaque eventually forms a bulge in the artery wall. The body sees it as a wound and forms a sort of scab, or cap, over it. If inflammatory chemicals eat away at the cap so that it bursts, the plaque's contents spew into the artery. The body sends a distress signal that triggers a clotting response. If a clot blocks the artery, a heart attack results.

Move over, cholesterol. Inflammation—measured by levels of C-reactive protein, or CRP—is now considered an even more significant heart attack risk factor.

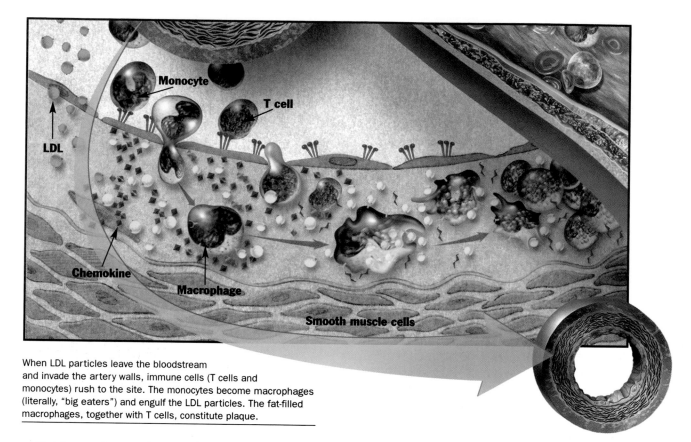

When LDL particles leave the bloodstream and invade the artery walls, immune cells (T cells and monocytes) rush to the site. The monocytes become macrophages (literally, "big eaters") and engulf the LDL particles. The fat-filled macrophages, together with T cells, constitute plaque.

Fast-forward to another meeting of heart specialists in the fall of 2002: There were no less than 100 papers discussing inflammation and heart disease, and Dr. Ridker ran himself ragged talking to colleagues and reporters who were eager for the latest news on CRP.

Just when we thought we knew the gang responsible for heart disease—cholesterol and other blood fats—comes word that they have an accomplice in hardening our arteries: our immune systems. Recent research has revealed that heart disease is as much about chronic inflammation—caused by overactive immune defenses—as it is about cholesterol. "This," says Dr. Ridker, "is a fundamental paradigm shift in how we cardiologists think about this disease."

That isn't all. Chronic, low-level inflammation has also been implicated in some other major plagues of our time, including diabetes, Alzheimer's disease, and cancer.

Our Defenders Attack Us

You know what happens when you get a splinter. The surrounding area of skin becomes puffy, red, and hot—in other words, inflamed. These are signs that your body's defenses have swung into action.

While you're working with tweezers and a needle to remove the offending object, your immune system is making its own efforts at a microscopic level. It's dispatching an army of infection-fighting white blood cells to contain the damage, destroy any bacteria that sneaked in with the sliver of wood, and start healing the wound.

This system evolved thousands of years ago, when humans scrambled for food, had few defenses against disease or injury, and lived 20 to 30 years at most. But what worked well in the Stone Age can be problematic in the twenty-first century. Today, the average American's immune system is less likely to be waging pitched battles against sudden invasions than to be engaged in continual skirmishes with chronic low-grade infections such as gum disease or herpes, and insidious insults wrought on our bodies by the habits and hazards of modern-day life— including steady diets of fatty and sugary foods, chronic lack of exercise, cigarette smoking, and unremitting stress.

The result can be chronic inflammation, a situation in which, as Harvard cardiologist Peter Libby, M.D., puts it, "our own defenses bombard us with friendly fire."

Heart Burn

The strongest evidence for the dangers of chronic inflammation shows up in studies of atherosclerosis, or hardening of the arteries. Until a few years ago, most cardiologists looked at heart disease as if it were a simple plumbing problem: Globs of cholesterol and fat stick to the inside surface of an artery, just like grease in a household pipe, until the deposit gets big enough to clog the pipe and cause a heart attack or stroke. But research by Dr. Ridker, Dr. Libby, and others has produced a more complex, more dynamic view of the process.

According to the new thinking, heart disease itself is a long, smoldering inflammation that causes plaque to accumulate not on the artery walls but within them. It's somewhat similar to that splinter in your finger: In your cardiovascular system, trouble starts when slivers of low-density lipoprotein (LDL), the bad cholesterol, dig into the wall of an artery. Once inside, the fatty particles start to oxidize—a process similar to rusting that results from an attack by damaging molecules called free radicals. The cells lining the artery wall (called endothelial cells) interpret oxidization as a sign of danger and rally the immune system troops.

To aid the defensive action, the endothelial cells puff out and grow sticky so they can snag passing white blood cells on guard duty in the bloodstream.

Reinforcements soon follow, and a class of hormones called cytokines takes charge, orchestrating the movements of the troops. On cue, some of the white blood cells transform into cells called macrophages, which gobble up the LDL. If there's too much for them to handle, the macrophages "ultimately become so packed with fatty droplets that they look foamy when viewed under a microscope," as Dr. Libby explained in a recent article. Those fat-filled "foam cells" combine with other immune cells to form the fatty streak known as plaque.

"This," says Dr. Ridker, "is a fundamental paradigm shift in how we cardiologists think about this disease."

Paul Ridker, M.D.

Once the immune system senses that it has contained the infection, it starts to heal the wounds of war. Perversely, though, that can create even more problems. Cells in the inflamed artery wall knit a tough, fibrous cap, much like a scab, over the plaque to seal it off. The plaque can remain stable for decades; indeed, some lucky folks live with it into their eighties. Often, however, a fresh bout of inflammation upsets the plaque, prompting the macrophages inside to secrete enzymes that chew away at the cap, creating what doctors refer to as vulnerable plaque. This plaque can rupture and spew sub-

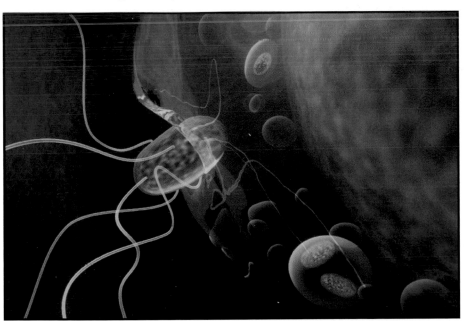

Bacterial infections are one cause of inflammation. Here, a white blood cell engulfs a bacterium. Germ-eating white blood cells also secrete inflammatory chemicals called cytokines, which direct other immune cells to the area as part of the immune response.

stances into the bloodstream that trigger blood clots. Next stop: the emergency room.

Not even Rube Goldberg could have designed a system so complex. Although the new model lends itself less easily to plumbing metaphors than the old, Dr. Libby and others think it explains many of the vexing riddles surrounding cardiovascular disease. The seemingly healthy 40-year-old who runs a 10K race one weekend and drops dead of a massive heart attack the next, for instance, or the fact that half of the approximately 1 million heart attacks that occur annually strike people with average cholesterol levels.

Cholesterol isn't the only irritant that triggers inflammation and, in turn, heart disease. Experts now believe that other well-known culprits such as smoking and high blood pressure do their dirty work in part by inflaming artery walls.

Another possible inflammation trigger is germs. Researchers have begun exploring an apparent connection between heart disease and chronic low-grade infections. For instance, studies have found that people with gum disease—15 percent of all adults under 50—are twice as likely to have heart disease as those with healthy gums. Another recent study showed that the risk of having a heart attack or dying of heart disease can double in people who've had past bouts of herpes simplex type 1 (the viral

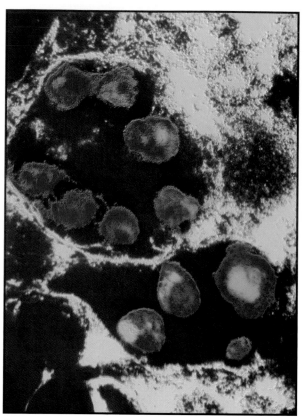

Chlamydia pneumoniae bacteria in a foam cell (yellow) of a coronary artery. Foam cells form plaque, and bacteria may increase plaque formation by triggering inflammation.

ARE STATINS
AN ANSWER?

Statin drugs were designed with one target in mind: LDL cholesterol. Until recently, experts thought that the reason medications such as atorvastatin (Lipitor), simvastatin (Zocor), and pravastatin (Pravachol) help prevent heart attacks is that they slow the liver's production of that fatty troublemaker. Recent evidence suggests, though, that statins also may work because they quell inflammation. For instance, lab studies show the drugs reduce the susceptibility of LDL to oxidation—the process that kicks off the inflammatory response—and inhibit the enzymes that cause plaque to rupture. Equally intriguing are studies showing that people who took statins to reduce their cholesterol also achieved, on average, a 15 to 25 percent drop in their CRP levels in as little as six weeks. There's a hitch, though: Not everyone gets that benefit, for reasons that are still unknown.

The big question is whether reducing CRP levels in a person with low cholesterol will buy protection against a heart attack. Paul Ridker, M.D., has just launched a study to answer that question. He's enrolling 15,000 men and women across the country who have low LDL levels but elevated CRP. Half will be put on a statin and half will get a placebo, then researchers will follow them for five years. "That will be the acid test," says Peter Libby, M.D. Until the results are in, Dr. Libby and others agree, there's no good reason to take these potent drugs simply to reduce your CRP. ■

strain that causes cold sores). One of the biggest germ threats may be *Chlamydia pneumoniae,* which causes the most common type of pneumonia. Most adults have been exposed to *C. pneumoniae* and carry antibodies to it. According to Dr. Libby, traces of the bacteria are also found in about 40 percent of atherosclerotic plaque.

Does this mean that we can prevent heart attacks by dishing out more antibiotics? Probably not. The largest studies to date have not found any such benefit from antibiotics. And since those antibiotics already in use are producing drug-resistant bacteria that are harder and harder to control, doctors are leery of over prescribing the drugs for fear of producing even more super-germs.

A Diabetes Trigger

Inflammation also appears to play a central role in type 2 diabetes. The incidence of this disease has skyrocketed in the past decade, especially among people in whom, until recently, it was rare—children, teens, and young adults. Some 17 million Americans now have diabetes, and an estimated 16 million more show signs that they're on the way to developing it.

Type 2 diabetes and the less common type 1 reflect problems with the body's use or production of insulin, the hormone that's needed to shuttle glucose from your bloodstream to your muscles and organs, which use it for fuel. When the insulin shuttle fails, blood sugar rises to dangerous levels. Type 1 diabetes is an autoimmune disease that strikes unpredictably, but there's no great mystery about the cause of type 2: It's usually a result of years of eating too much and moving too little.

Typically, type 2 develops gradually. At first, your body is merely less responsive to insulin—just as someone who's hard of hearing might miss a knock at the door. But if untreated, that unresponsiveness, known as insulin resistance, forces your pancreas to churn out more and more insulin, until its insulin-producing cells burn out and stop making enough to keep blood sugar in check. At that point, you'll probably need to take medication or insulin injections.

It's long been known that inflammation can play havoc with how the body regulates insulin production. When people get sepsis—a massive blood infection—their blood sugar levels soar. Likewise, lab studies show that when muscle, fat, or liver tissue is inflamed, it becomes less responsive to insulin.

Experts now believe that inflammation explains why the incidence of type 2 diabetes has shot up as Americans' waistlines have ballooned. Fat tissue, it turns out, releases cytokines, the hormones that help guide the immune system troops involved in inflammation. Recent research with lab animals suggests that cytokines can also muck up the intricate signaling process of insulin regulation. Elevated cytokine levels "create static on the line," explains Steven Shoelson, M.D., head of cellular and molecular physiology at the Joslin Diabetes Center in Boston. The fatter someone is, the more cytokines are produced, and the less that person's body tunes in to insulin's knock at the door. "It may be as simple as that," says Dr. Shoelson.

If obesity itself causes inflammation, so do the kinds of foods that make us pack on pounds, according to Paresh Dandona, M.D., Ph.D., professor of medicine at the State University of New York at Buffalo. In a series of studies, he measured various indicators of inflammation after feeding doses of sugar or cream or fatty foods—the essences of junk food—to volunteers with diabetes. All three, he found, triggered the production of free radicals, damaging oxygen molecules that activate cytokines and proteins involved in the inflammatory response. The resulting inflammation persisted for 3 to 4 hours. It's not hard to imagine how the immune system reacts to a diet loaded with junk food: It goes into a state of near-constant readiness, like police repeatedly rushing out in response to a broken burglar alarm.

According to the new thinking, this inflammatory process may account for the fact that people with diabetes are two to four times more likely to have a heart attack or stroke than those with normal blood sugar levels. "Almost everyone with diabetes ends up dying of a heart attack," says endocrinologist John Buse, M.D., Ph.D., director of the Diabetes Care Center at the University of North Carolina in Chapel Hill. And, he adds, a Scandinavian study published in September 2002 confirmed his gut belief that most people with heart trouble either have diabetes or harbor early signs of the disease. In that study, researchers tested the blood sugar of patients who had had heart attacks. Twenty to 30 percent already knew they had blood sugar problems, and another two-thirds tested positive for diabetes or pre-diabetes.

The Cancer-Inflammation Link

Researchers are identifying more and more cancers associated with ongoing inflammation caused by infection, irritation (by the body's own stomach acids, for instance), or a chronic inflammatory condition. The chart below represents some of these cancers.

CANCER	INFECTIOUS AGENT OR IRRITANT
B-cell non-Hodgkin's lymphoma	Epstein-Barr virus
Bladder, liver, rectal cancer	Schistosomes (parasites)
Colon cancer	Liver flukes (Opisthorchis viverrini)
Esophageal cancer	Gastric acids
Gallbladder cancer	Helicobacter pylori bacteria
Non Hodgkin's lymphoma	Human immunodeficiency virus, human herpesvirus type 8
Ovarian cancer	Gonococcus (gonorrhea), chlamydia, human papillomavirus
Stomach cancer	Helicobacter pylori bacteria

CANCER	INFLAMMATORY CONDITION
Bladder cancer	Cystitis, bladder inflammation
Colorectal cancer	Inflammatory bowel disease, chronic ulcerative colitis
Lung cancer	Bronchitis
Oral squamous cell cancer	Gingivitis

Suspicions about Alzheimer's

Could inflammation also be at work in Alzheimer's disease? That possibility emerges from a slew of studies showing that people who take nonsteroidal anti-inflammatory drugs (NSAIDs) such as aspirin and ibuprofen regularly for many years have a 30 to 40 percent lower risk of developing the dreaded dementia than people who don't use those drugs.

Now researchers are working backward to determine whether there's a biological cause for that effect. In autopsies, the brains of Alzheimer's patients inevitably show two abnormalities: beta-amyloid plaques (clumps of protein and dead brain cells) and neurofibrillary tangles (twisted skeins of the same material). On closer inspection, scientists in recent years have also detected signs of inflammation. Some experts speculate that when the brain's defense squad—made up of immune cells known as microglia—mounts an attack on the invading plaques and tangles, it also destroys healthy neurons (nerve cells). But, says John Breitner, M.D., professor and head of the division of geriatric psychiatry, psychiatry, and behavioral sciences at the University of Washington in Seattle, "it's not clear whether the inflammatory response is responsible for the loss of function in Alzheimer's disease or whether it's just adding insult to injury."

Cancer: Wounds That Never Heal

As long ago as 1863, German pathologist Rudolf Virchow hypothesized that cancer springs from sites that are chronically inflamed, but the idea fell by the wayside until recently. Now, both population studies and lab studies support the notion that some tumors are essentially wounds that failed to heal. One of the strongest examples is colon cancer. People with a history of inflammatory bowel diseases have as much as a 60 percent higher risk of developing colorectal cancer than people who haven't had the bowel problems. What's more, rheumatoid arthritis patients who regularly take NSAIDs (which counter inflammation) "almost never get colon cancer," says Dawn Willis, Ph.D., scientific advisor to the American Cancer Society.

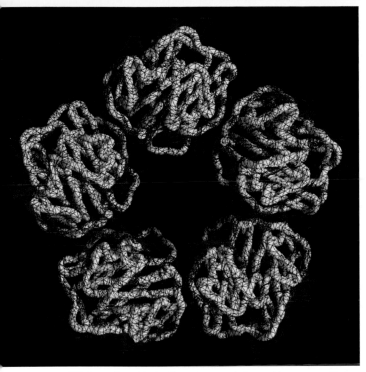

CRP is produced in the liver whenever inflammation occurs. If your arteries are under attack, your CRP level rises. People with elevated CRP levels are more likely to have a heart attack or stroke, even if their cholesterol levels are normal.

Bacterial or viral infections may also be implicated. According to one estimate, infections cause some 15 percent of cancers worldwide. The bug that causes stomach ulcers, *Helicobacter pylori,* is linked with gastric cancer, for example. Genital warts, which are caused by the human papillomavirus, are a primary cause of cervical cancer. Both hepatitis B and C raise the risk of liver cancer. As Dr. Willis puts it, "chronic inflammation sets up an environment that's very conducive to cancer."

Early Detection: The CRP Test

These theories are all well and good, but since chronic inflammation operates below your body's radar— it's there, but you don't feel it—how do you know whether you have something worrisome brewing?

Enter C-reactive protein, a molecule produced by the liver in response to inflammation. If you have an acute infection—say, pneumonia—your blood levels of CRP shoot up several hundredfold. But as Harvard's Dr. Paul Ridker and others have shown in a wealth of studies, tiny rises in CRP are also significant because they're signs of silent inflammation. (There's even growing evidence that CRP not only indicates inflammation but also contributes to it by helping to accelerate the oxidation of LDL particles.)

The study that put CRP on the medical map was a 1997 report in which Dr. Ridker and his colleagues analyzed the CRP levels of 1,086 men who were being monitored over several years for their incidence of heart problems. The researchers found that the men who had the highest CRP levels at the outset of the study were three times more likely to have heart attacks and twice as likely to have strokes as the men with the lowest levels. Dr. Ridker found an equally striking difference in a later study that tracked 28,000 women for eight years: The women with the highest CRP levels were nearly 2 1/2 times more likely than those with low levels to have heart attacks or strokes. Even if they didn't smoke or have particularly high cholesterol or a family history of heart disease, their odds of heart disease or stroke were still higher.

That study also suggested that a CRP reading may be an even better predictor of risk for cardiovascular disease than cholesterol numbers. The women most likely to have heart attacks or strokes were those with high levels of both CRP and LDL. No surprise there. But the second highest risk occurred

The Risk of High CRP

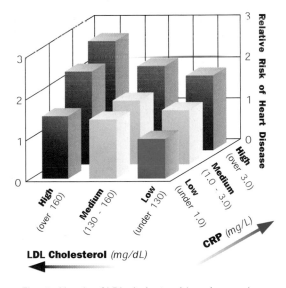

Elevated levels of LDL cholesterol (purple arrow) or CRP (green arrow) raise the risk of a heart attack. A person with high CRP but normal cholesterol is still at increased risk for a heart attack, and vice versa. High levels of both cause the greatest risk.

Source: Circulation 107: 363, 2003

in women with low LDL levels and high CRP. When it comes to identifying people at risk for heart trouble, the current cholesterol-oriented guidelines totally miss this group, says Dr. Ridker. And that's no minor omission, since some 25 to 40 million healthy, middle-aged Americans are in the same boat, he says. That doesn't mean you can forget about having your cholesterol measured, however. Dr. Ridker's point is that measuring CRP adds vital information to existing tests.

CRP may be an equally useful predictor of type 2 diabetes. For instance, Georgia researchers measured CRP levels in 5,888 healthy men and women. Checking back with the subjects three to four years later, they found that the people with elevated CRP were twice as likely to have developed diabetes as those with lower readings. It's still not clear whether the protein serves as a marker for Alzheimer's and cancer, however.

CRP isn't the only way to gauge inflammation. Other proteins and cytokines circulating in the blood can also signal that something is amiss. Still, many doctors think that CRP is the most reliable and most easily obtained marker. What has really pushed it into the limelight is that there's now a good test for CRP. It's easy (a simple blood draw)

and inexpensive ($20 to $25). You'd think that doctors would want to include it in every standard exam.

The experts are urging caution, however, trying to head off what they fear will be a stampede of demand. "It's not a test for everyone," says cardiologist Thomas Pearson, M.D., Ph.D., chair of the department of community and preventive medicine at the University of Rochester in New York. Dr. Pearson headed a panel convened by the American Heart Association and the Centers for Disease Control and Prevention to come up with a policy on CRP. In February 2003, the panel recommended that the only people who should be screened for CRP are those who already have mild cause for concern.

That group includes people who by current medical reckoning have as little as a 10 to 20 percent chance of having a heart attack in the next decade because they already have some of the classic risk factors. They're 20 pounds overweight or their blood pressure is a tad high; their LDL is a little high or their HDL (good cholesterol) is low. In those borderline cases, says Dr. Pearson, the test can help a doctor decide whether to treat a patient, and how. "If the CRP is high, I might be more aggressive. If it's normal, I might decide not to do anything," he says. Otherwise, a CRP test shouldn't be used for

TAKE THE TEST
C-REACTIVE PROTEIN

A simple blood test can tell you your CRP level. You don't need any special preparation for the highly sensitive CRP assay that's used to assess heart disease risk. (A less sensitive CRP test has long been used to evaluate inflammation in people with rheumatoid arthritis.)

A reading of 1 milligram per liter (mg/L) of blood or less is considered low risk. A level of 2 to 3 mg/L indicates intermediate risk—a sign of potential trouble. A finding of 3 mg/L or higher is a waving red flag, a warning of the sort of smoldering inflammation that doubles your risk of heart disease. If your level is 10 mg/L or higher, it could be a sign of acute infection, and you should repeat the test once the infection subsides.

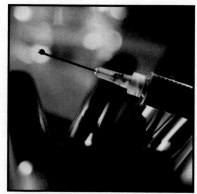

There's no significant difference between men's and women's CRP levels, although postmenopausal women should know that taking hormone replacement therapy can nudge CRP up slightly.

While your baseline CRP is fairly stable, levels can vary on any given day. A viral infection such as a cold or the flu, an infected tooth, or even a bad cut can raise levels above normal. That's why cardiologist Robert Superko, M.D., medical director of the Berkeley HeartLab in Burlingame, California, argues that people should not rely on the results of a single test. "If I'm going to use it to make a clinical decision about a patient, I do it at least two or three times," he says. ∎

widespread screening, he says, and ticks off some of the reasons:

- **Too many unknowns:** Participants in the CRP studies to date have been mostly white. No one knows yet what a healthy CRP level is in African-Americans, who tend to have higher rates of heart disease, or in other ethnic groups.
- **Too many false positives:** An infected tooth or a bout of bronchitis can drive up CRP levels, which could lead to expensive and unnecessary follow-up tests.
- **Too few solutions:** A high CRP reading isn't going to change the treatment for someone who already has heart disease. And if someone has no other risk factors besides a high CRP reading, there's nothing to treat. "If I'm not going to use the information, why collect it?" Dr. Pearson asks. What's

Exercise is one way to lower your CRP levels. One study found that men who were the fittest tended to have the lowest levels of CRP, while those who were the least fit tended to have the highest levels. Just 30 minutes of moderate exercise a day can boost your fitness level.

more, as even CRP's biggest boosters readily admit, no one knows yet whether reducing your CRP translates into lowering your odds of heart attack, stroke, or diabetes. Studies designed to answer that question are only now getting under way.

Nehama Beer, a 52-year-old piano teacher in Cupertino, California, learned first-hand about the test's limitations. In the fall of 2002, Beer's doctor suggested that she be tested when her cholesterol levels suddenly shot up into the danger zone, soaring to more than 250. The test showed her CRP was 3.7—frighteningly high (see "Taking the Test" on page 22). Beer decided to see what she could do on her own before trying medication. She rejoined her gym, changed her eating habits—no more cheese or red meat—and lost 5 pounds. By her next checkup some three months later, her cholesterol had dropped back to a healthy level of 184, but her CRP hadn't budged. She had more tests, including a heart scan, that showed her pipes were clean as a whistle. That left Beer, as well as her nurse practitioner, in a quandary. Beer didn't want to start a

cholesterol-lowering statin drug because of the risk of liver damage, and she feared that taking an NSAID (like aspirin) on a regular basis would upset her stomach.

She suspects that the high reading reflects her mild arthritis. Although not deeply worried, she hasn't stopped wondering about the source of her elevated CRP. "But I really don't know. I'm in a really odd situation. I want to know where it's coming from." In the meantime, she says, "I'm going to keep the diet and exercise. *Que sera, sera*. What else can I do?"

Healthy Living Is Still Your Best Defense

When you listen to Dr. Ridker, Dr. Libby, and other architects of the inflammation hypothesis, there's no missing the excitement in their voices. They're thrilled not only to be charting new scientific territory but also to see their discoveries pointing at new ways to curb some of the biggest killers today.

A number of drugs now on the market are being studied anew for their potential in fighting inflammation. There's some evidence that the potent cholesterol-lowering drugs known as statins can quiet inflamed arteries (see "Are Statins an Answer?" on page 18). And it appears that the drugs now used to treat type 2 diabetes and boost insulin sensitivity are effective because they have anti-inflammatory effects. Researchers are exploring possible new roles for aspirin, long known as an inflammation fighter, or aspirin-related compounds, as well as their nonsteroidal anti-inflammatory kin such as ibuprofen and the latest arrivals, the COX-2 inhibitors rofecoxib (Vioxx) and celecoxib (Celebrex). Meanwhile, drug makers are frantically searching for new compounds that may short-circuit the inflammatory response in a safer and more targeted way than the medicines now available.

In the absence of any magic pills, the best bet for keeping those inner fires damped is that old standby-healthy living. What does that mean?

Quit smoking. Smoking is associated with higher CRP levels. The smoke particles themselves irritate your lungs and arteries, not to mention the 55 other chemicals you inhale with every puff.

Lose weight. The heavier you are, the more likely you are to have elevated CRP, thanks to the inflammatory molecules produced by fat tissue. There's no question, says diabetes expert Dr. Steven Shoelson, that someone who gains 30 pounds is more likely to become insulin resistant than someone whose weight stays steady. When you shed the weight, the insulin resistance goes away.

Exercise. The fitter you are, the lower your markers for inflammation, research has shown. For example, in a study of 3,638 healthy men and women, researchers at Emory University School of Medicine in Atlanta found that those who worked out 22 or more times a month were 37 percent less

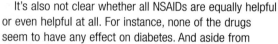

KEEP THE LID ON
NSAIDS

If heart disease, diabetes, Alzheimer's, and cancer all stem from chronic inflammation, you'd think the ideal antidote would be the over-the-counter nonsteroidal anti-inflammatory drugs (known as NSAIDs) that we all have in our medicine cabinets. Alas, it's not that simple.

Yes, studies suggest that NSAIDs may help to prevent these maladies. But such studies demonstrate only a correlation, not proof that the drugs' anti-inflammatory properties produce the results. Something else could be responsible. Studies to nail down a connection are only just beginning. The National Cancer Institute, for instance, has begun trials to see if one of the new COX-2 inhibitors, celecoxib (Celebrex), can prevent cancer of the colon, bladder, and esophagus or the precancerous lesions that lead to a type of skin cancer. A similar study is under way for Alzheimer's: Researchers will give healthy middle-aged adults either a placebo, celecoxib (Celebrex), or naproxen (Aleve), and then watch for signs of dementia in the participants.

It's also not clear whether all NSAIDs are equally helpful or even helpful at all. For instance, none of the drugs seem to have any effect on diabetes. And aside from aspirin, the older NSAIDs appear to do little to prevent heart attacks. There's also some suggestion that the newer COX-2 inhibitors can worsen matters, increasing the risk of blood clots and heart attacks.

Finally, it's no minor matter to take an NSAID every day. The older drugs such as ibuprofen can be irritating, causing stomach upset, bleeding ulcers, and liver and kidney problems in some people. One of the researchers in the Alzheimer's study, Joseph Rogers, Ph.D., president of the Sun Health Research Institute in Sun City, Arizona, put himself on a daily dose of ibuprofen—acting as a guinea pig in his own experiment. "I started having stomach problems," he says, "so I had to stop."

The best advice, experts say, is to talk to your doctor. Don't take matters into your own hands and start taking an NSAID to ward off future health threats. ■

Fish rich in omega-3 fatty acids can help lower your CRP levels, which may be one reason that people who take fish-oil supplements are less likely to die from a heart attack.

likely to have elevated CRP levels than their sedentary brethren. Exercise not only helps you drop pounds, it also helps keep blood vessels supple, makes muscles more sensitive to insulin, and helps your body use glucose more efficiently. "It's a cure-all," says Dr. Shoelson.

Eat well. No single food can cure inflammation, but some nutrients help reduce it—for instance, the omega-3 fatty acids found in walnuts, flaxseed, and cold-water fish such as salmon and sardines, and antioxidant vitamins C and E, which are abundant in dark-colored fruits and vegetables. Conversely, certain foods, such as bacon, hot dogs, and sausage, can help inflammation along. People who dine daily on processed meats have elevated CRP, says Frank Hu, M.D., Ph.D., associate professor of nutrition and epidemiology at the Harvard School of Public Health. Also, starchy, highly refined foods such as white bread, doughnuts, and mashed potatoes tend to drive up inflammatory markers (not to mention triglycerides, blood fats that increase the risk of heart disease and diabetes). A diet heavy in those foods has been linked to increased risk of insulin resistance, diabetes, and heart disease.

If your diet is in need of revision, don't make the mistake of trying an overnight overhaul. Instead, see if you can move step by step toward what Dr. Hu and his colleagues call "the healthy eating pattern"—lots of fruits and vegetables, whole grain breads and cereals, fish, poultry, and low-fat dairy products. Change one meal at a time or replace a single type of food—whatever you can handle comfortably—so it becomes not a will-testing heroic gesture but a lasting improvement. People who pack their plates with the kinds of foods Dr. Hu recommends have lower CRP levels and about a 30 percent lower risk of heart disease and diabetes than those who follow the traditional Western-style meat-and-potatoes diet.

True, changing your eating habits may be harder than popping a pill. On the other hand, it's safe and free of side effects. Why not give it a try? Your body will benefit when its defending armies get their new orders: at ease and stand down. ■

what does it mean to you?

Inflammation, marked by high CRP levels, can double your risk of a heart attack—even if you don't have high cholesterol—and contribute to type 2 diabetes. A simple blood test measures CRP, but unless you have other risk factors for heart disease, you may not need it. Currently, there are no simple ways to reduce chronic inflammation. There are, however, ways to protect yourself.

■ If your cholesterol is low but you have other risk factors for heart disease—overweight and/or high blood pressure—talk to your doctor about whether you should have a CRP test.

■ Exercise and lose any extra weight. Both can be as effective as the best medications in keeping your immune system defenders in line.

■ If you have a chronic inflammatory condition such as bowel disease or acid reflux, be sure to have the relevant cancer screening tests regularly.

■ Take good care of your teeth. Brush and floss to prevent germs from setting up shop in your gums, since gingivitis is linked to heart disease.

REBUILDING THE FOOD PYRAMID

The Food Guide Pyramid, an icon seen on everything from cereal boxes to health manuals, has had a longer shelf life than most other advice about what's good for you. Now, though, prominent nutrition experts insist that it has gone stale. They're pushing to replace the pyramid with one designed around new data on the benefits—and risks—of carbohydrates, fats, fiber, and other nutrients.

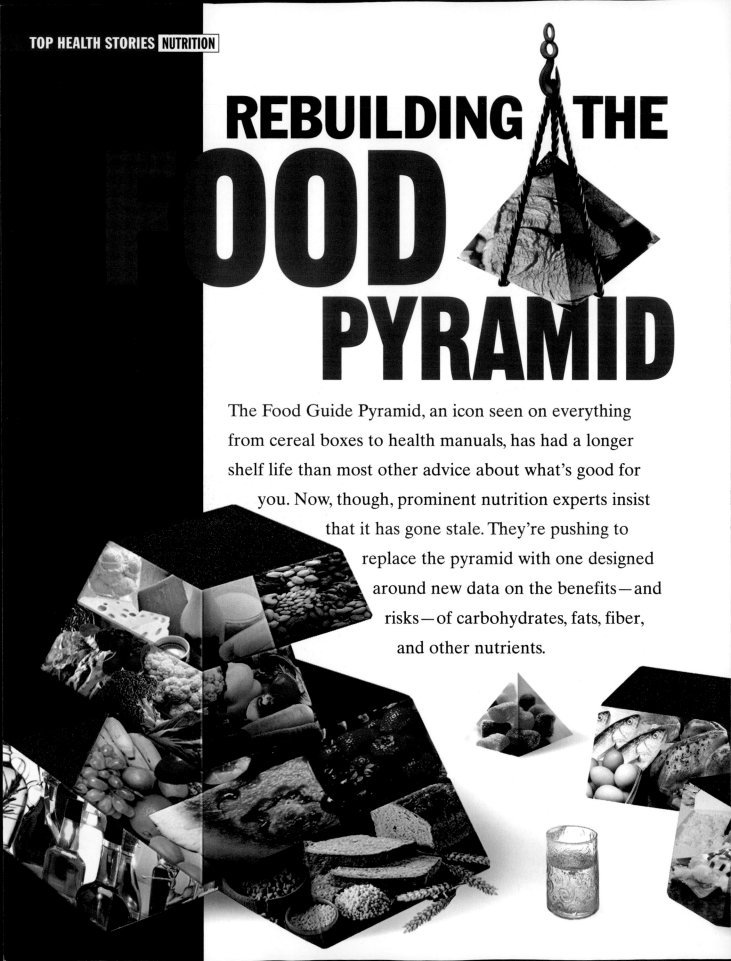

Want to lose weight? Be healthier? Live longer? Until a couple of years ago, many of those same experts would have guided you to the good old U.S. Department of Agriculture (USDA) Food Guide Pyramid. Introduced in 1992 to help consumers make wise choices about what to eat, the pyramid depicts a diet with a clear hierarchy of virtues.

At its base—the foundation of good health—are bread, cereal, rice, pasta, and other carbohydrates. Next come vegetables and fruits, then dairy foods and the group comprising meats, fish, dry beans, eggs, and nuts. Perched at the tip, where prudent people should rarely venture, are fats, oils, and sweets.

The high-carbohydrate, low-fat focus seemed logical during the 1980s and 1990s. But as time passed, the pyramid starting showing cracks. Studies began to cast doubt on the standard nutritional guidelines, and some respected experts proposed a heresy: Such a diet may actually promote weight gain, heart disease, and diabetes. There's no getting around the fact, they pointed out, that in the 12 years since the pyramid was unveiled, the U.S. population has become less healthy, with more than half of all adults now overweight.

So—what's next? Even while debate rages about what constitutes healthy eating, many experts agree on what does not: the pyramid. Researchers point to study after study showing that not all fats are bad for your health or waistline. Possibly more important, not all carbohydrates are good for you. As a result, there's a movement afoot to completely overhaul the government's guidelines and the pyramid that symbolizes them.

The USDA plans to update the pyramid by early 2005 to reflect new research completed since 1992, says John Webster, director of public information and governmental affairs for the USDA Center for Nutrition Policy and Promotion. The news has researchers, nutrition educators, and industry groups clamoring for a chance to shape the next pyramid.

Fat: No Longer All Bad

Leading the charge is Walter C. Willett, M.D., professor of epidemiology and chair of the nutrition department at the Harvard School of Public Health. To encourage debate about the pyramid, Dr. Willett unveiled his own Healthy Eating Pyramid in his book *Eat, Drink, and Be Healthy* (see "Will the Real Pyramid Please Stand Up?" on page 34).

"There is a lot of misinformation out there," says Dr. Willett. "The Food Guide Pyramid is tremendously flawed. It says that all fats are bad and that all complex carbohydrates are good. That's not accurate. The biggest nutritional mistake people can make is getting rid of all of the fat in their diets. Not all fats are bad, and some are required for good health."

Dr. Willett has spent much of the past 20 years researching the relationship between carbohydrates, fats, and good health. He and others at Harvard have tracked the eating, exercise, and lifestyle habits of thousands of health professionals and published hundreds of studies based on their data. Their research has helped to change the basic understanding of human nutrition, mostly as it pertains to fat consumption.

As it turns out, rather than clogging arteries and packing on the pounds, the monounsaturated and polyunsaturated fats found in fish, avocados, flaxseed, soybeans, olives and olive oil, and nuts

> The biggest nutritional mistake people can make is getting rid of all the fat in their diets. Not all fats are bad.
>
> **Walter C. Willett, M.D.**

and nut butters seem to improve cholesterol ratios and help with weight loss. Monounsaturated fats have been shown to help raise levels of high-density lipoprotein (HDL, or "good") cholesterol and lower levels of low-density lipoprotein (LDL, or "bad") cholesterol. They also seem to be involved in controlling hunger and burning fat.

Surprised? A lot of people are, considering some basic facts about fat. It is a fact that a gram of fat contains 9 calories, compared with 4 calories in a gram of carbohydrate or protein. And it's a fact that the body stores energy from fat more efficiently than from carbohydrates and protein. Thus, the overriding message of the 1990s was that you get fatter from eating fat. It seemed to follow, then, that if you wanted to lose weight, you could do it just by cutting back on fat.

It's just not that simple. According to Liz Applegate, Ph.D., professor of nutrition at the University of California-Davis and author of *Bounce Your Body Beautiful*, among other books, monounsaturated and polyunsaturated fats may help keep blood sugar and insulin levels steady, which reduces hunger and promotes fat burning instead of fat storage. In fact, a recent investigation that compiled the results of 147 different studies on nutrition and health found that fats are downright necessary for good health.

Even saturated fat—the kind found in steak, butter, and ice cream and long considered a dietary villain—may not be quite as bad for us as we thought. Recent studies published in the *New England Journal of Medicine* and elsewhere have found that the Atkins Diet, rich in protein and saturated fat, promotes more weight loss and better cholesterol levels than high-carbohydrate, low-fat diets (see "Study Finds No Beef with High-Protein Diets" on page 118).

The bottom line. "Not all fats are bad, and some are absolutely essential," says Dr. Willett. Numerous studies of healthy populations in places such as the Greek island of Crete have convinced him that you can safely get a whopping 40 percent of calories from fat—as long as nearly all of it is "good" fat from fish, avocados, nuts, olives, flaxseed, and soybeans. Not all experts agree on that point, but just about all are in accord that some fats are indeed good for your heart and your waistline, so they shouldn't be relegated to the pyramid's tippy-top.

There is one kind of fat that just about everyone now agrees we should avoid: the synthetic type known as transunsaturated fatty acids, or trans fats. Harvard studies conducted during the 1990s revealed that these fats, found in margarine and countless packaged foods, may be especially bad for the heart. Trans fats, which are produced when liquid vegetable oil is hydrogenated to make it solidify, are used to prolong the shelf life of processed foods and contribute to the taste and

fats

Experts agree that the trans fats in many processed and fried foods are particularly bad for you. Most also agree that the saturated fats in animal products are less healthful than unsaturated fats.

out

Researchers now believe that monounsaturated and polyunsaturated fats are essential to good health.

in

texture of the crackers, chips, baked goods, and fried foods that so many of us know and love.

Until the 1990s, we were told that such man-made trans fats were healthier than saturated fats, so many people switched from butter (a saturated fat) to margarine. Yet Dr. Willett and his colleagues showed that trans fats raised levels of LDL and triglycerides, the molecules that make up fat, while lowering levels of HDL. Raising the ratio of LDL to HDL increases the risk of heart disease. Although controversial at the time, the "trans fats are bad" message is now mainstream. In late 2002, the National Academy of Sciences Institute of Medicine (IOM) declared trans fats unsafe, and the FDA now requires manufacturers to list the amount of trans fats on labels of packaged foods.

Carbs: No Longer All Good

When people cut back on fat during the 1990s, many replaced it with carbohydrates. That would have been fine if the carbohydrate foods had been mostly fruits, vegetables, and whole grains, but they weren't. Instead, a lot of people reached for processed foods such as white bread, bagels, candy, snack chips, fat-free cookies, and soft drinks.

"It doesn't do any good to replace the fat in your diet with foods that are high in sugar or refined carbohydrates," says Dr. Willett. "A lot of people think that a plain bagel with jam can be a healthy thing to eat in the morning, but actually that's one of the unhealthiest breakfasts you can consume. You'd be better off with scrambled eggs."

Just as you can split fats into "good" and "bad" categories, you can now do the same with carbohydrates. Unprocessed carbohydrate foods that are high in fiber—such as fruits, vegetables, and whole grains—generally rate as "good." Those that are processed, low in fiber, and digested quickly—such as sugar, soft drinks, white pasta, and jam on a bagel or any other bread made from refined flour—fall into the "bad" category.

Here's the reasoning. Fruits, vegetables, and whole grains not only contain important disease-fighting plant chemicals, they also have fiber, which is highly effective at slowing digestion, reducing hunger, and lowering cholesterol levels. One 10-year study published in the *Journal of the American Medical Association* in 1999, for example, found that people who ate diets high in fiber tended to gain about 10 pounds less, on average, than those who consumed low-fiber diets.

On the other hand, processed, vitamin-vacant, low-fiber carbohydrates that the body digests quickly—such as snack foods, refined-flour breads, and sugary desserts—have been shown to cause blood sugar swings that can lead to weight gain.

Eating processed carbohydrates isn't a problem for lean, fit people. In these people, the hormone insulin can easily keep glucose (blood sugar) levels under control by shuttling it out of the bloodstream and into muscle cells, which use it for energy. The typical American, however, is neither lean nor fit.

In many sedentary, overweight people, insulin can't do its job properly, so too much glucose stays in the blood, and the pancreas may respond by cranking out more of the hormone. High insulin levels prompt the liver to convert sugar into fat, which is eventually shuttled into fat cells. Blood

The better breakfast?

out

in

A bagel with jam is a breakfast of sugar and refined carbohydrates, which lacks fiber and leads to blood sugar swings that cause you to overeat. Protein (in scrambled eggs) and whole grains (in whole-wheat bread) don't have the same effect.

sugar levels suddenly drop too low. In an attempt to bring them back to normal, your brain calls for food, making you feel hungry even though you don't actually need the calories.

Chronically high levels of blood sugar and insulin do more than make you fat; they've also been linked to heart disease. In one of Dr. Willett's studies on thousands of nurses, those who consumed the highest amounts of quickly digested carbohydrates also had the highest incidence of heart disease.

Generally, the more fiber a food contains and the less refined the food, the less it will affect blood sugar. Because foods loaded with refined carbohydrates, such as white bread and snack crackers, raise blood sugar levels and lack nutrients, a growing number of nutrition experts now lump them into the same category as junk food. The World Health Organization and the IOM now promote high-fiber, slow-to-digest carbohydrates such as beans, whole grains (including brown rice, whole-wheat breads and pastas, and bran or whole-wheat cereals), and many fruits and vegetables over refined carbohydrates.

Grains currently make up the base of the food pyramid, and no one is arguing that we should eat less of them. We should, however, eat less of some types (refined) and more of other types (whole or minimally processed). Since refined carbohydrates such as pancake syrup, high-sugar breakfast cereals, and cookies are a major part of many people's diets, this switch may be the most important one to make.

carbs

Sugar and other refined carbohydrates cause insulin levels to spike, which encourages fat storage. They cause blood sugar swings that trigger hunger. And they lack fiber and may contribute to heart disease and diabetes risk.

Fruits, vegetables, beans, and whole grains—all sources of complex carbohydrates—contain fiber (which keeps blood sugar levels steady) and other nutrients.

out

in

Potatoes Are Singled Out

Some fats and carbs are better for you than others—on that many nutrition experts agree. But that's where the agreement stops. Once they start talking about how to fix the Food Guide Pyramid to reflect those differences, the debate becomes very heated.

One of the more controversial issues is what to do with the potato. The pyramid recommends three to five servings of vegetables a day. While few people eat even the minimum of three, most do eat potatoes. And the potato, according to Dr. Willett, is a vegetable that should be relegated to the "use sparingly" category at the tip of the pyramid. He includes it with white bread, sugar, candy, and other refined carbohydrate foods, arguing that because potatoes are digested quickly, they tend to cause blood sugar to spike.

Are Potatoes as Bad as Table Sugar or Soft Drinks?

Here, Dr. Applegate doesn't agree with Dr. Willett. She eats potatoes almost every day. She mashes together different types—particularly the purple and blue varieties known to contain cancer-fighting chemicals—and includes the skins, which contain heart-healthy fiber and other nutrients. Also, all potatoes aren't digested at the same speed. For example, new potatoes (picked when they're young) break down more slowly, so their sugar hits the bloodstream less rapidly than that of mature whites and russets—and, of course, any type that's mashed or instant. Yams, sweet potatoes, and red potatoes such as La Soda, La Touge, and Red Norland are also digested more slowly.

No one knows for sure why potatoes vary so much in terms of their effect on blood sugar, although some nutritionists suspect that the amount of starch a potato contains may come into play. The body quickly converts starch, a form of stored carbohydrate, into sugar. New potatoes contain less starch than more mature potatoes, and deeper-colored varieties (yellows, reds, and blues) contain less starch than white potatoes. Eating the skin can further slow the digestive process.

Dr. Applegate agrees that high-sugar diets are bad for certain people, but she maintains that because potatoes are, after all, a plant food containing fiber and nutrients, they're certainly not as bad as soft drinks and other vitamin-vacant processed foods.

Red Meat Fights for Redemption

As with the potato debate, the arguments over red meat consumption can also get heated. During the 1990s, nutritionists often put red meat in the same category as butter, cream, and other foods high in saturated fat. To fight back, the meat industry began promoting cuts of beef that rivaled chicken and turkey for leanness.

"Certainly the concern has been raised about saturated fat, but there are 13 cuts of beef that meet government guidelines for lean or extra lean, meaning that they are considered low-saturated-fat

Dangerous or benign? Meat may not raise your cholesterol levels, but some experts now suspect a cancer connection.

foods," says Mary Young, R.D., executive director of nutrition at the National Cattlemen's Beef Association in Centennial, Colorado.

Although lean red meat was enough to placate some nutritionists, Dr. Willett and others say it still belongs at the pinnacle of the pyramid. Not only is heart disease a concern, he says, but there are colon and prostate cancer to consider as well.

"There are many studies indicating a higher risk of colon cancer with higher red meat consumption," he says. "It doesn't just seem to be about the fat. It may be how it's cooked, usually at high temperatures, which produce a lot of carcinogens. Or it may even be the amount of iron. A lot of research suggests that high iron concentration can accelerate cell growth."

Young counters that for every study that links beef to cancer, she can produce a study that finds no connection. She points out that red meat contains two nutrients—the antioxidant selenium and a fat called conjugated linoleic acid—that have been shown to fight cancer. "The most conclusive thing you can say about the cancer issue is that it is inconclusive," she says. "I believe it's not what we are eating that's the problem, but what we aren't eating and aren't doing. We are not being physically active enough, we are not eating enough fruits and vegetables, and we are not eating whole grains."

Dr. Willett would like to see beef separated from other high-protein foods. You don't have to ban red meat from your menu, he says, but you should limit yourself to no more than two servings a week. Young, of course, wants the pyramid's protein category to remain at the current recommendation of two to three servings a day.

Dairy Falls from Grace

Finally, there's the dairy debate. When most of us were growing up, we were taught that dairy products are rich sources of calcium, making them essential for building strong bones. Yes, dairy products also contained a lot of artery-clogging saturated fat, but not if you switched to fat-free milk and yogurt and low-fat cheeses.

Now it seems that as with other building blocks in the pyramid, the dairy story may not be quite what it originally seemed.

First, the issue of bone health. In a startling study published in the *American Journal of Clinical Nutrition* in February 2003, Harvard researchers reported that they found no link between high calcium consumption, or milk consumption, and bone strength. After tracking hip fractures and eating habits in 72,337 women for 20 years, they failed to find a correlation between consuming more than 700 milligrams of calcium a day and stronger bones. They did find an association between higher intake of vitamin D and a lower risk of fractures, however.

"There really is no requirement for dairy in the diet," says Amy Lanou, Ph.D., nutrition director for the Physicians

Dairy was once considered by Westerners to be essential to healthy bones, but that thinking is beginning to change.

Committee for Responsible Medicine in Washington, D.C. "The countries with the highest rates of osteoporosis are the ones where people drink the most milk and have the most calcium in their diets. The connection between calcium consumption and bone health is actually very weak, and the connection between dairy consumption and bone health is almost nonexistent."

Dr. Willett agrees. "How much calcium do we need? It's probably greatly overstated by our current recommendations," he says, referring to the U.S. government's 1,000- to 1,500-milligram daily allowance. "The British government just reviewed their recommended daily allowance for calcium and came up with 700 milligrams. From all the evidence I've seen, it looks as if the British number is closer to the right one."

Of course, the dairy industry strongly disagrees. In 2003, it began promoting a "3-a-Day of Dairy for Stronger Bones" campaign. "The contention that we need less than 1,000 milligrams of calcium a day — boy, I disagree," says Greg Miller, Ph.D., senior vice president of nutrition and scientific affairs for the National Dairy Council. "The dairy industry didn't come up with those numbers. The Institute of Medicine and the National Academy of Sciences put together a prestigious panel of experts who came up with recommendations of 1,000 to 1,500 milligrams of calcium a day."

As for Dr. Lanou's statement that countries with high dairy consumption have high rates of osteoporosis, Dr. Miller suggests that some confounding factors are at work. For example, Asians may not drink a lot of milk or consume a lot of calcium, but they get a lot more exercise than the average Westerner. And besides inactivity, factors such as smoking, alcohol consumption, caffeine, and high protein intake—all common in Western dairy-consuming countries—have been shown to weaken bones.

UC-Davis's Dr. Applegate says that, yes, some people—fit people who don't smoke—could probably get away with just 700 milligrams of calcium daily. But, she adds, most people need more.

Regardless of the calcium requirements, dairy opponents also point to the health risks of this food group. For example, a number of studies have linked dairy consumption with an increased risk of prostate and ovarian cancer. In Harvard's Health Professionals Follow-Up Study of 51,529 men, those who drank two or more glasses of milk a day were nearly twice as likely to develop prostate cancer as those who didn't drink milk.

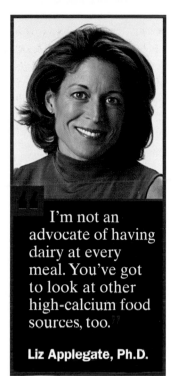

" I'm not an advocate of having dairy at every meal. You've got to look at other high-calcium food sources, too. "

Liz Applegate, Ph.D.

Although no one knows for sure why this is, Dr. Willett suspects that high amounts of calcium may interfere with vitamin D's role in slowing cell division in the prostate.

Dr. Miller cautions that such population-based studies show only correlations, not cause and effect, and that some other factor could be at work. "The clinical data that are available suggest that calcium is not a problem and that it may even be advantageous for cancer prevention," he says.

Even Dr. Willett isn't convinced that dairy should be relegated to the tip of the pyramid. His own pyramid recommends one or two calcium-rich foods a day. "You get different kinds of answers depending on which data you look at," he says. "Because there are many more studies showing harm and almost none showing benefit, it seems to me that we should be cautious about encouraging people to consume high amounts of dairy. Let's hope that in a few years we will have better data."

WHITE RICE AND HEALTH:
THE CHINESE PARADOX

If refined carbohydrates are so bad, how can people in China eat white rice two or three times a day and stay so healthy? The answer: They can't.

For many years, the Chinese lived in an agrarian society where, in the natural course of a day, they got plenty of exercise. Food was also scarce. Due to the regular exercise and low calorie intake, most people just didn't get fat.

Those conditions began to change in the 1950s as parts of China became more metropolitan. This was particularly true in Beijing, where heart disease is now the number one cause of death, and rates of diabetes have skyrocketed.

Life in Beijing is now similar in many ways to life in Western cultures. People work at desk jobs and move very little during the day. During the late 1950s, the average Chinese person took in just over 2,000 calories a day. Today, that number is closer to 2,300, yet energy expenditure has gone down. The result: weight gain.

Harvard's Walter Willett, M.D., believes that if you're going to eat refined carbohydrates, your body handles them best when you are lean and get plenty of exercise. Exercise helps keep muscle cells abundant and active, allowing them to more easily sop up blood sugar. As soon as you stop exercising, your metabolism undergoes complex changes that allow starchy, refined carbohydrates to spike insulin levels, raising blood cholesterol and encouraging fat storage.

"That's been a really important finding," Dr. Willett says. "If you are sedentary and overweight, your muscle cells are probably resistant to the hormone insulin, so your metabolism won't be able to deal with these foods."

Lack of exercise isn't the only factor in the declining health of the Chinese. As they have adopted a more metropolitan lifestyle, they've also switched to a more Westernized diet. People in China now eat much more animal protein and saturated fat than they did many years ago, a change that also could be affecting rates of heart disease and diabetes. ■

Is the Pyramid Really Flawed?

The USDA pyramid recommends 6 to 11 servings a day from the grains group and 3 to 5 servings of vegetables. Surveys show that in the United States, just one person in three eats the recommended amount of vegetables or grains, and fewer than one of every five gets the minimum amount (two servings) of fruit. At the same time, Americans seriously overeat foods from the pyramid's "use sparingly" category that includes fats, oils, and sweets. That begs the question: What if we did eat according to the pyramid? What if we actually ate five to nine servings of fruits and vegetables, for example, and followed a diet based on whole grains?

"Then we would not be having some of these problems, such as our obesity epidemic. I don't care which pyramid we use," says Jeanne Goldberg, R.D., Ph.D., director of the Center for Nutrition Communication at Tufts University in Boston. Dr. Goldberg served as the primary investigator for a study done in 1991 to determine whether the pyramid graphic could be understood by average Americans. "The point is that we've all got to eat lots of fruits and vegetables and whole grains," she says. "The real challenge is how to move the behavioral needle and get people to change their diets."

And for all its flaws, other experts agree, the old pyramid was a step in the right direction. "What I think is good about the existing pyramid is that it is clearly hierarchical—it makes it very clear that you are supposed to eat more of some foods than others," says Marion Nestle, Ph.D., professor and chair of the department of nutrition and food studies at New York University in Manhattan and author of *Food Politics*. "This in itself is an enormous step forward in nutritional advice. So now the question is how to deal visually with the nuances of good fats and bad fats and good carbs and bad carbs. There are a lot of things wrong with the pyramid—that's true. But it may be hard to fix, in large part because it's difficult to figure out how one piece of paper can deal with all the complexities of nutrition." ■

Will the Real Pyramid Please Stand Up?

As controversy has grown over the content of the USDA's Food Guide Pyramid, plenty of people have chimed in with their ideas of what a revised pyramid should look like. Here are three popular versions, along with the current pyramid.

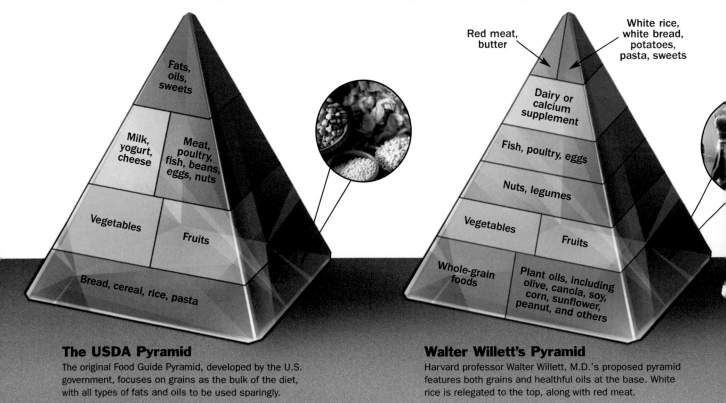

The USDA Pyramid
The original Food Guide Pyramid, developed by the U.S. government, focuses on grains as the bulk of the diet, with all types of fats and oils to be used sparingly.

Walter Willett's Pyramid
Harvard professor Walter Willett, M.D.'s proposed pyramid features both grains and healthful oils at the base. White rice is relegated to the top, along with red meat.

what does it mean to you?

Although researchers and industry groups may not agree yet on what the next Food Guide Pyramid should look like, there's a strong consensus on the cornerstones of a healthy diet. They include:

■ **More vegetables.** Few of us eat enough. Vegetables are packed with fiber, vitamins, and phytochemicals (plant-based compounds) that help guard against heart disease, cancer, and other serious ailments. If you currently eat one serving a day, aim for two. If you eat two, aim for three.

■ **A bigger variety of foods.** We're talking primarily about the diversity of fruits and vegetables you eat—not the types of junk food. Even if you eat the recommended three to five servings of vegetables a day, are you eating three to five different ones? Different vegetables contain nutrients that can fight disease in different ways. If you eat five servings of baby carrots a day, for example, you're not doing your body as much good as if you had a serving of carrots (for beta-

carotene, essential to good vision and resistance to infection), a helping of broccoli (for its anti-cancer chemicals and fiber), some red bell peppers (for more beta-carotene and vitamin C for the immune system), and some dark leafy greens (for fiber and folate for the immune system and health in pregnancy).

■ **Beans.** Like vegetables, beans are one of nature's power foods. They're packed with two types of fiber that are important not only for heart health but also for bowel health. Plus, more and more research is finding that beans contain chemicals similar to those in fruits and vegetables that help fend off disease. Add canned beans to dishes that you already eat, such as salads, soups, and casseroles.

■ **Whole foods.** As much as possible, eat your grains unprocessed. Look for 100 percent whole-wheat bread, for instance, and whole-grain cereals. Make switches in areas that aren't so obvious, such as choosing whole-grain pasta instead of plain.

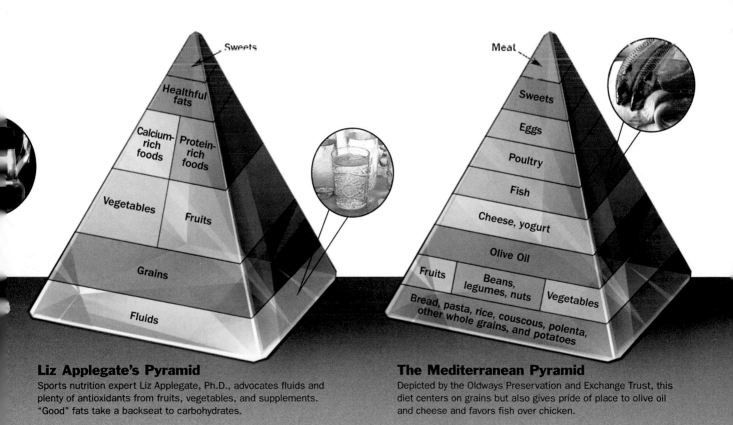

Liz Applegate's Pyramid
Sports nutrition expert Liz Applegate, Ph.D., advocates fluids and plenty of antioxidants from fruits, vegetables, and supplements. "Good" fats take a backseat to carbohydrates.

The Mediterranean Pyramid
Depicted by the Oldways Preservation and Exchange Trust, this diet centers on grains but also gives pride of place to olive oil and cheese and favors fish over chicken.

CANCER VACCINES

ON THE VERGE OF VICTORY

By the time John L. Willey, then 53, joined one of the first clinical trials for the prostate cancer vaccine GVAX, he'd already undergone surgery, only to find that the cancer had moved into his lymph nodes. His PSA level, an indicator of how fast the cancer is growing, was rising so fast that it "was giving me nosebleeds," he says. It had skyrocketed from 3.5 to 6.4 in just a year. Levels like that "mean you've all of a sudden entered another realm," Willey says—where your life is measured in months, not years. So when his doctor told him about the trial, he had one question: "Where do I sign up?"

John L. Willey credits an experimental prostate cancer vaccine with saving his life. It's one of many so-called therapeutic vaccines poised to control cancer with a simple injection.

Over eight weeks, he had 224 shots, two daily in each arm or leg. The only side effect was small, itchy, raised nodules where the shots were given, similar to mosquito bites. Six months after the first injections, Willey's PSA had plummeted to 1.2, which is quite normal for a man his age. "The vaccine saved my life," says the 58-year-old real estate developer from Poolesville, Maryland. "My chances of making it this far without this therapy were minimal."

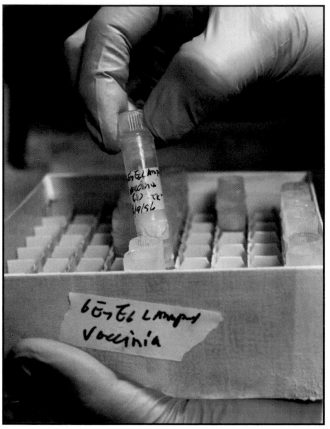

This cervical cancer vaccine uses a genetically engineered virus (*Vaccinia*) to insert a molecular tag in cancer cells to alert the immune system to kill them.

Stories like Willey's are becoming less exceptional as the research on cancer vaccines moves into high gear, and as several companies prepare to submit final applications to the FDA for approval of their vaccines in late 2003 or early 2004.

Could it be that after years of hype and hope, the much-vaunted cancer vaccine is finally poised to become a reality? "I think that it is," says Christopher G. Wood, M.D., assistant professor of urology and cancer biology at the University of Texas MD Anderson Cancer Center in Houston.

In the past five years, hundreds of human clinical trials of cancer vaccines have been conducted around the world, and cancer conferences these days are chockablock with posters, abstracts, and presentations on the results of those trials, as well as animal studies.

Still, there's a long way to go. While a few very simple therapeutic vaccines—those that stimulate the patient's immune system to fight the cancer—have been approved in Canada and Europe, none have yet been approved in the United States, and only a small handful have reached Phase III clinical trials, the last stage before submission to the FDA for approval.

Part of the problem is that early trials designed to test the safety of vaccines can be conducted only in people with advanced disease, for whom there is little hope. These are also the patients who are least likely to show any benefit from the vaccine, says Jeffrey Schlom, Ph.D., chief of the National Cancer Institute's Laboratory of Tumor Immunology and Biology. "The fact that we're seeing *some* clinical responses and *some* increased survival in advanced patients bodes well for the field," he says. And now, after years of early trials to test safety and effectiveness, some vaccines are finally moving into Phase III trials, which can be conducted with people whose cancer isn't as advanced. "I think we have extremely potent vaccines now," says Dr. Schlom. "It just takes time and a lot of energy moving through the regulatory process and getting things up and moving."

A "Vaccine" of a Different Color

When you think of a vaccine, you probably think of the shots kids get to protect them from measles, mumps, and a host of other infectious diseases. These are called prophylactic—or preventive—vaccines, meaning they work by training the immune system to attack the disease-causing organism if it ever turns up. Some cancer vaccines are designed this way, most notably the hepatitis B vaccine, which protects against the virus known to cause liver cancer, and the experimental HPV vaccine, which guards against the virus that causes nearly all cases of cervical cancer. However, most cancer vaccines are therapeutic in nature, meaning they're designed to bolster the immune system's battle against existing cancers.

One major advantage of cancer vaccines is that unlike chemotherapy or radiation, which work by poisoning cancer cells and healthy cells alike, vaccines are essentially harmless to healthy cells, so side effects are practically nil. "It's like taking a flu shot, only with fewer side effects," says Dr. Woods.

Researchers don't expect these vaccines to be a magic bullet for cancer. Rather, they predict that vaccines will be used to turn an often-fatal disease— in which current treatments may be worse than the disease itself—into a chronic condition that's easily controlled with a simple injection every three or four months.

To understand how cancer vaccines work, it helps to grasp the wily nature of cancer cells. They are masters at evading detection. Because the immune system doesn't recognize them as a danger, it doesn't try to destroy them. That's why early cancer vaccines rarely worked—researchers simply took a piece of a patient's tumor, ground it up, nuked it with radiation so it couldn't divide, then injected it back into the patient, hoping its mere presence would stimulate the immune system to attack it. But the immune system, which never recognized the original cancer cells, did no better with the injected cells. Cancer cells also send out signals to turn off the body's immune response, the equivalent of turning off the sprinkler system as flames lick at a building.

Thus, even 10 years ago, vaccines were a very minor area of cancer research. That's all changed. In the late 1990s and early 2000s, scientists unearthed new clues about cancer cells' ability to evade the very system that should destroy it. At the same time came fresh insights into how that system could be prompted to go after the cells.

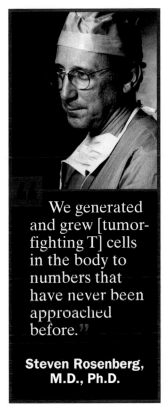

We generated and grew [tumor-fighting T] cells in the body to numbers that have never been approached before."

Steven Rosenberg, M.D., Ph.D.

Mounting Success Stories

Scientists from the privately held Dendreon Corporation told their peers at an international prostate cancer meeting in February 2003 that they had a patient with late-stage, rapidly spreading prostate cancer who has been disease-free for 3 1/2 years after injections of their vaccine—a "remarkable" response. And in a study published in the February 2003 issue of the *Journal of Clinical Oncology*, Boston doctors presented the results of their vaccine therapy on 25 patients with non-small-cell lung cancer, which accounts for 80 percent of all lung cancers. Each patient had less than half a year to live when they received the vaccines; three were still alive more than four years after treatment.

One of the biggest headline grabbers came in September 2003, when researchers from the National Cancer Institute (NCI), led by Steven A. Rosenberg, M.D., Ph.D., published news of their success in treating metastatic melanoma, the deadliest form of skin cancer, with a vaccine. In an unusually dramatic move, the researchers replaced patients' entire immune systems with specially targeted killer cells developed to attack the cancer. The treatment either stopped the cancer cells from growing or destroyed them altogether. Dr. Rosenberg performed it on 13 patients, some of whom had only months to live despite previous highly aggressive treatment. One 16-year-old boy, who'd been given just two months to live, was still free of disease two years later. Overall, the treatment shrank the tumors by half in six of the patients, with no growth or

Immune cells called T lymphocytes (orange) attach themselves to a cancer cell (pink) to induce it to undergo cell death. Cancer vaccines aim to help the body recognize cancer cells.

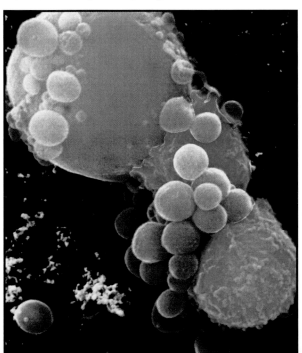

appearance of new tumors, while tumors disappeared completely in four patients.

The growing number of successes is possible in large part because scientists figured out exactly how cancer cells differ from normal cells. These differences are often too small for the immune system to notice, says cancer researcher Antoni Ribas, M.D., of the University of California-Los Angeles Jonsson Cancer Center. For instance, cancer cells make certain proteins that normal cells don't, or they make more of them than normal cells do. These proteins should have the same effect on the immune system as waving a red flag at a bull—if only there were a way to get the immune system to realize the danger.

The goal of much of today's cancer vaccine therapy, then, is to teach the immune system to recognize

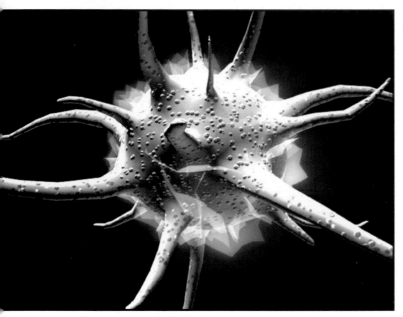

Dendrites are white blood cells that alert other immune cells to launch an attack. Dendritic cell vaccines use dendrites loaded with a tumor antigen to prompt the immune system to seek and destroy cancer cells.

these chemical markers as foreign—to stop "tolerating" cancer cells rather than attacking them. The process is known as breaking tolerance.

Researchers are focusing on three main types of cancer vaccines:

● Dendritic vaccines use immune cells called dendritic cells that have been made to carry proteins from a tumor. These cells then train other immune cells to recognize the protein—and therefore the cancer cells—as bad.

● With heat shock protein vaccines, doctors isolate "red flag" proteins called heat shock proteins from a patient's cancer cells. These proteins are then injected back into the patient after the tumor is removed to spur the immune system to attack any remaining tumor cells.

● Viral vector vaccines use a harmless virus to carry tumor proteins into the patient in a kind of biological Trojan Horse.

Arming the Generals: Dendritic Vaccines

Dr. Ribas uses a military analogy to explain the dendritic cell vaccine he's testing in people with melanoma. He tells his patients that the dendritic cell is like the general of the immune system army. Its job is to tell the army of fighter cells, specifically cytotoxic (toxic to cells) T lymphocytes, or T cells, what to attack. By loading dendritic cells with a protein that the tumor cells make, scientists make the generals "command" the T cells to recognize this protein, or antigen, as bad, and then attack it.

To make the vaccine, researchers grow a patient's own dendritic cells in the lab. Then they either insert the cancer antigen into the cells or fuse it to them using electricity. Sometimes they insert the gene responsible for making the cancer protein into the dendritic cell so the cell itself becomes a little antigen-making factory, spewing out future generations of dendritic cells that also carry the cancer protein.

And it works—sometimes. "We do have occasional, rather spectacular, responses with dendritic cells, where we have patients with late-stage melanoma cancer in whom the cancers just disappear," says Dr. Ribas. Some of those patients are still cancer-free three years after treatment.

Given the fact that every other treatment for these patients has failed, saving 1 out of 10 or 1 out of 5 is no small feat. "It's something we need to build on," says Dr. Ribas, "because it proves that we can rationally design vaccines tailored to the patient's tumor antigens using the body's system to fight these bad things."

More important, he notes, is that in most trials, patients have an immune response against the cancer. In other words, the dendritic cells are doing their job. The big question, then, is why can't the immune system destroy the tumors? Dr. Ribas thinks one reason may be the cancer cells themselves. "Cancer cells are very intelligent. They make a huge array of proteins that try to turn off the immune system, and they evade the immune system by turning off the dendritic cells so they don't pick up the antigens." Researchers are looking for ways to prevent immune system cells from being "turned off."

Because it's generally difficult to extract enough dendritic cells from children to make a vaccine, researchers from the Children's Hospital of Philadelphia are investigating the use of different immune cells, called B cells, to deliver genetic material from tumors in order to stimulate an immune response. In the lab, at least, it worked, according to research presented at a conference in May 2003. The researchers say the finding could lay the groundwork for future cancer vaccines for children.

"Shocking" the Immune System into Action

A second type of vaccine targets heat shock proteins (HSPs), also called stress proteins, which are present in all cells. HSPs are created when a cell undergoes any of various types of environmental stresses, such as heat, cold, and oxygen deprivation. They're also made by healthy cells to "chaperone" other proteins in the cell so they wind up in the right place. HSPs are normally found *inside* cells, but when a cell is sick, they move outside to the cell's surface. There they act as red flags, triggering an immune response. HSP vaccines mimic the "danger signal" sent by these extracellular HSPs.

One of the most advanced vaccines, called Oncophage (produced by Antigenics), is created by extracting HSPs from the patient's cancer cells and capturing from them the cancer's unique "fingerprint," made of peptides, or pieces of proteins attached to the HSPs. The peptides are then injected back into the patient's bloodstream—where the immune system can find them—after the tumor is removed. The hope is that they will prompt the immune system to go after any remaining tumor cells, which contain the same peptides.

Oncophage is one of the few vaccines in Phase III clinical trials—the last phase before FDA approval. At MD Anderson, where the vaccine is being used in patients with renal cell carcinoma, a type of kid-

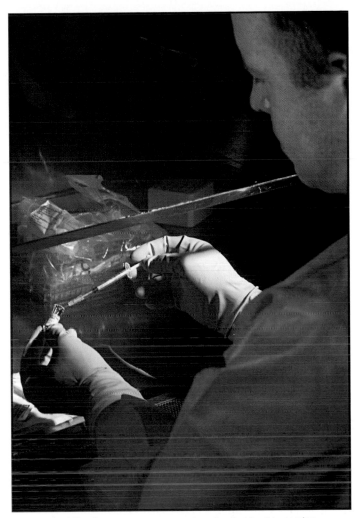

Dr. J. Michael Hamilton prepares a cancer vaccine that targets carcino-embryonic antigen (CEA), a protein made by many different cancer cells. The vaccine marks for destruction any cancer cells that express CEA.

ney cancer, earlier trials stopped the growth of tumors in patients in advanced stages of the disease.

"That's significant," says Dr. Woods, "because although the disease didn't go away, it didn't grow, either." He presented data on those trials at the May 2003 meeting of the American Society of Clinical Oncologists. Antigenics is also conducting Phase III trials of Oncophage for metastatic melanoma.

In September 2003, the FDA put enrollment for the Phase III trials on hold while it sought more information on the potency and purity of the protein in the vaccine. Safety was not an issue, and patients already enrolled in the trials were allowed to continue with the treatment. Antigenics expected to have the additional data ready for the FDA by the end of 2003.

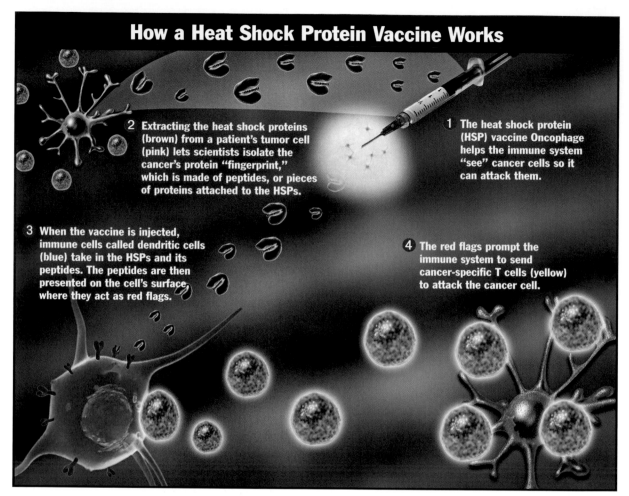

How a Heat Shock Protein Vaccine Works

2 Extracting the heat shock proteins (brown) from a patient's tumor cell (pink) lets scientists isolate the cancer's protein "fingerprint," which is made of peptides, or pieces of proteins attached to the HSPs.

1 The heat shock protein (HSP) vaccine Oncophage helps the immune system "see" cancer cells so it can attack them.

3 When the vaccine is injected, immune cells called dendritic cells (blue) take in the HSPs and its peptides. The peptides are then presented on the cell's surface, where they act as red flags.

4 The red flags prompt the immune system to send cancer-specific T cells (yellow) to attack the cancer cell.

The Trojan Horse Vaccine

Another type of cancer vaccine, called a viral vector vaccine, is similar to the dendritic cell vaccine, but instead of the antigen (tumor protein) being put into the patient's dendritic cells—a very time-consuming, labor-intensive, expensive method—it's put into a carrier, also known as a vector.

This is the approach that pharmaceutical giant Aventis Pasteur has taken with its ALVAC colorectal vaccine, which was in Phase II testing at several sites in the United States and Canada in the spring of 2003. The vector is a virus called canarypox, which is found only in canaries and is harmless in humans. The antigen is a protein called carcinoembryonic antigen (CEA), found in about 95 percent of colon cancers.

In one trial, the vaccine stabilized the disease in 40 percent of colon cancer patients in whom it was tested. That's pretty good, says Neil Berinstein, M.D., professor in the department of medicine at the University of Toronto and assistant vice presi-

dent/oncology of the Aventis vaccine program. As with most vaccine trial participants, these were the sickest of the sick. Some had undergone an unusual six rounds of chemotherapy treatments.

Current trials being conducted at several sites in Canada and the United States mesh the vaccine with chemotherapy, hoping the two together will have a stronger effect than either one alone. "We're so optimistic that we're already designing those Phase III trials," says Dr. Berinstein.

Cancer Vaccines on Deck

Other vaccines in late-stage trials as of summer 2003 included treatments for the following cancers.

Breast cancer. Theratope, from the Canadian Biomira Corporation, combines an immune system enhancer, interleukin-2, with cancer-associated antigens. Phase III trials, now completed, involved 1,030 women at more than 120 clinical sites around the world. The company expects to submit its data to the FDA for approval in 2004.

Melanoma. Canvaxin, from Carlsbad, California–based CancerVax, is in the midst of two international Phase III trials in patients with late-stage melanoma. Earlier studies found that the vaccine significantly increased overall survival in these patients. Another melanoma vaccine, Melacine, is already used in Canada. In the summer of 2003, Seattle-based Corixa Corporation, its manufacturer, was discussing with the FDA the design of a second round of Phase III trials in the United States.

Pancreatic cancer. Avicine, from Avi Biopharma, was to begin Phase III trials for pancreatic cancer in 2003. The vaccine spurs the immune system to attack cells that express human chorionic gonadotropin (hCG), a hormone commonly associated with pregnancy and fetal development and one that most cancer cells also express.

Prostate cancer. A dendritic cell vaccine called Provenge, from Seattle-based Dendreon, completed a Phase III clinical trial that showed the drug significantly slowed progression of prostate cancer and delayed onset of pain from the disease. Enrollment for a second Phase III trial was to continue into early 2004. At least one participant in the Phase II trials, who had advanced, progressive, metastatic cancer, experienced a complete remission following treatment and was still disease-free 3 1/2 years later, the company reported in February 2003 at the 13th International Prostate Cancer Update meeting in Vail, Colorado.

Another vaccine aimed at prostate cancer, GVAX, from Foster City, California–based Cell Genesys, was expected to enter Phase III trials in

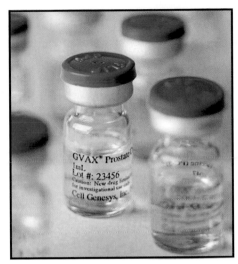

GVAX is the vaccine that appears to have cured John L. Willey of prostate cancer.

2003. This is the vaccine that John Willey credits with saving his life.

Heading into the Future

For every cancer vaccine that makes it to a Phase III clinical trial, a dozen or more begin Phase I trials, so it's obvious that this is a field that will only continue to grow. Already, researchers are exploring a "generic" cancer vaccine, one that could be used on all cancers because it targets the telomerase protein, an enzyme that helps prevent natural cell death and is thought to be involved in cancer.

To speed the process along, several powerhouse cancer research centers have combined to form the Cancer Vaccine Collaborative. The group, which includes New York Weill Cornell Medical Center, Columbia-Presbyterian Medical Center, Mount Sinai School of Medicine, and Memorial Sloan-Kettering Cancer Center, plans to openly share findings and explore vaccines using the same criteria and research rules.

"The field is moving very, very rapidly, building on itself in terms of what is right and not right and moving ahead with the things that are right," says the NCI's Dr. Schlom. "That's why I'm fairly optimistic that there are going to be some cancer vaccines that will be used early on in the management of a whole range of human cancers."

It won't be tomorrow, he and other researchers warn—but wait a couple of years. "It won't be like a light switch going on," says Dr. Schlom, "but like a dimmer being turned. Slowly, the room gets brighter and brighter." ■

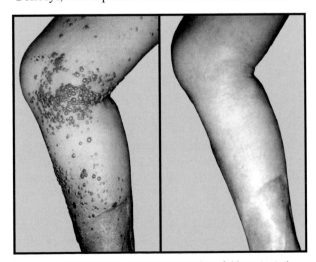

Oncophage triggered the complete regression of this metastatic melanoma 32 months after treatment with the vaccine.

SARS: A WARP-SPEED MEDICAL DRAMA

The doctor from Singapore did what doctors do: He treated sick patients. In this instance, the patients were sick with a mysterious form of pneumonia, but when the doctor flew to New York City in early March with his pregnant wife and his mother-in-law, he thought nothing of it. Then he began experiencing the same symptoms as his patients: high fever, shortness of breath, and coughing.

We had an international outbreak which was spreading over continents in a short period of time.

Klaus Stöhr, Ph.D.

Just before he boarded a flight back to his home country on March 15, the doctor told a colleague how sick he felt. The fellow health care worker alerted officials at the World Health Organization (WHO), who were already mobilized to identify and attack an unknown illness responsible for the deaths of at least four people since it had emerged in late February.

The plane had about 300 passengers and crew who were bound for 15 countries. After much debate, WHO officials grounded the plane in Frankfurt, Germany, quarantining the doctor and his family. (All of them eventually recovered.) Within hours, the agency had issued a rare global travel alert, calling the newly named severe acute respiratory syndrome (SARS) "a worldwide health threat."

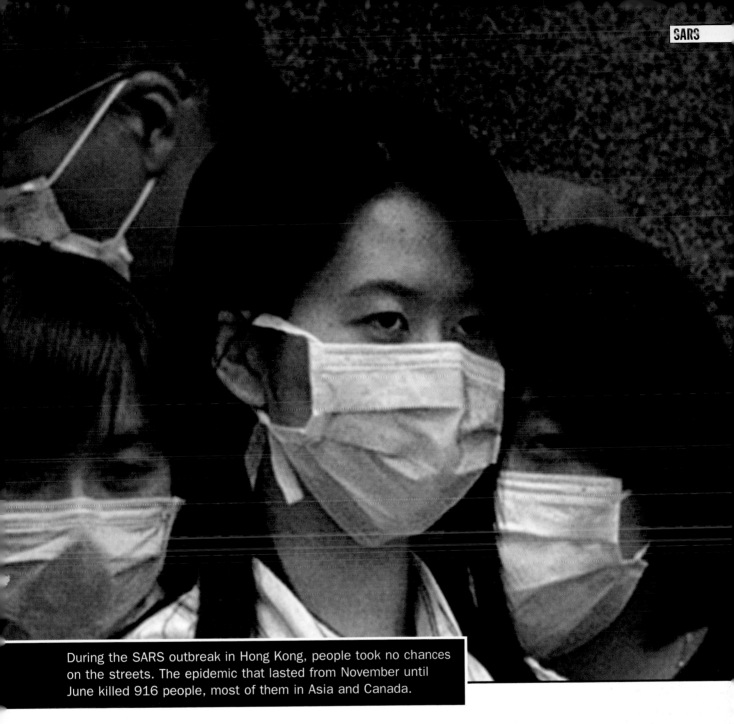

During the SARS outbreak in Hong Kong, people took no chances on the streets. The epidemic that lasted from November until June killed 916 people, most of them in Asia and Canada.

"We not only had a disease with an unknown causative agent, but we had no treatment, no diagnostic test, and now we had an international outbreak which was spreading over continents in a short period of time," says Klaus Stöhr, Ph.D., who is coordinating global research on the SARS virus for the WHO. What had been an emergency was now a crisis with global implications. Dr. Stöhr picked up the telephone to make the first of what would be 12 critical calls, each one to a member of the WHO's global influenza network laboratories. "We need your help," he told laboratory officials.

The Incredible Shrinking Timeline

Anyone frustrated by the snail's pace at which medical research often seems to move should consider the story of the SARS virus, responsible for the deadly disease that terrified much of the world in early 2003. Just 23 days after the first confirmed case of the unknown disease and 8 days after the first

WHO medical alert, researchers identified a new strain of coronavirus as the cause. Three weeks later, the virus's entire genome—the genetic code that defines it—had been sequenced and posted on the Internet for scientists around the world to use. Only three months after the first confirmed case, the Centers for Disease Control and Prevention (CDC) in Atlanta had already submitted a diagnostic test to the FDA for approval.

Compare that with the two years it took to identify the human immunodeficiency virus (HIV) after AIDS was first recognized in 1981. The HIV genome wasn't sequenced until the mid-1980s, a commercially available blood test didn't exist until 1985, and the first treatment for the disease wasn't approved until two years after that.

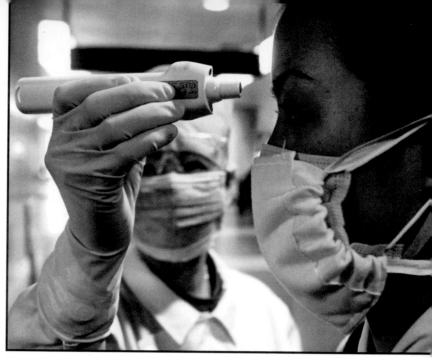

At the airport in Beijing, China, a flight attendant has her temperature checked. Airlines also screened passengers for SARS symptoms.

With SARS, researchers took a "shock and awe" approach. They had little choice. Today, we live in a global environment, where one passenger on a packed 747 can spread a virus to nearly every continent within a few hours.

The unprecedented speed in identifying the virus and sequencing its genome was possible, say those familiar with the process, because of a confluence of technology, new communication techniques (Web pages, list servers, and e-mail didn't exist in 1981, when AIDS first struck), and a greater appreciation of the risks posed by new infections in a global environment. "It shows that complementary work in a

competitive environment, knowing a public health emergency exists, can propel research much better than working in a closed, confined laboratory and doing these things all by oneself," says Dr. Stöhr.

That's a good thing, for although officials deemed the crisis over by the early summer of 2003, they knew the reprieve was most likely temporary. SARS is expected to roar back to life, like the conventional flu, sometime in early 2004.

Hunting Down the Mystery Virus

The first inkling that something might be wrong came in early February 2003, when Chinese officials reported an outbreak of some form of virulent flu in the southern province Guangdong, with 305 cases and five deaths. They assured WHO officials that the outbreak was under control, but by February 20, reports of atypical pneumonia began coming out of Hong Kong. WHO officials figured the illnesses were caused by a form of the influenza virus called H5N1, an avian flu that had supposedly struck the Chinese in Guangdong as early as November 2002.

As reports of more cases began trickling into the WHO, however, along with blood and saliva samples that showed no evidence of flu, worry mounted. WHO labs in Hong Kong, the United States, and Japan began testing the samples, to no avail. "We looked for hemorrhagic fevers, for every possible virus we could think of," says Dr. Stöhr, "and we could not find any of them."

SARS FAST FACTS

■ SARS is a respiratory illness that, by end of July 2003, had been reported in 32 countries and affected 8,099 people, 774 of whom died.

■ The cause is a new form of coronavirus, a member of the same family of viruses that causes colds, which is thought to have jumped from wild animals—probably civets, which are sold in southern China—to humans.

■ Symptoms include fever, headache and muscle aches, cough, and shortness of breath.

Until then, officials thought the outbreak was regional, confined to the Chinese mainland and Hong Kong. But on March 10, 2003, a WHO doctor reported a cluster of similar cases in Vietnam, most affecting health care officials who had treated a patient there with the disease. The next day, officials in Hong Kong reported that their health care workers were falling ill. Cases also began turning up in

Joseph DeRisi, Ph.D., a researcher at the University of California, San Francisco, holds a slide containing every known viral sequence. His lab identified the virus behind the SARS outbreak.

Singapore and Canada. On March 12, the WHO issued a global health alert, warning of an outbreak of atypical pneumonia and urging medical officials to report cases to authorities in their countries.

Then came the Singapore Airlines flight and Dr. Stöhr's phone calls. The day after the calls, he followed up with e-mails, and the network of influenza labs held its first conference call on March 17. To get the labs working together and swiftly sharing information, Dr. Stöhr set up a Website and arranged for twice-daily conference calls.

By March 24—barely a week after they started working on the problem—labs in Hong Kong and at the CDC had identified the probable culprit: a mutated form of the common coronavirus, the second leading cause of colds in humans. Sure enough, antibodies found in patient samples were able to neutralize the suspect virus. Like calling cards, the antibodies represented the immune system's past response to the virus, proving that the patients' bodies had done battle with it before. But additional tests were needed to complete the multi-step checklist that researchers use to definitively identify a virus as the cause of an illness.

That same day in March, members of the CDC team sent samples of the virus to researchers at the University of California, San Francisco (UCSF), who had recently developed a sophisticated gene chip that could quickly identify viruses. It took just one day to verify that this one was indeed a never-before-seen coronavirus, and the UCSF researchers e-mailed CDC officials coded sequences of genetic material confirming the identification.

By April 2, the CDC began sequencing longer stretches of the virus's genome, posting results on the WHO Website so that other labs could use the information. A few days later, the genome center at the British Columbia Cancer Agency in Vancouver received a minuscule amount of the genetic material to begin its own decoding process, and the center pulled nearly half of its 90 staffers off other projects to work on SARS. They hit pay dirt. At 2:25 A.M. on April 12, researchers had completely sequenced the genome for the SARS coronavirus. They posted the virus's genetic map on the Website later that day, and the CDC got its own map up on the Web two days later. On April 16, the WHO formally announced that SARS was caused by the new coronavirus.

There were several reasons for the unprecedented teamwork on this investigation and the speed with which it occurred, says Dr. Stöhr. First, the labs had all worked together before, so they trusted each other and the WHO. Also, the WHO has the neutrality necessary to lead such a project. For instance, unlike the CDC, which participated in the research, the WHO wasn't competing to find the virus with its own experiments—it was just coordinating the effort. Perhaps most important, it insisted that credit would go to whichever laboratory found the virus.

"Of course we played a catalyzing role," says Dr. Stöhr. "Of course we gave strategic direction and initiated certain research which the laboratories might not have started on their own. But we felt it was important that the laboratories saw themselves as equal partners, with no one trying to dominate their efforts or impose opinions."

Now for the Hard Part: Treatment

Unfortunately, the same approach probably won't work quite as well in the search for treatments and a vaccine for SARS, says Dr. Stöhr. "Drugs are commodities that cost money to produce and which will have a price. That changes the whole ball game." But the WHO still has a critical role to play. "What we can do is play the public health card," he says. "We can say, 'What do you need? Is there anything we can do to help you? Any obstacles we can help you overcome?'"

For instance, early in the crisis, the WHO created a repository of virus samples from which researchers may draw, including stool, blood, urine, and respiratory samples from people who were infected. It also negotiated with the Genomic Institute in Singapore, which created one of the first diagnostic tests for the virus, to provide 25,000 free test kits to China. The WHO will continue to use this bargaining power, providing free viral samples in return for a guarantee that tests, treatments, and vaccines will be provided at reduced cost to developing countries, not only for SARS but for other infectious diseases as well, Dr. Stöhr says.

In the United States, the National Institutes of Health (NIH) has taken a leading role in coordinating the search for treatment and a vaccine. It's awarding grants to researchers already working in the field of coronaviruses to find drugs to combat the virus and is working with private industry to develop genetically engineered antibodies that could potentially be used in a SARS vaccine. By early June, thousands of compounds had been screened

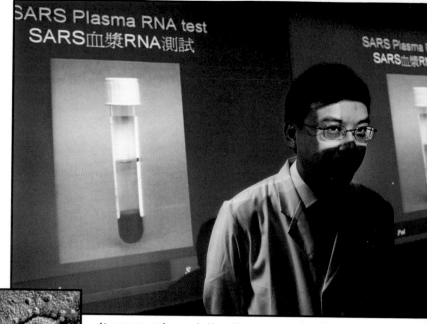

At a press conference in Hong Kong, a University of Hong Kong pathologist talks about a rapid new diagnostic test for SARS. The test checks for the presence of the virus's RNA in a nasal swab or throat culture. University of Hong Kong scientists were among those to identify a strain of the coronavirus (left) as the cause of SARS.

for their potential use in fighting the virus. The NIH said it planned to screen as many as 100,000 compounds.

This search for a treatment wouldn't be possible without the genetic sequencing of the virus, says Earl G. Brown, Ph.D., professor at the University of Ottawa in Canada and an expert on viruses. With the genetic code in hand, scientists can compare it with that of other viruses, including coronaviruses, looking for similarities. If an existing drug already works on a virus with a similar genetic code, that drug could be modified to work against the SARS virus. Or, as Dr. Brown puts it, "Maybe we could cut the tail off here, and fold the corners over there, and then it's going to be a good drug." That way, researchers aren't starting from scratch.

SARS Timeline

2002

Nov. 16. A mysterious illness strikes the southern Chinese province of Guangdong. By early February 2003, 5 people have died and more than 800 are infected.

2003

March 10–11. The disease is reported in Hong Kong and Canada as well as mainland China.

March 12. The WHO issues a global alert about a new infectious disease of unknown origin in both Vietnam and Hong Kong.

March 15. The WHO issues a heightened global alert about atypical pneumonia, now called SARS. The alert includes a rare emergency travel advisory to international travelers, health care professionals, and health authorities. An international network of laboratories is established to determine the cause of SARS and develop potential treatments.

March 24. CDC officials present the first evidence that a new strain of the coronavirus, a virus most frequently associated with upper respiratory infections and the common cold in humans, may be the likely cause of SARS.

In September 2003, researchers in Canada reported a promising breakthrough: SARS patients who were treated with interferon, an anti-viral protein, showed dramatic improvement, and 15 out of 19 of the seriously ill patients who were treated with it survived. The doctors used a highly potent version of interferon called Infergen. Earlier test tube studies conducted by the U.S. Army had shown that Infergen was extremely active against the SARS virus, and the CDC and the NIH are planning to conduct a large clinical trial of interferon during the next SARS outbreak. If it is indeed effective against the virus, the treatment could be available immediately.

The Holy Grail: A Vaccine

The best defense against an infectious disease is a vaccine, says Gary Nabel, Ph.D., chief of the Vaccine Research Center at the National Institute of Allergy and Infectious Diseases (NIAID), because the effects of the vaccine are global.

Consequently, NIAID is pursuing its own "shock and awe" approach to the SARS virus, spearheading a campaign designed to produce a vaccine in the unheard-of timeframe of 3 to 5 years instead of the 10 to 15 years it normally takes. It's doing that by using a form of research called parallel tracking, in which animal and human studies are conducted simultaneously once the vaccine is deemed safe. (Drug companies typically take an experimental compound through animal studies first, determining its effectiveness before putting the time and money into producing the compound to be used in human studies.)

Researchers at NIAID as well as private companies such as vaccine maker Aventis are also pursuing two lines of research simultaneously: They're developing an old-fashioned virus vaccine, such as the ones used for polio and smallpox, as well as a cutting-edge, gene-based vaccine in which pieces of the SARS virus are inserted into harmless viruses or other carriers, then injected into people in the hope it will stimulate an immune response.

Dr. Nabel thinks the latter approach may be the winner. Genetic vaccines, he says, tend to induce both a cellular response, helping cells resist the virus, and an antibody response, creating antibodies that attack it.

Overall, he says, he's cautiously optimistic about the eventual development of a vaccine, even though more than 20 years after the identification of HIV, there is still no vaccine to combat that virus. SARS has two things going for it that HIV doesn't, he says: Many patients recover from SARS, meaning that scientists can study their immune responses and compare them with the responses triggered by experimental vaccines. Also, the SARS outbreak was contained fairly quickly, which was not the case with HIV. The quick containment means the virus had fewer chances to mutate—and the less a virus mutates the more likely that a vaccine can be developed to attack it.

As with the early efforts to identify the SARS virus, the campaign to develop a vaccine is also taking place globally, says Dr. Nabel. There are collaborators in mainland China, Hong Kong, and Singapore, among other countries. "I've sensed that when there is a perceived biological threat, the biomedical research community seems to be stepping up to the plate," he says.

Unfortunately, he says, today's researchers have had a lot of practice in this kind of teamwork, what with recent threats of smallpox, anthrax, and West Nile virus. "I actually think that SARS is another example where the biomedical research community wants to apply their knowledge to help solve the problem. It really is the ultimate confluence of science, medicine, and technology, where we can have an impact on people's health." ■

April 12. Canadian researchers announce completion of the first successful sequencing of the genome of the coronavirus believed to cause SARS.

April 16. A new form of coronavirus never before seen in humans is confirmed as the cause of SARS. (In order for any new pathogen to be confirmed as the cause of a disease, it must meet four specific conditions, called Koch's postulates.)

April 14. CDC officials announce that their laboratories have sequenced a nearly identical strain of the SARS-related coronavirus.

June 12. Just seven new SARS cases are reported worldwide, and the WHO says the outbreak may be coming to an end.

Statins have reaped plenty of glory in the past few years. After all, millions of people worldwide are taking these drugs to lower artery-clogging cholesterol and prevent heart attacks. In addition, experts believe that millions of other people—even those who don't have high cholesterol—should be taking them to prevent heart attacks.

STATINS:
THE NEXT ASPIRIN

But the story doesn't end there. In 2003, statins approached star status as new research revealed a host of other potential benefits, including protection from diabetes, cancer, osteoporosis, and Alzheimer's disease.

In May 2003, two doctors from the University of Texas Southwestern Medical School won the third annual Albany Medical Center Prize—called "America's Nobel Prize"—for their groundbreaking work on cholesterol and the role of statins. By June, dozens of studies that suggested medical uses for statins far beyond the original objective of lowering cholesterol levels had been published in major journals or presented at major medical meetings. In mid-June, diabetes experts began proclaiming that most people with diabetes, regardless of their cholesterol levels, should take statins to protect against heart disease.

With all this new evidence of statins' potential, it's no wonder that doctors around the world are calling them "the next aspirin" and jokingly suggesting that they be added to the drinking water. It seems that someday, statins just may surpass the ubiquitous white tablets in usefulness.

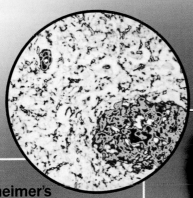

Alzheimer's and Multiple Sclerosis

Statins reduce levels of a blood marker for brain cholesterol, implicated in the brain plaques characteristic of Alzheimer's. The drugs could also work against multiple sclerosis.

Cancer

Tantalizing new evidence suggests that people who take statins are less likely to develop cancer. And drugs similar to statins may one day have a role in cancer treatment.

Diabetes

Statins slash the risk of heart problems in people with diabetes, regardless of their cholesterol levels. They also reduce the risk of complications such as eye and kidney disease.

Cardiovascular Disease

Statins lower LDL cholesterol and help prevent arteries from narrowing. Studies have shown a 30 percent reduction in overall deaths among people who take certain statins.

Currently prescribed for high cholesterol, statins are showing beneficial effects that reach far beyond the heart.

Osteoporosis

Statins could be the next wonder drug for bones. They not only slow the rate of bone breakdown but also speed the formation of new bone.

Like aspirin, statins have wide-ranging effects. They block an enzyme called HMG-CoA, which the liver uses to form cholesterol. And although cholesterol has a reputation as the "bad boy" of modern lifestyles, it might also be called "the stuff of life," because it's required by every cell in the body. That's why statins' exploding potential is not that surprising to researcher Gloria L. Vega, Ph.D., professor of clinical nutrition at the University of Texas Southwestern Medical Center at Dallas, who is examining their role in preventing Alzheimer's disease. "Statins appear to be a 'wonder drug' simply because their target is a key molecule in the life of cells."

> **"Statins appear to be a 'wonder drug' simply because their target is a key molecule in the life of cells."**

Arresting Alzheimer's

Scientists weren't looking for a cure for Alzheimer's when they studied the effects of statins on cholesterol, but they couldn't ignore tantalizing clues that suggested that people taking the drugs were less likely to develop the debilitating brain disease. Researchers began publishing articles about their

Exercise, antioxidants, and now statins are thought to help stave off the development of Alzheimer's.

observations as early as 2000, but it was too early to draw any direct links.

Then, in April 2003, Dr. Vega and her colleagues published the first major study to show clearly that statins reduced levels of a blood marker for brain cholesterol. Brain cholesterol is thought to drive the production of beta-amyloid protein, which is implicated in the development of the characteristic brain plaques found in people with Alzheimer's.

In Dr. Vega's study, published in the journal *Archives of Neurology*, researchers gave 44 people with Alzheimer's either one of three different statin drugs or a dose of extended-release niacin, which also lowers cholesterol. After six weeks, those taking the statins had a 20 percent drop in the markers for brain cholesterol, compared with 10 percent for those taking niacin. The study suggests one way in which statins may work on Alzheimer's and opens the way for much larger studies, says Dr. Vega.

Growing Bone

With the news on hormone replacement therapy getting worse by the minute, women and their doctors are on the lookout for other ways to protect bones. They may have found one in statins.

In an Italian study of 60 postmenopausal women, researchers gave 30 women with high cholesterol 40 milligrams a day of simvastatin (Zocor). Another group of 30 women, who had normal cholesterol, weren't given the drug. After a year, the researchers found that bone density in the spines, legs, and hips of the women taking Zocor had significantly increased, while bone density in the other women had significantly decreased. The study was published in the April 2003 issue of the journal *Bone*.

It seems that statins not only slow the rate at which bone breaks down (as shown in animal studies) but also actually increase bone density. That's critical, because until early 2003, all drugs approved for osteoporosis worked by preventing further breakdown of bone and were of little use to women who already had fragile bones. A new drug, teriparatide (Forteo)—approved by the FDA in November 2002 and on the market in early 2003—does build bone, but it's very expensive, has significant side effects, and requires regular injections.

No one really knows how statins help build bone, but animal studies suggest two possibilities, says Douglas Bauer, M.D., associate professor of medicine, epidemiology, and biostatistics at the University of California-San Francisco. One method is promot-

Statin Drug Stimulates Bone Formation

After 14 days of treatment with the drug cerivastatin, cultures of small pieces of bone showed remarkable growth compared with untreated bone.

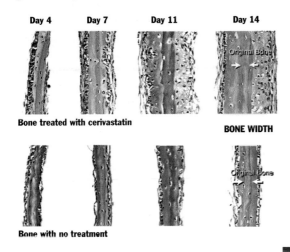

Day 4   Day 7   Day 11   Day 14

Original Bone

Bone treated with cerivastatin

BONE WIDTH

Original Bone

Bone with no treatment

Source: Dr. I. R. Garrett, OsteoScreen

ing production of a protein called BMP2, which stimulates bone-building cells called osteoblasts, and the other is reining in bone-destroying cells called osteoclasts.

Despite the drugs' promise for treating osteoporosis, doctors aren't writing prescriptions for statins to prevent fractures just yet, says Dr. Bauer. "I think the story is that people are optimistic that statins are going to turn out to be a useful clinical intervention," he says—someday.

Conquering Cancer

Cancer specialists are accustomed to using cancer drugs that are essentially poisons, with side effects that sometimes kill the patient before the cancer can. But at the American Society of Clinical Oncology meeting in May 2003, the specialty's largest conference, statins took a starring role as Dutch researchers presented a study showing that people who used statins were 20 percent less likely to develop cancer.

The greatest risk reduction occurred for prostate and kidney cancer, according to the study, which compared medical records of 3,219 people with heart disease who took statins with those of 16,976 who didn't. The connection was also strongest in people who had been taking the drugs for at least four years. Once they stopped taking statins, their

cancer risk returned to what it had been prior to taking the drugs.

One theory about how statins may reduce cancer risk stems from their effect on the enzyme HMG-CoA. In addition to helping the liver form cholesterol, this enzyme reduces production of a protein called mevalonate, which in turn lowers the activity of genes that play a role in cancer development. Statins also appear to block epidermal growth factors and blood vessel growth factors, which are critical in creating the blood vessels that feed tumors.

Two studies published in the spring of 2003 looked at a statin's action on breast cancer cells. In one, French researchers found that cerivastatin (Baycol) damped down mechanisms that cause breast cancer cells to divide aggressively. Although Baycol is no longer on the market because it was linked to a rare muscle disorder, other statins would most likely have similar effects on cancer cells.

In another study, scientists from the University of Texas MD Anderson Cancer Center in Houston found that both Zocor and lovastatin (Mevacor)

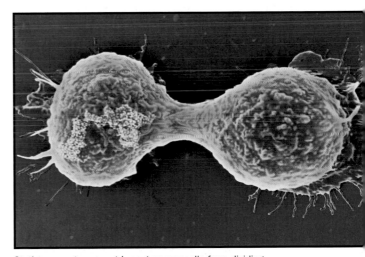

Statins seem to prevent breast cancer cells from dividing aggressively. People who take the drugs may also be less likely to develop cancer in the first place.

have a unique side effect. Namely, they allowed cells to maintain high levels of proteins that stop cancer cells from growing. Interestingly, researchers noted that it's the "inactive" part of a statin, which remains in the body after most of the drug has been taken up by the liver (where it reduces cholesterol production), that seem to have the anti-cancer effect. "Because these statins have the ability to kill tumor cells, they have a potential role in the future treatment of a number of cancers when used in combination with other drugs," says Khandan Keyomarsi, Ph.D., associate professor and lead author of the study.

Defeating Diabetes

Statin drugs work so well at preventing heart disease in people with diabetes—regardless of their cholesterol levels—that in June 2003, some experts began recommending that all people with diabetes take them.

The remarkable pro-statin stance came about after a major study involving 6,000 people with diabetes found that using statins cut the risk of cardiovascular problems by about a third, even in those with normal cholesterol levels. This is especially important because people with diabetes are two to four times more likely to develop heart disease than people who don't have the disease. In fact, some 80 percent of people with diabetes ultimately die of heart attacks. Overall, researchers said, statins could prevent a major cardiovascular problem, such as angina or a heart attack, in 45 out of every 1,000 people with diabetes. The study was conducted by Pfizer Inc., the pharmaceutical company that manufactures and sells the statin drug atorvastatin (Lipitor); Diabetes UK; and the department of health in the United Kingdom. The results were reported in the British journal *Lancet* in June 2003.

"Based on the data," says Robert Eckel, M.D., professor at the University of Colorado School of Medicine in Boulder and chairman of the American Heart Association Nutrition Committee, "a statin should be seriously considered in all adults with diabetes, independent of their LDL ['bad' cholesterol] level." How interchangeable the different statin drugs are is unclear, he says, but he believes all statins provide similar protection to people with diabetes.

Other research on diabetes and statins found that the drugs reduced the risk of leg ulcers, kidney disease, and the eye disease diabetic maculopathy, all of which are common complications of diabetes. One of the most intriguing findings of the year was the discovery that statins may actually prevent the development of diabetes in high-risk people.

> Based on the data, a statin should be seriously considered in all adults with diabetes, independent of their LDL ['bad' cholesterol] level.
>
> **Robert Eckel, M.D.**

How might statins prevent diabetes? By increasing the body's production of nitric oxide. Without sufficient levels of this important chemical, your risk of diabetes, as well as diabetes complications, increases. Studies find that people with type 1 and type 2 diabetes have a decreased ability to generate nitric oxide from food. Increasing the body's production of the chemical, the thinking goes, will reduce the risk of insulin resistance, a precursor of diabetes. That's just what happened when Swiss researchers fed a high-fat diet to mice that lacked part of a gene necessary to make nitric oxide (and were insulin resistant) and then gave them Zocor. The levels of nitric oxide increased significantly in the mice, improving their sensitivity to insulin and thus reducing their insulin resistance.

"One potential mechanism behind this effect," says Peter Vollenweider, M.D., the lead author of the study, "is that nitric oxide increases blood vessel dilation partly in response to insulin. This increased blood flow (particularly in muscles) probably plays a role in insulin sensitivity, as it increases delivery of insulin and glucose to target tissues, thereby

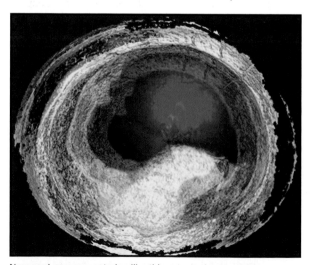

Narrowed coronary arteries like this one are heart attacks waiting to happen. Statins reduce heart attacks and heart disease deaths mainly by lowering levels of LDL cholesterol.

increasing the amount of glucose cells can take up." So if you're not making enough nitric oxide, your cells may not be able to use the insulin you make very well, resulting in insulin resistance, a major risk factor for diabetes.

The results of the study, conducted by Dr. Vollenweider and other researchers at the Institute of Cellular Biology and Morphology in Lausanne, were presented at the April 2003 American Physiological Society meeting.

Managing Multiple Sclerosis

Early studies on statins suggested that the drugs may be able to tone down an overactive immune system, leading hopeful researchers to conduct a plethora of studies on their effects on a variety of autoimmune diseases. In one study, published in the journal *Neurology* in October 2002, researchers discovered that statins appear to reprogram the immune cells that attack myelin, a protective sheath that covers many nerves in the brain and spinal cord and is damaged in multiple sclerosis (MS). Another study, conducted in mice and published in the November 2002 issue of the journal *Nature*, found that a week of treatment with Lipitor reversed or prevented relapses of MS and curbed brain inflammation, which is a hallmark of the disease.

> **One of the most intriguing findings of the year was the discovery that statins may actually prevent the development of diabetes in high-risk people.**

Scientists also think that statins may help organ transplant recipients, who typically take huge doses of immune-suppressing drugs to prevent their bodies from rejecting donor organs. In one recent study, researchers found that lung transplant patients who took statins at any point after their operations had a six-year survival rate of 91 percent, compared with a rate of 54 percent for those who didn't take the drugs.

Someday, then, instead of highly expensive immune-suppressing drugs that carry a multitude of side effects, transplant recipients may be able to pop a statin to protect not only their arteries but their new organs as well. ■

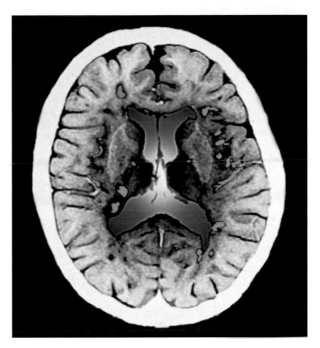

Statins could help reverse or prevent multiple sclerosis. One study found that the drugs reduced brain plaques caused by the disease (shown above in pink) by 40 percent.

what does it mean to you?

Researchers are discovering unexpected applications for the drugs called statins, typically prescribed to lower cholesterol. Someday they may be used to prevent or treat diseases such as Alzheimer's and other dementias, cancer, osteoporosis, and multiple sclerosis. Meanwhile, keep these tips in mind.

■ If you have diabetes, ask your doctor whether you should consider taking a statin drug to lower your risk of heart disease, even if your cholesterol levels are normal.

■ Don't start taking your spouse's statins. You need to talk to your doctor first about whether they're right for you. (After all, no drug is without risks.) Your doctor will consider your health history, your family's health history, and any risk factors for heart disease, including smoking, high blood pressure, low levels of "good" HDL cholesterol, and your age. Men 45 and over and women 55 and over are at increased risk.

■ Whether you have heart disease or diabetes, you can't rely on medication to resolve the disease for you. Diet and exercise will still play an important role.

Dig deep into the recesses of your memory and recall your high school biology lessons. Chances are, you'll remember at least a little about DNA, the strands of matter that carry the blueprint for life. But you probably won't recall much, if anything, about RNA, its humbler cousin. Back then, we were told that RNA amounted to little more than a chemical UPS man whose job was to carry directions from the DNA to another part of the cell, where it could be turned into proteins.

RNA BIOLOGY'S NEW SUPERSTAR

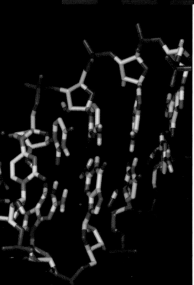

Molecules of small RNA like this one can be used to "turn off" individual genes.

My, how things change. In the past two years, RNA has become more popular than a prom queen with loose morals and a winning lottery ticket. In December 2002, *Science* magazine named recent discoveries about one type of RNA, called small RNA, the Breakthrough of the Year. Scientists involved in the research are being talked about as shoo-ins for a Nobel Prize, and more than 50,000 researchers around the world are now using a technique called RNA interference (RNAi) to figure out what the 30,000 or so genes mapped in the Human Genome Project actually do.

"To see this level of activity over just a two-year period has been awesome," says Gary Ruvkun, Ph.D., professor of genetics at Harvard Medical School and one of the leaders in the field. "In terms of research, there's no question that it's incredibly important."

What exactly is all the commotion about? In simple terms, small RNAs are short stretches of RNA that function as a kind of natural "off" switch for genes. If scientists can use them to turn off individual genes, they can better understand the role of those genes in the body. That's critical. But what's far more tantalizing is this: By using small RNA to turn off the genes responsible for certain diseases—such as HIV, hepatitis C, or a particular type of cancer—we may be able to cure them.

"There is essentially an almost limitless number of applications for this kind of technology," says Gregory Hannon, Ph.D., a professor at Cold Spring

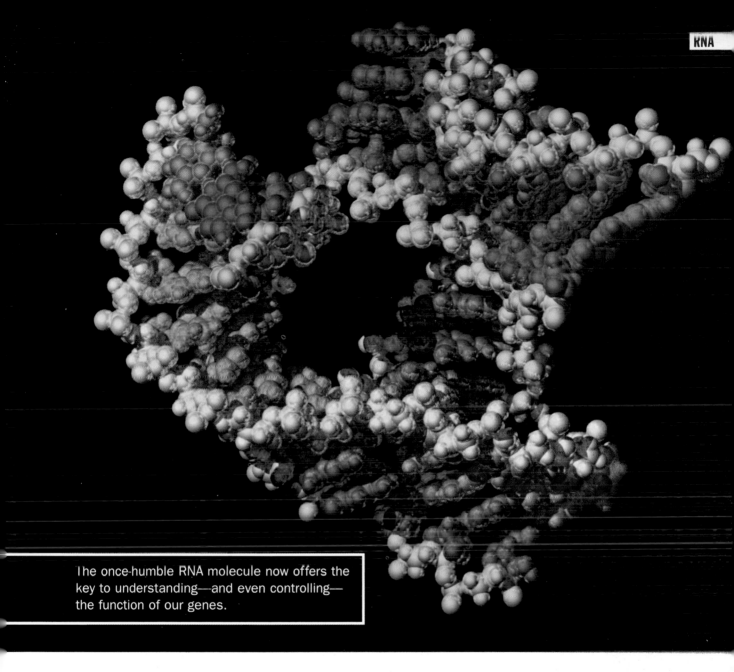

The once-humble RNA molecule now offers the key to understanding—and even controlling—the function of our genes.

Harbor Laboratory in New York, who was instrumental in the development of this scientific arena. "That's why people are so excited about it."

The ABCs of RNA

To appreciate RNA's recent rise to stardom, it helps to recall some more basic biology. We all have 23 pairs of chromosomes—one set from each parent. Each pair contains DNA, which holds the genetic instructions that dictate our eye color, height, and everything else about us. DNA is essentially a code for making proteins, the worker bees of cells.

Turning that code into proteins involves a type of RNA called messenger RNA, which makes a copy of the code and delivers it to cellular protein factories called ribosomes. Scientists have long searched for a way to interfere with this information hand-off in order to keep faulty, disease-causing genes from being translated into proteins.

Enter small RNA. It turns out that this RNA can ambush "complementary" bits of messenger RNA, interfering with them and thereby inhibiting a gene's function—hence the name *RNA interference*. Biologists think that in plants, and probably also in animals, RNAi is an organism's way of blocking bad DNA or viruses that threaten the genome.

What's so exciting about RNAi, says one of its pioneers, Andrew Fire, Ph.D., of the Carnegie

Institute of Washington in Baltimore, is that it's a totally natural cellular function that scientists can manipulate for their own purposes. Because it's natural, it could be easier to work with than the artificial methods that researchers had been trying.

The Case of the Purple Petunias

RNA's new role was discovered quite by accident back in 1989, when plant researcher Richard Jorgensen, Ph.D., tried to make purple petunias more purple by adding an extra copy of the purple pigment gene. But the flowers came out white, or purple streaked with white. Somehow, the extra gene had turned *off* the color-making genes. Dr. Jorgensen didn't know it at the time, but the gene he inserted into his flowers triggered the plant to make small RNA that interfered with the very process he was trying to enhance.

A few years later, Dr. Fire and Craig Mello, Ph.D., of the University of Massachusetts Medical School, along with several of their colleagues, injected double-stranded RNA into worms. (RNA is typically single-stranded, but sometimes it kinks up, putting complementary sequences of the "letters" that "spell" the RNA beside each other.) They found that the doule-stranded RNA dramatically inhibited the genes the scientists were targeting. Voilá! RNAi was born.

The only problem was that the double-stranded RNA didn't work in mammals, including humans. Other researchers trimmed the double-stranded RNA molecules, creating their own small RNA

This flower is streaked with white because small RNA interfered with the purple-making gene.

and enabling scientists to use RNAi in human and other mammalian cells. A patent on the use of RNAi as a technique was issued in January 2003, and it has since been widely licensed in the United States, Europe, and Japan to address a broad range of research questions.

By allowing scientists to turn off genes, RNAi may help them figure out what specific genes do. Until now, explains Dr. Fire, to determine the role of a gene, researchers had to breed "knockout" organisms—that is, organisms (usually mice) with that particular gene "knocked out," or disabled. The process took a year or more, and if the disabled gene was critical for development, the mouse would never grow properly. Also, once the animal was born, other genes couldn't be turned off.

Now, scientists are taking bits of RNA, modifying them to turn off specific genes, and setting them loose in cells. A paper published in the January 2003 issue of the journal *Nature* describes how Dr. Ruvkun and his colleagues, along with collaborators in the United Kingdom, used the RNAi technique to turn off almost all of a worm's genes, one at a time, to discover those linked to obesity. If you figure out the genes responsible for obesity in humans, goes the thinking, you could develop drugs to interfere with the actions of those genes. Even better, you could send a modified form of RNA into human cells to turn them off.

If you figure out the genes responsible for obesity in humans, goes the thinking, you could develop drugs to interfere with the actions of those genes.

A Future Cure for Cancer?

Researchers are already considering ways to use RNAi technology to treat diseases, many of which are caused when genes produce too much of the protein they're designed to make—a situation called gene overexpression. The beauty of RNAi, note researchers, is that it isn't an all-or-nothing approach. Instead of turning a gene completely off, RNA can act as a dimmer switch, reducing the gene's expression a little or a lot.

Researchers have used the technology to turn off just one copy of a disease-causing gene and leave the healthy gene alone. (Remember, everyone has two copies, one from Mom and one from Dad.) Such efforts have great potential in treating diseases such as Huntington's chorea and several forms of cancer.

Cold Spring Harbor Laboratory's Dr. Hannon and his colleagues used RNAi in mouse stem cells to manipulate the tumor suppressor gene p53, involved in suppressing the development of lymphoma (cancer of the lymph tissue). The scientists destroyed the

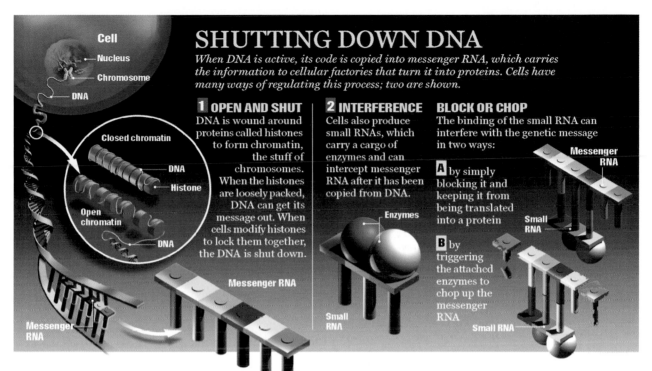

SHUTTING DOWN DNA

When DNA is active, its code is copied into messenger RNA, which carries the information to cellular factories that turn it into proteins. Cells have many ways of regulating this process; two are shown.

1 OPEN AND SHUT
DNA is wound around proteins called histones to form chromatin, the stuff of chromosomes. When the histones are loosely packed, DNA can get its message out. When cells modify histones to lock them together, the DNA is shut down.

2 INTERFERENCE
Cells also produce small RNAs, which carry a cargo of enzymes and can intercept messenger RNA after it has been copied from DNA.

BLOCK OR CHOP
The binding of the small RNA can interfere with the genetic message in two ways:

A by simply blocking it and keeping it from being translated into a protein

B by triggering the attached enzymes to chop up the messenger RNA

---

mice's own stem cells, then injected the mice with cells engineered to produce low, medium, or high levels of the proteins that p53 codes for. The mice reacted just as expected: Those that got "dimmed" versions of p53 developed a highly aggressive form of lymphoma, while those that got genes that were "turned up" showed a more benign form of the cancer. "This will let us examine in more detail the steps through which a tumor arises," says Dr. Hannon. "A better understanding of those steps could reveal ways to detect developing lesions and might lead to new methods to treat cancers at an early stage."

Don't look for clinical applications any time soon, though, cautions Dr. Ruvkun. "Medicine takes a long time," he says. "It's like turning around a giant aircraft carrier." He compares the RNA revolution to the molecular biology movement, which began more than 25 years ago but is just now resulting in clinical applications (such as the cancer drugs Herceptin and Gleevec).

As of late 2003, all RNAi experiments had been conducted in small animals or petri dishes. Human trials aren't expected to begin until at least 2006. One challenge will be finding a way to stabilize RNA in the lab, since it's fragile and breaks apart quickly in solution. Another problem, says Dr. Fire, will be figuring out how to get the relatively large RNA molecule into human cells and how to get it

into the *right* cells. "Delivering even small molecules to cells is a whole art form," he says. Pharmacologists are working on the technique.

Researchers are targeting their RNAi efforts to specific diseases, including:

- **HIV.** Several groups of researchers have coaxed human cells to produce double-stranded RNA that matches RNA sequences from the virus. The strands prevent infected cells from making HIV proteins.
- **Hepatitis C.** At Harvard, researchers reported that they had successfully cured the disease in mice by using injected small RNA.
- **RNA-linked chromosomal defects.** Scientists have found that Prader-Willi and Fragile X syndromes (chromosomal abnormalities that result in mental retardation) and chronic lymphocytic leukemia may be linked to RNA defects. The finding suggests that if researchers can figure out what goes wrong genetically and fix it early in a fetus's development, it may be possible to avoid the defects altogether.

Dr. Fire describes the mood among researchers in the field as "cautiously optimistic"—cautious because scientists have been burned once too often by grandiose predictions of where genetic biology would lead, and optimistic because, if RNAi lives up to its promise, they will have the power to control the very seed of life. ∎

FINGERING THE REAL ALZHEIMER'S CULPRIT

For nearly 100 years, medical researchers have been trying to unravel a mystery that German doctor Alois Alzheimer first described back in 1907. In the past year, they've made some huge strides—and their new understanding about the nature of the mind-robbing disease that bears the doctor's name may have brought truly effective treatments within reach for the first time. Just as exciting are advances in screening that may soon allow doctors to diagnose the disease much earlier, before any mental decline is even evident, and start treatment when it can help the most.

The origins of the Alzheimer's puzzle date to 1901, when a 51-year-old woman named Auguste D. was taken to a psychiatric hospital in Frankfurt, Germany, by family members who were alarmed by how disoriented and forgetful she had become. She was placed in the care of Dr. Alzheimer, who could do little but watch as her condition steadily worsened. She spent five years at the hospital, unable to remember her husband's name or to care for herself. After her death, Dr. Alzheimer examined her brain and found a "peculiar substance" in her cerebral cortex—thick clumps of fibers lodged between a marked paucity of brain cells.

Sister Nicolette Welter, born in 1907, is one of the nuns at the School Sisters of Notre Dame in Mankato, Minnesota, taking part in a study on Alzheimer's. New insights into the cause of the disease may lead to drugs to treat or even prevent it.

These are the defining anatomic features of Alzheimer's disease, and in the years since Auguste D.'s death, they've been seen in the brains of many thousands of Alzheimer's patients. Over the years, medical detectives around the world have worked to understand what causes them and what they have to do with the ravages of Alzheimer's. To pathologists peering through microscopes, these clumps, known as plaques, look like smoking guns in a crime scene littered with the corpses of brain cells. Clearly, the death of brain cells must be the problem and the unwelcome plaques the underlying cause. Or so went the prevailing wisdom.

Gunk in the Brain

"You see that gunk lying in the brain there between the neurons, and you think, 'That must be bad for your brain,' " says Eliezer Masliah, M.D., a neuro-

Eliezer Masliah, M.D., has studied the brain autopsies of many Alzheimer's patients. He is currently investigating how fragments of amyloid-beta protein in the brain may rob people of precious memory stores.

An Inside-Outside Job

"The real bad guys, the toxic guys," Dr. Masliah says, are now thought to be the sticky fragments of a protein called amyloid-beta (or A-beta) that are produced and secreted by brain cells. Over time, these tiny fragments join, forming the large clumps or plaques first seen by Dr. Alzheimer. But in the early stages of the disease, Dr. Masliah and others believe, they do damage by interfering with communication across the synapses, the tiny gaps between neurons that must be bridged for brain signals to be transmitted. Amyloid-beta does this, he suggests, from both inside and outside the neurons. "It's like a double whammy," he says.

Inside, Dr. Masliah believes, mini-clusters of A-beta molecules accumulate in the borders of the synaptic membranes and prevent the exchange of neurotransmitters, the brain chemicals that help signals cross the gap.

Outside the cell, says Lennart Mucke, M.D., director of the Gladstone Institute of Neurological Disease at the University of California-San Francisco, "small assemblies of these A-beta proteins float around like cruise missiles, disrupting the complex networks of neurons in which our memories are formed and stored." Dr. Mucke and other researchers are still not certain exactly

pathologist at the University of California-San Diego. "It looks pretty nasty. So for years, based on that imagery, people thought, 'That's the toxic agent. That's the bad thing in the brain.' "

A few years ago, however, Dr. Masliah and a colleague, Robert Terry, M.D., noticed that the number of plaques in the brains of autopsied patients had very little to do with how demented the people had been. Some patients whose memory impairment had been mild had extensive plaques, while some whose dementia had been severe had few. "There was really no correlation," Dr. Masliah says. Subsequent studies in mice supported these findings.

Over time, the lack of a direct correlation between plaques and dementia helped shift the prevailing wisdom about the cause of Alzheimer's disease. Today, mounting evidence suggests that a furtive loss of memory may actually begin long before plaques ever form—even, many experts now think, before brain cells start to perish. The "paradigm shift" in thinking about Alzheimer's disease—as Harvard associate professor of neurology David Teplow, Ph.D., called it in an article in the September 2002 issue of the *Journal of Neuroscience Research*—is that the infamous plaques may not be the real culprits at all.

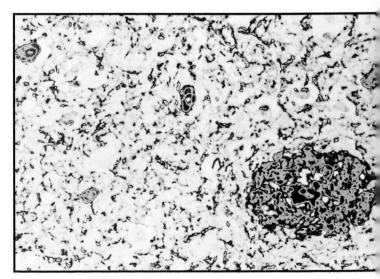

Made of amyloid-beta protein, brain plaques like the five above are the hallmark of Alzheimer's disease—but they may not be the actual cause.

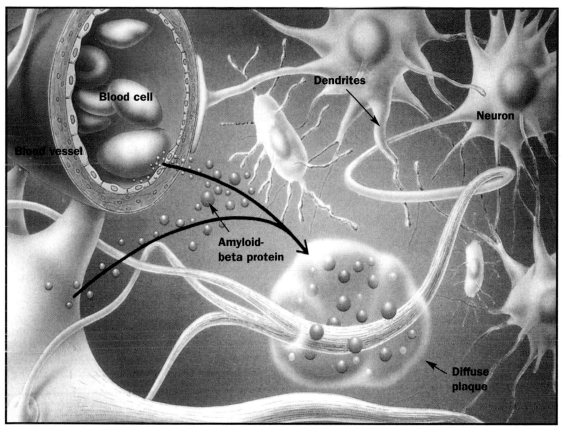

Amyloid-beta proteins are secreted by brain cells. They can also enter the brain from the bloodstream. Even before they form plaques, they appear to disrupt communication between nerve cells (neurons).

how these floating missiles attack, but they are excited by their belief that in as few as 5 to 10 years, new treatments may be able to prevent or even reverse the devastating effects of Alzheimer's. Drug companies, eyeing a huge potential market, are pouring billions of dollars into the effort to develop effective treatments.

The treatments could take different forms. One approach is to try to prevent the production of A-beta by using a drug, similar to those used against HIV, to inhibit the enzymes that help make the protein. Another strategy, says Dr. Mucke, is to take advantage of the body's immune system by triggering antibodies and clean-up cells to devour and degrade the toxic proteins that exist in the brain.

The Big Tease

That was the theory behind what amounts to the most exciting tease to date in the brief history of Alzheimer's treatments. In 1999, researchers from Elan Pharmaceuticals announced successful tests of a vaccine that greatly reduced the creation of

amyloid plaques in mice that had been genetically altered to produce human A-beta. Even more amazing was the fact that the mice, which had developed a form of Alzheimer's, showed rapid improvement in memory and learning ability.

With great excitement, Elan researchers tried the vaccine on 300 people with Alzheimer's. With even greater disappointment, they had to call off the study in early 2002 after 15 of the patients developed inflammation in their brains. Despite the setback, Dr. Mucke says, the experiment wasn't a complete failure. It provided additional evidence that A-beta is indeed the primary agent of brain damage in Alzheimer's. And, if the vaccine can be reengineered, it still may prove to be a useful treatment. (For more news on vaccine-like strategies, see "New Approach to an Alzheimer's Vaccine" on page 87.)

Another promising treatment also passed the mouse test recently. In a study published in a March 2003 issue of the *Journal of Neuroscience,* a group of researchers, including Dr. Masliah and investigators from the Salk Institute for Biological Studies in San

A PUNCTURED HEART
A DARING REPAIR

> Interventional cardiologists are a very aggressive bunch. When a potential treatment like stem cells comes up, we don't sit around in an ivory tower wondering how we're going to approach it. We just do it.

Emerson Perin, M.D., Ph.D.

In the Michigan town of Almont, Dimitri Bonnville spent the summer of 2003 doing the things that teenagers do in the summer: hanging out with friends, going to parties, playing a little basketball, and enjoying being young. There's nothing special about that—except that a few months earlier, the boy had been shot through the heart by a nail gun on a construction site, leading to a massive heart attack that destroyed a third of his cardiac cells. His heart was left pumping so weakly that surviving to adulthood was an iffy proposition.

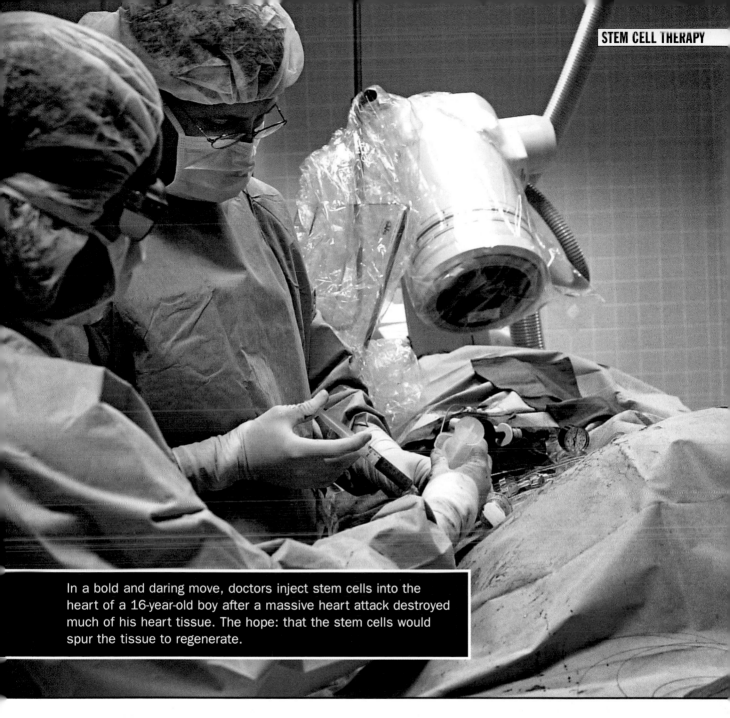

In a bold and daring move, doctors inject stem cells into the heart of a 16-year-old boy after a massive heart attack destroyed much of his heart tissue. The hope: that the stem cells would spur the tissue to regenerate.

Convinced that the condition of the 16-year-old's heart would only grow worse, surgeons at Beaumont Hospital in Royal Oak, Michigan, made the bold decision to use an experimental procedure. They took millions of stem cells—immature cells that can transform themselves into almost any kind of tissue cell—from Bonnville's blood and injected them into his heart to stimulate its repair. "This treatment was Bonnville's only option, aside from a heart transplant," Beaumont's chief of cardiology, William O'Neill, M.D., told the press afterward.

Four months later, it looked like a good call, since Bonnville's heart function had improved enough for him to hit the basketball courts. More specifically, in that time, his "ejection fraction"—the percentage of blood pumped out of the left ventricle, the heart's main pumping chamber—had shot up to 40 percent from a low of 25 percent after his heart attack. Although still short of a healthy person's ejection fraction of 50 percent or higher, the boost was far greater than would be expected without the stem cell treatment, according to Bonnville's doctors.

Dimitri Bonnville at a March 5, 2003 press conference announcing the United States' first stem cell transplant to treat a heart attack.

The success of that operation moved heart repair by stem cell therapy out of the "future possibility" category and into the "now."

Adult Stem Cells Step In

The stunning success of Bonnville's treatment represents the crest of a two-year wave of progress in stem cell heart repair. In the United States and Europe, a flurry of formal studies have begun to test the ability of stem cells to get failing cardiac function back up to speed, or at least closer to it. In 2003, reports of successful stem cell procedures that resulted in measurable boosts in blood-pumping power proliferated across the globe, notably in Germany, France, Brazil, and the United States.

"Stem cells are going to have an impact on treating heart disease," says James T. Willerson, M.D., president of the University of Texas Health Science Center at Houston and medical director and chief of

cardiology at the Texas Heart Institute. Such optimism is now the norm in cardiology circles.

That's quite a turnaround from just a few years ago, when the public imagination was first stirred by the idea that days-old human embryos contain "master cells" that are capable of becoming any kind of cell. Scientists were already able to harvest these stem cells from lab-created embryos left over from in vitro fertilization (the "test-tube baby" procedure that joins sperm and egg in a petri dish). The goal was to treat certain diseases by manipulating these all-purpose cells to re-create destroyed cells or tissue—to grow new nerve cells for people with Alzheimer's or Parkinson's disease, for example, or develop new kidney tissue for people with kidney disease.

Using stem cells to repair damaged heart tissue seemed a distant dream at the time. For one thing, it wasn't known for sure whether the heart was capable of regenerating itself under any circumstances. Then, in 2001, President Bush severely restricted stem cell research in the United States, responding to a faction of the anti-abortion movement that considers the medical use of any part of an embryo—even "spare" lab embryos that would never see the inside of a uterus—to be a destruction of human life. One avenue left open for the development of stem cell therapy was adult stem cells, which are similarly adaptive, early-stage cells that are entirely noncontroversial. There was little indication, however, that any of these adult stem cells were capable of turning into heart cells.

Diligent lab work and animal research paid off with the discovery that the heart can indeed regenerate itself—with the help of stem cells. Furthermore, it turned out that the body's adult stem cells, especially those from bone marrow and muscle tissue, can get the job done after all, without ethical issues, research restrictions, or any danger of rejection of "foreign" cells by the immune system.

"I'm not too worried about the embryonic stem cells," says Emerson Perin, M.D., Ph.D., a cardiologist at the Texas Heart Institute who has personally injected adult stem cells into human hearts. "Embryonic stem cells might be more potent, but these adult cells are pretty good. I've never been let down by them."

Something else helped turn stem cell therapy into a reality: pure necessity. Each year, the United States sees 550,000 new cases of heart failure, a deadly condition marked by the inability of the heart to pump sufficient blood. Even if you're lucky enough to survive a heart attack, the damaged heart tissue you're left with makes you a prime candidate for advancing heart failure—precisely the reason that Bonnville's doctors resorted to stem cell therapy. Unfortunately, the best existing treatment for end-stage (that is, near-death) heart failure patients is a hard-to-get heart transplant. The newer "assist devices" that help the left ventricle with its pumping duties are "hardly a panacea," in Dr. Willerson's words. "Heart failure is going to be a larger problem, not smaller, until we find a way to arrest it at an early stage," he says. "Stem cells may be the way to do it."

Revival in Rio

While Bonnville's transplanted cells were just beginning to multiply in his heart, another amazing stem cell story was playing out at the other end of the Western Hemisphere. Cardiologists from the Texas Heart Institute, including Dr. Willerson and Dr. Perin, had tested stem cell transplantation on 14 people at the Hospital Procardiaco in Rio de Janeiro, Brazil. All had had heart attacks and suffered from heart failure so severe that stem cell therapy wasn't just a clinical experiment to them; it was their last chance.

It was a chance well taken. "I saw what bad shape the patients were in before the procedure, and it's unbelievable to see how well they're doing now," Dr. Perin says. "I mean, they were bedridden and couldn't even walk outside the house, and now these guys are jumping around, going in the water, and climbing stairs." Here's how that happened.

On the day of the procedure, surgeons sucked out a bit of bone marrow with a needle and sent it to a

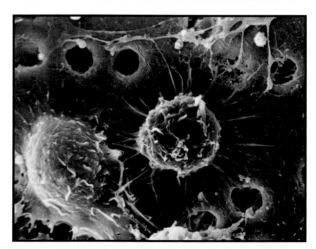

Most experts agree that certain stem cells can turn into heart muscle cells, although it's not known whether that's exactly what happened in Dimitri Bonnville's case.

A MASTER GENE FOR MASTER CELLS

Picture a not-too-distant future with an endless supply of powerful, heart-healing embryonic stem cells—that don't come from embryos. Imagine that instead of harvesting these cells from embryos, scientists reprogram normal body cells in the laboratory to function the way embryonic stem cells do. Then they direct them to create precisely the kind of tissue your heart needs in order to be healthy.

Such a medical marvel became possible in May 2003, when Scottish and Japanese researchers announced the discovery of the gene that gives stem cells their extraordinary power to transform themselves into any kind of cell in the body. Now that this master gene has been identified (it was christened Nanog, after a mythical land of eternal youth in Celtic folklore), the next step is to learn the conditions that activate and deactivate it. Once researchers are armed with that knowledge, they will be within reach of a Holy Grail of medical science—the ability to duplicate stem cells' regenerative powers to cure disease. ■

nearby lab to filter out what's not needed (red blood cells and fat cells, among others) and keep the mononuclear cells, a class of bone marrow cells that includes the stem cells. Within a few hours, the stem cells were ready. "We only used the fresh stuff," Dr. Perin says. "We didn't culture them up or grow a colony or even isolate specific types of mononuclear cells. All we did was filter and purify." (Bonnville's doctors, some 8,000 miles to the north, varied this technique by using a drug to coax the desired cells out of the bone marrow and into the bloodstream, from which they were extracted.)

Before they delivered the cells, the surgeons threaded a special 3-D camera through a catheter (a long, narrow tube) up an artery to the heart. This let them identify which areas of the heart muscle were healthy, damaged, or dead. Using the same catheter, Dr. Perin then aimed the stem cell solution at the damaged (but not dead) tissue and injected 0.2 cc. That's no more than a drop or two, but it contained about 2 million stem cells. Each Rio subject got 15 injections, for a total of 30 million stem cells.

According to results published in the May 2003 issue of the journal *Circulation*, in just two months,

Dr. Yong-Jian Geng of the Texas Heart Institute did research on stem cells that helped lead to a new treatment for heart failure.

the subjects' ejection fraction improved a whopping 31 percent on average. Their treadmill test scores improved, their incidence of angina (chest pain) decreased, and their blood flow improved. The gains held steady for the next two months. Dr. Willerson was confident that there would be no regression at the one-year mark, and perhaps there'd be even more improvement. Clearly, stem cells had helped these ailing hearts.

New Blood to Power the Heart

Bonnville's surgeons and the Brazilian study cardiologists doubt that the transplanted stem cells from the blood or bone marrow are actually turning into heart cells. "The reason we're putting those stem cells in there is to stimulate the growth of new blood vessels in the heart itself, not necessarily to create new heart muscle tissue," Dr. Perin says. "That's why we insist on planting a colony of stem cells on what we call hibernating myocardium—heart muscle that's

damaged but not dead. Get that hibernating heart muscle tissue a better blood supply, and it will wake up and start working again. That's what these bone marrow cells have done."

The new blood vessels may not even be formed by the implanted stem cells and their offspring. It's just as likely that the mere presence of the cells stimulates processes in the heart that recruit other circulating cells to become blood vessel cells.

Other researchers, though, are pursuing a version of stem cell heart therapy that does seek to turn stem cells into heart cells and grow new heart muscle tissue. Rather than filtering out adult stem cells from bone marrow, these scientists are culling adult stem cells out of skeletal muscle—the kind of muscle we tone up at health clubs. Unlike embryonic stem cells or even bone marrow stem cells, these young skeletal muscle cells, called myoblasts, are already committed to being a certain kind of cell—a muscle cell. But (and here's the breakthrough) they are not necessarily committed to being skeletal muscle cells. Recent research has indicated that myoblasts can make themselves right at home as a different kind of muscle—heart muscle.

Sure enough, German tests with humans in 2001 showed that myoblasts injected directly into the heart during open-heart surgery improved the pumping power of the patients' weakened hearts. In 2002, researchers from the Arizona Heart Institute transplanted myoblasts into more than a dozen failing hearts and also got the desired boosts in pumping power. Also, imaging equipment picked up indications of tissue regeneration—that is, new live tissue was seen in the area of dead tissue. The hearts were apparently regrowing.

Myoblast transplanters go about their business a little differently than the bone marrow researchers. They take a pinch of calf or thigh muscle, tease out the myoblasts, and grow them in a culture for a few days to get enough. Once they're ready, the myoblasts are shot into and around dead heart

PRE-INJECTION   POST-INJECTION

A PET scan shows scar tissue becoming living tissue after a stem cell transplant.

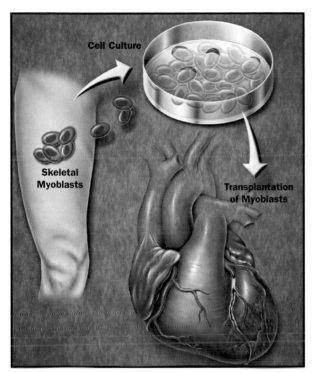

Cell Culture

Skeletal
Myoblasts

Transplantation
of Myoblasts

Skeletal muscle stem cells (myoblasts) are being used to revitalize damaged heart tissue to save patients with severe heart failure.

tissue, the "scar" tissue formed after a heart attack. The idea is to replace that tissue with new, live, honest-to-goodness heart muscle. And they've shown they can do it.

A Heartening Future

Bonnville's case, the Rio results, and several successful myoblast treatments tell us that stem cell therapy already exists as a viable option for people with heart failure. What doesn't exist is approval by the FDA, without which stem cell therapy can't be performed in the United States, except in clinical studies. (The Beaumont Hospital team that operated on Bonnville actually got a scolding from the FDA for using an unapproved procedure.)

To move toward that approval, the Texas Heart Institute started a second study in 2003 in Rio de Janeiro, where they have a working relationship with the Procardiaco Hospital. This time, they've doubled the number of heart patients receiving stem cells and fine-tuned their bone marrow cell selection by cherry-picking the specific kinds of mononuclear cells that they suspect will do the most for heart repair.

The results from the second Rio study should be announced sometime in 2004, followed closely by results from a similar study by the same team in

Houston. And the Texas Heart Institute is already drawing up plans for a much bigger study that will involve hundreds of patients in various medical centers across the United States. This would be a Phase III study—usually the last step before FDA approval. With many other institutions gearing up for (or already performing) similar studies, it's conceivable that the FDA could approve some form of cell therapy for heart repair as early as 2005.

Dimitri Bonnville and his fellow patients in Brazil have brought real hope for heart patients around the world. As Dr. Perin points out, adult stem cells are a remarkable source of renewable life that lies within us. Our newfound ability to tap that force to save failing hearts can't help but stimulate optimism about conquering heart disease. It even inspired Dr. Perin to slip this jaunty line into the normally solemn medical journal *Circulation*: "The future's so bright we've got to wear shades." ■

what does it mean to you?

Stem cells' unique ability to transform themselves into any kind of body tissue will deliver powerful treatments for failing hearts. If the current successes in heart repair via stem cell therapy are repeated in ongoing studies, heart patients can start taking advantage of stem cells in a number of ways.

■ Stem cells transplanted from your bone marrow can stimulate the formation of new blood vessels inside the heart, reactivating damaged cardiac tissue to improve your heart's pumping capacity.

■ Adult stem cells culled from your own thigh or calf muscles can turn into heart cells and grow into new heart muscle, replacing dead scar tissue caused by a heart attack. This also boosts your heart's pumping power and reverses heart failure.

■ Cardiologists expect to soon develop a technique for sending selected genes inside stem cells to failing hearts. This combination of cell therapy and gene therapy will build blood vessels or new tissue in the heart. It also will either replace damaged genes or deliver new genes that are specially altered to improve heart function.

■ In the more distant future, scientists may be able to manipulate stem cells in the lab to grow into an exact replica of your own heart (as well as other organs). If you need a heart transplant, there will be no need to wait for a compatible donor—there's a perfect heart waiting for you.

Doctors protested the cost of malpractice insurance at a rally in Abington, Pennsylvania, in April.

The White Coats Borrow a Blue-Collar Tactic: Walk Out

New Year's Day 2003 brought an unusual sight to the evening news as surgeons at four West Virginia hospitals walked off the job. Over the ensuing two months, New Jersey physicians also left their posts in protest, and well-publicized "white coat rallies" took place in Florida, Missouri, and Mississippi. At issue was the skyrocketing cost of malpractice insurance. Rates shot up more than 50 percent on average in 2002 alone.

Doctors need malpractice insurance for the same reason you need liability coverage for your car. As careful as you try to be, accidents can happen. But while you may grudgingly accept paying a bumped-up premium after a fender-bender, doctors have been getting hit with drastic premium hikes whether they've been involved in malpractice cases or not.

The American Medical Association (AMA) never endorsed the walkouts (which were temporary and didn't interrupt emergency services), but it did voice alarm about the malpractice insurance situation. What's at risk, the AMA contends, isn't so much the financial well-being of individual doctors as the availability of adequate medical care in at least 12 "crisis" states. Fear of malpractice suits has already led some surgeons to abandon higher-risk proce-dures, including delivering babies. Now, many are packing up their stethoscopes and retractors and moving out of high-premium specialties. The number of obstetricians and neurosurgeons practicing in New Jersey (a crisis state) shrank by an estimated 25 percent in 2002.

The insurance companies say they need to raise their rates because they're paying out much more money these days to malpractice victims who take their cases to court. In their view, the real culprits are greedy trial lawyers who are too quick to sue at the drop of a surgical clamp and are too successful at winning excessive monetary awards for their clients. (The lawyers get to keep a sizable chunk of the awards, often 40 percent.)

The medical profession agrees. With damage awards of a million dollars or more becoming increasingly common (there were 50 percent more of them in 2000 than in 1996), doctors are demanding a legal limit on how much a malpractice victim can get for "pain and suffering" damages. That's the only way, they insist, to stabilize insurance rates and put an end to the crisis.

Not everyone supports that strategy, however. Patient advocates and consumer groups maintain that medical malpractice awards have been remarkably steady over the past 30 years when measured against inflation. They contend that the real reason insurance companies are hiking rates so sharply is to make up for profits lost to a sagging economy and their own poor investments. Instead of penalizing the victims of malpractice, they ask, why not take more aggressive steps to reduce medical errors in the first place?

At press time, Congress was working on a solution to the malpractice insurance crisis. In March 2003, the House of Representatives gave doctors (and President Bush) exactly what they wanted by approving legislation that puts a $250,000 limit on malpractice compensation awards arising from lawsuits. Victims of medical errors would still be able to collect more than that amount to offset medical bills and make up for lost income, but compensation for the damage itself—such as blindness or unnecessary mastectomies—would be capped at $250,000 unless individual states pass higher limits. ∎

Britain Launches Huge Genetic Census

Genetic information on thousands of people will be stored as part of U.K. Biobank.

One-shot gene therapy to cure Alzheimer's and cancer. A DNA-based early warning system to head off heart disease. Personalized medicine that works in cooperation with your genetic traits. When are ordinary people going to reap these and other health benefits promised by publication of the rough draft of the human genome in 2001? A half-million Britons are volunteering to make certain that it happens sooner rather than later.

The completion of the human genome—a blueprint of the vast genetic information that creates a human being—was a stunning achievement. But the human body is not a blueprint. Genetically speaking, it's a messy affair complicated by outside influences, lifestyle choices, genetic differences among individuals, and genes that don't follow the plan. For us to reap the genome's full practical benefits, researchers need to see how all of these factors interact and play out over time. And they need to see it in lots of different people.

That's what British officials had in mind when, in 2003, they launched a staggeringly ambitious research project that will follow for decades—at the most intimate, molecular level—the health of 500,000 middle-aged Britons. The mega-project, dubbed U.K. Biobank, is a good, old-fashioned "prospective" study, the kind that observes a group of people over time to look for correlations between what they do (or what's done to them) and how healthy they are. What gives this one a cutting edge, though, is that the precise genetic makeup of each of the subjects will be known. Not only will environmental influences such as smoking, medication, exercise, diet, and stress be tracked, but every individual gene variation or other personal genetic trait will be collected, evaluated, and stored.

Blood samples given by Biobank volunteers may eventually reveal how individual gene variations contribute to certain diseases.

Other "genetic censuses" are planned or under way around the world—most notably in Iceland and at the Mayo Clinic in Minnesota—but none match the scope of U.K. Biobank or focus as broadly on both nature (genetics) and nurture (environment and lifestyle). The final 500,000 study subjects will be culled from an original volunteer pool of more than a million Britons ages 45 to 69 who started signing up early in 2003. People in this age range were chosen because they're the ones most likely to get sick in the next 10 to 20 years. The participants will give blood samples to reveal their DNA, the molecular structure that contains all of the genetic information. They'll also answer questions about everything from what they normally eat and drink to how much they earn. Then they'll go about their lives as anyone else would, except that all of their ensuing health records—doctor's visits, diagnoses, medications, and such—will be entered into the Biobank database.

This means that researchers in the near future will have access to an enormous databank that will help them finally answer vexing questions about the origin of disease. What combinations of gene variations predispose us to heart disease or cancer? How exactly do those variations team with environmental and lifestyle factors to cause disease, and how can those elements be manipulated to prevent or cure it? These are big questions that require study on the huge scale envisioned by U.K. Biobank.

How will it all pay off for you once U.K. Biobank has gathered enough information to be useful—sometime around the year 2014? Here's one simplified scenario: By then, it should be more practical and economical, if not yet routine, for plain folks to have their personal genomes read. If so, your doctor may be able to match your particular gene variations with study results made possible by U.K. Biobank. If 80 percent of Biobank volunteers with your variations developed heart disease over the course of the study, that's a strong indication that aggressive preventive treatment is a good idea for you. If almost all of the remaining 20 percent practiced yoga every day...well, you always wanted to give yoga a try, didn't you?

Personal genetic information is a double-edged sword. In the hands of your doctor, it's a blessing, but you probably don't want your insurance provider or employer to have it. Such privacy concerns have surrounded U.K. Biobank from the beginning, but project organizers say they have it covered, at least for the volunteers in their study. Unlike similar projects, U.K. Biobank is a public sector endeavor, operated by the government's department of health and two grant-making charities—the Medical Research Council and the Wellcome Trust. By law, it must operate only for the public benefit. An oversight body will make sure that access to the data is limited to scientists and medical researchers and that even they won't know the names of the subjects. ■

Live Tissue, Hot Off the Presses

Desktop computer printers are now capable of turning out products that are far more impressive than plain old paper with letters on it. They can print glossy photos, round labels for compact disks, and even usable postage stamps. But those capabilities aren't nearly as impressive as what some South Carolina scientists are doing with their printers. They're printing three-dimensional, living animal tissue.

A report published in the April 2003 issue of the journal *Trends in Biotechnology* details how a modified ink-jet printer—similar to the kind that may be hooked up to your personal computer—can produce tubes made of hamster ovary cells. Thomas Boland, Ph.D., assistant professor of bioengineering at Clemson University and one of the paper's coauthors, says that he and his fellow researchers are the first to print living cells in this way, although other scientists have printed more basic substances, such as proteins and DNA. Here's a simplified explanation of how the process works.

The researchers clean out an ink-jet cartridge and fill it with the living cells. Another clean cartridge is filled with a liquid that turns into a gel when it's sprayed onto a surface. Scientists can't just print cells onto any surface and expect them to stay in place, Dr. Boland explains, so they use the gel as a sort of scaffolding to hold the cells together in a particular shape.

Using special software on the computer that's connected to the printer, they print a thin layer of the gel onto a glass or plastic slide, then print a ring of cells on top of the gel. Then they repeat the process, printing another layer of gel and another ring of cells, and so on. Eventually, they have many

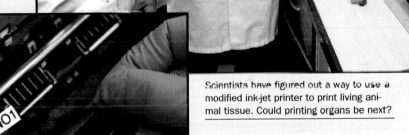

Scientists have figured out a way to use a modified ink-jet printer to print living animal tissue. Could printing organs be next?

layers of stacked rings in the shape of a tube, which is embedded in the gel.

The printers they use have been specially modified to work in three dimensions. The cartridge moves back and forth across a surface like a normal cartridge, but it also moves up and away from the surface as the printed object grows taller.

Once the stack of rings is printed, the researchers pop it into an incubator for up to 72 hours. The incubator feeds the cells the nutrients they need to stay alive, such as protein and sugar. The rings fuse, and the researchers then wash away the supporting gel, leaving a tiny tube of living cells. Currently, the cells can be kept alive for several weeks, Dr. Boland says.

The scientists have been working on this process for two years. "While we've made good progress, we're still at the beginning of this research," Dr. Boland says. His next step is to print out a mouse blood vessel, which is more complicated since it requires two types of cells.

This technology could someday be a boon to pharmaceutical companies, which could print out large amounts of complex tissues to use while testing new drugs. Even further down the road—at least 10 years, Dr. Boland estimates—doctors could use printers to turn out complete new organs for people in need of transplants. ■

Snack Foods in Trans-ition

An artery-clogging ingredient that has long been lurking in many of our foods was dragged into the spotlight in 2003. In July, the FDA ordered food makers to begin listing the amount of trans fatty acids—also known as trans fats—that foods contain. Manufacturers have until 2006 to incorporate this information into the Nutrition Facts box that lists the nutrition content of packaged foods on their labels, though some will do so sooner. It will appear below the listing for saturated fat.

Trans fats most often work their way into our diets through snack foods, such as crackers, chips, and French fries, and store-bought baked goods, such as doughnuts, cookies, pies, and frozen waffles. Vegetable shortening and some margarine (especially stick margarine) also contain trans fats. The stuff results from a process called hydrogenation, in which manufacturers add hydrogen to vegetable oil used in foods. This solidifies the oil, making it more resistant to spoiling, and contributes to the food's texture. Until the FDA ruling, the only way to know that trans fats were present in a food was to look for a phrase such as "partially hydrogenated vegetable oil" in the ingredient list.

Trans fats were once thought to be better for your health than artery-clogging saturated fats. In fact, they may be even worse. They raise levels of "bad" cholesterol (LDL) in your blood without giving a similar lift to "good" cholesterol (HDL). LDL is the chief culprit in the formation of dangerous plaques inside your artery walls that cause heart attacks and strokes. HDL, on the other hand, is believed to protect against cardiovascular disease by preventing plaque from accumulating.

The new nutrition labels will show how many grams of trans fats a food contains, but they won't put that into a context of what quantity of trans fats you can have each day. Therefore, it may be hard for the average consumer to tell if a product contains a little or a lot. According to the FDA, research hasn't determined a Daily Value, or a healthy limit, for trans fats—but many nutritionists believe there is no "safe" amount.

Trans fats were once thought to be better for your health than artery-clogging saturated fats. In fact, they may be even worse.

The consumer group Center for Science in the Public Interest had urged the FDA to use the existing Daily Value for saturated fat—20 grams per day—as the new combined Daily Value for saturated fat plus trans fat. Other experts recommend keeping combined levels of saturated fat and trans fat to 10 percent or less of total daily calories—which works out to 20 grams for someone who eats 2,000 calories a day. According to *Consumer Reports*, a Dunkin' Donuts glazed doughnut contains 4 grams of trans fat; a serving of Nabisco Chips Ahoy! cookies, 1.5 grams; and chocolate Jell-O Pudding Snacks, 1.5 grams.

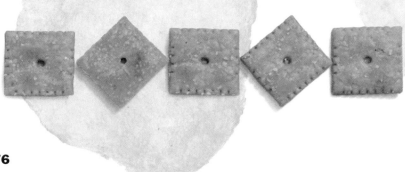

Nutrition Facts

Serving Size 1 cup (228g)
Servings Per Container 2

Amount Per Serving

Calories 260	Calories from Fat 120

	% Daily Value*
Total Fat 13g	**20%**
Saturated Fat 5g	**25%**
Trans Fat 2g	
Cholesterol 30mg	**10%**
Sodium 660mg	**28%**
Total Carbohydrate 31g	**10%**
Dietary Fiber 0g	**0%**
Sugars 5g	
Protein 5g	

Vitamin A 4%	•	Vitamin C 2%
Calcium 15%	•	Iron 4%

*Percent Daily Values are based on a 2,000 calorie diet. Your Daily Values may be higher or lower depending on your calorie needs:

	Calories:	2,000	2,500
Total Fat	Less than	65g	80g
Sat Fat	Less than	20g	25g
Cholesterol	Less than	300mg	300mg
Sodium	Less than	2,400mg	2,400mg
Total Carbohydrate		300g	375g
Dietary Fiber		25g	30g

Calories per gram:
Fat 9 • Carbo... ...otein 4

Trans fats were already in the news well before the FDA ruling. In September 2002, McDonald's announced that it would reduce the amount of trans fats in its French fries. The company later put that change on hold, citing product quality issues. In May 2003, a California lawyer sued Kraft, the maker of Oreos, over trans fats in the cookies. He reportedly dropped the lawsuit upon learning that Kraft was exploring ways to reduce trans fats in the product. Frito-Lay has removed partially hydrogenated oils from its Doritos, Tostitos, and Cheetos snacks and started using corn oil instead. Company nutritionists had been following trans fat research since 1992 and decided to remove the fat once they became convinced that the science was strong enough to merit the change and the manufacturing technology became available.

Keep in mind that even foods that are low in trans fats may still be high in calories and other types of fat. ■

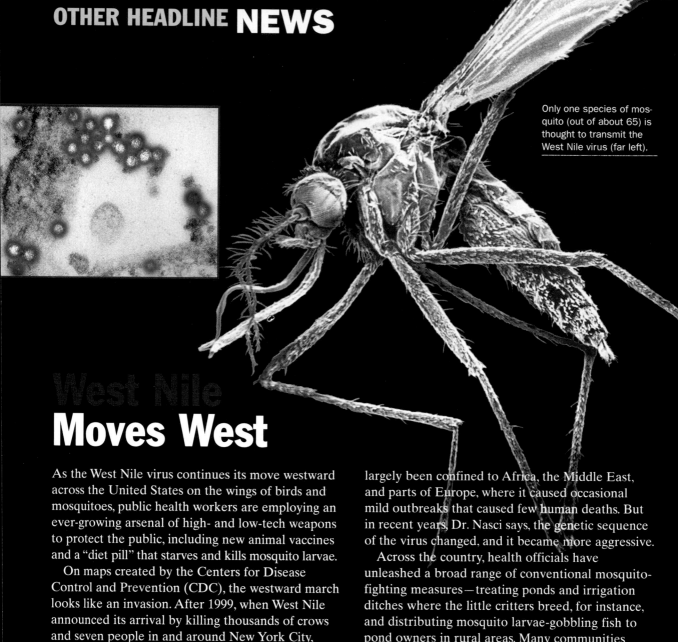

Only one species of mosquito (out of about 65) is thought to transmit the West Nile virus (far left).

West Nile
Moves West

As the West Nile virus continues its move westward across the United States on the wings of birds and mosquitoes, public health workers are employing an ever-growing arsenal of high- and low-tech weapons to protect the public, including new animal vaccines and a "diet pill" that starves and kills mosquito larvae.

On maps created by the Centers for Disease Control and Prevention (CDC), the westward march looks like an invasion. After 1999, when West Nile announced its arrival by killing thousands of crows and seven people in and around New York City, only a few red diamonds appeared on the map. By the end of 2002—a year when the virus exploded—almost the entire country was colored in; more than 4,000 Americans had been infected, and 284 had died. In October of 2003, the death toll for the year was at 115 and climbing.

"The virus seemed to spread very, very quickly—faster than most of us expected," says Roger Nasci, Ph.D., a research entomologist with the CDC. West Nile spreads when mosquitoes pick up the virus by biting infected birds, then transmit it with another bite to birds, people, or animals. First detected in the West Nile district of northern Uganda in 1937, it had

largely been confined to Africa, the Middle East, and parts of Europe, where it caused occasional mild outbreaks that caused few human deaths. But in recent years, Dr. Nasci says, the genetic sequence of the virus changed, and it became more aggressive.

Across the country, health officials have unleashed a broad range of conventional mosquito-fighting measures—treating ponds and irrigation ditches where the little critters breed, for instance, and distributing mosquito larvae-gobbling fish to pond owners in rural areas. Many communities have posted "sentinel chickens"—birds that aren't killed by West Nile but develop antibodies when infected, thus warning of the virus's spread. Over the past couple of years, Pennsylvania officials have merged satellite climate data (to identify areas where mosquitos will flourish) with virus infection reports to decide how to focus the efforts of mosquito control staff.

But some new tactics may soon come to the rescue as well. Researchers at the University of Florida have discovered a protein that is produced in the ovaries of female mosquitoes. When eaten by mosquito larva, the protein prevents them from digesting food. "It's a perfect diet pill," says its discoverer, biochemist Dov Borovsky, Ph.D. "They eat and eat and don't digest. After a few days, they starve to death." Dr. Borovsky found a way to genetically insert the protein into yeast, which mosquito larvae love to eat. The product is awaiting approval by the Environmental Protection Agency.

New vaccines may protect some of the country's hard-hit animal population. To the shock of wildlife experts, the virus has killed tens of thousands of crows, bluejays, and other birds, and by early 2003 it had infected some 14,000 horses and a host of other animals, from alligators to emus, rabbits to reindeer.

Horse owners are being urged to inoculate their steeds with a new equine vaccine, approved by the U.S. Department of Agriculture in February 2003. In tests, it prevented infection in 95 percent of horses exposed to the virus. It is also being used by some zoos to protect their exotic birds.

Another experimental vaccine, made from DNA taken from the virus, reduced West Nile deaths by 60 percent in the American crow, a species that has been devastated by the virus. Mice and horses injected with the vaccine "were completely protected from West Nile virus," says Jeff Chang, Ph.D., the CDC microbiologist who developed it. The DNA vaccine is not yet approved but is being used on an

The Spread of West Nile Virus

The mosquito-spread West Nile virus made an amazingly fast march across the United States. The first case was reported in 1999 in New York state. By 2002, the virus had sickened more than 4,000 and killed 284 people. It continued to spread westward in 2003.

Total human cases

Year	Cases
1999	62
2000	21
2001	66
2002	4,071

Months cases reported

1999	J	F	M	A	M	J	J	A	S	O	N	D
2000	J	F	M	A	M	J	J	A	S	O	N	D
2001	J	F	M	A	M	J	J	A	S	O	N	D
2002	J	F	M	A	M	J	J	A	S	O	N	D

■ Counties with human cases
□ States with no human cases

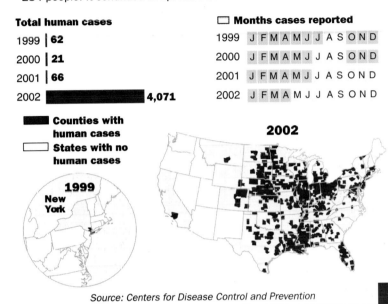

1999
New York

2002

Source: Centers for Disease Control and Prevention

emergency basis in an attempt to protect the last 200 California condors. Human vaccines are also under development but they are several years away from being approved for public use.

A natural end? In the long run, West Nile virus may finally be controlled by a process of natural decline. Most female mosquitoes bite only twice, when they seek the blood meals they need to lay eggs. (Males don't bite at all.) In order to transmit the virus, both of the mosquito's two bites have to be into the flesh of a host that isn't immune. If the person, bird, or animal that it bites on either occasion has immunity to West Nile, the chain of transmission will be broken.

"What will ultimately help control this virus is that more birds will become infected but survive, and they'll become immune in the process," says Andrew Spielman, Sc.D., an entomologist at Harvard University and author of *Mosquito: The Story of Man's Deadliest Foe.*

Meanwhile, the standard means of protection are still advised: Wear long sleeves and long pants and use a mosquito repellent that contains DEET. ■

Mosquito fish, which devour mosquito larvae, are being introduced into ponds to control the spread of West Nile virus.

Surgical Solution
Washing Away Memory Loss

Can a tiny implanted device preserve memory for Alzheimer's patients? A Stanford University neurosurgeon and his research team think so. They invented a special shunt—essentially a drainage tube—that appears to stop Alzheimer's disease in its tracks by speeding up the natural "flushing" of the liquid that fills the space between the brain and the skull.

Like many drug treatments under study, this surgical approach seeks to prevent proteins called tau and beta-amyloid from clumping together in the brain to

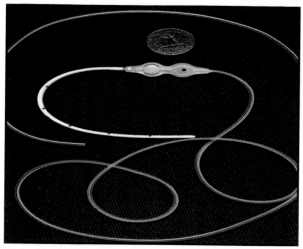

The shunt system, next to a quarter to show its size. Could it be a simple answer to Alzheimer's?

Shunt's Inventor Could Need His Own Device One Day

Pursuing a breakthrough medical treatment is the opposite of committing a crime, but both bold acts require the same three elements: motive, means, and opportunity. As the leader of the research team developing a new shunt implant to stop Alzheimer's disease, Stanford University neurosurgeon Gerald Silverberg, M.D., has the strongest of motives.

"It's self-preservation," he says. "My grandmother died of what was then called senile dementia, which may have been Alzheimer's. Anybody with a relative who develops Alzheimer's disease has a higher likelihood of getting it himself. And that might be me."

Dr. Silverberg created the means by becoming a neurosurgeon with special expertise in the fluid that surrounds the brain. The opportunity came in the mid-1990s, when other researchers started noticing that people with hydrocephaly, a brain disease caused by an overaccumulation of cerebrospinal fluid, often had Alzheimer's as well.

"A group of us sat down to think about what the common denominator of those two diseases could

be," Dr. Silverberg says. The theoretical culprit: poor circulation of the fluid and a failure to wash away the tau and amyloid proteins that clump together in the brain. "We did some experiments, and sure enough, it turned out to be true."

A shunting system to drain excess fluid from around the brain is already an accepted treatment for hydrocephaly. Dr. Silverberg's team set out to adapt the shunt, turning a pressure-relieving drainage device into a constant, low-flow circulation booster. Anti-dementia shunting had been tried as far back as the 1960s, but it was abandoned because of mixed results and dangerous side effects. To avoid the same pitfalls, Dr. Silverberg and his colleagues created a product development company and worked with engineers to build a better mousetrap—specifically, a safe shunt system designed for Alzheimer's treatment. The company, appropriately enough, is called Eunoe—the "river of returning memory" in Dante's *Divine Comedy*.

The treatments available now, Dr. Silverberg points out, provide only temporary memory improvement by inhibiting enzymes that break down a chemical that's crucial to memory. They do nothing to brake Alzheimer's progress and the death of brain cells that goes with it. "If the shunt is as successful as we expect it to be, it will be the first treatment that actually alters the course of the disease," he says.

Does that mean Dr. Silverberg would consider having a shunt implant himself? "I'm 65 years old," he says. "If I start losing my memory, you bet I would." ■

form the plaque deposits associated with dementia in Alzheimer's patients. But instead of getting rid of the proteins through chemical means, the shunt literally washes them away before they can enter the brain, much as the circulating water in a fish tank keeps scum off the glass.

To test the shunt, the research team assembled 29 people who were at similar early stages of Alzheimer's. Twelve of them were fitted with the device. After a year, those 12 scored better on mental capacity tests than those who didn't have the drains. The results of this pilot study were published in the October 2002 issue of the journal *Neurology*.

How it works. Aging normally slows the rate at which cerebrospinal fluid (the liquid surrounding the brain) refreshes itself. Just as stagnant water can turn into a mosquito breeding ground, the sluggish circulation makes it easy for tau and amyloid proteins to mass outside the brain and eventually enter it to do their dirty work. The shunt gets the flow going again by draining fluid through a tiny catheter, or tube, that the surgeons thread down from the implant site in the skull, through the neck and chest, and into the abdomen, where the fluid is easily absorbed. A specially engineered valve at the top of the shunt and the natural pressure difference between the head and the abdomen maintain a controlled flow that constantly removes old cerebrospinal fluid. This makes way for fresh fluid produced by the body.

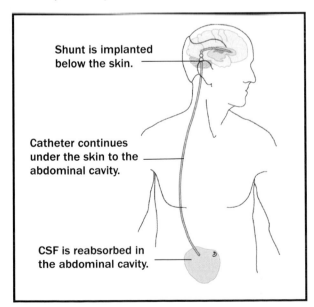

Shunt is implanted below the skin.

Catheter continues under the skin to the abdominal cavity.

CSF is reabsorbed in the abdominal cavity.

The shunt allows fluid from the brain to drain all the way to the abdomen, where it is absorbed.

Availability. Principal study author Gerald Silverberg, M.D., considers the successful pilot study a promising beginning for two new concepts in treating Alzheimer's. One of those is preventing formation of tau and amyloid plaque by boosting the circulation of cerebrospinal fluid; the other is using a shunt to do it. What's needed now is a much larger study to ensure that the positive results were no fluke. That study, already under way, will test the shunt in more than 250 Alzheimer's patients at about 25 sites across the United States. Results are expected in 2005. ■

RESEARCH ROUNDUP

Odd Walks Could Mean Dementia Down the Road

Almost half of all cases of dementia, or mental impairment, in the elderly have nothing to do with Alzheimer's. How do you know if someone you love is at risk? Watch how they walk.

According to study results published in a November 2002 issue of the *New England Journal of Medicine*, certain abnormal gaits are reliable predictors that a person will develop dementia 10 years or more down the road. Such unusual walks are almost never associated with Alzheimer's, only with non-Alzheimer's dementia. The researchers discovered the connection by evaluating the walking styles of 422 people age 75 and older who did not have dementia. Over the next 10 years, 55 of them developed non Alzheimer's dementia, and those identified with abnormal gaits at the outset were more than twice as likely to be among those 55.

Three specific gait variations were the best predictors. One, unsteady gait, is marked by swaying, loss of balance, or placing one foot directly in front of the other, as in a sobriety test. The second (called the frontal gait) is the classic "senior shuffle"—taking short steps with the feet wide apart and without lifting them off the floor. The third (hemiparetic gait) involves swinging the legs outward in a semicircle. The researchers hope their discovery will provide an early warning to at-risk older people and spur development of ways to prevent the onset of dementia. ■

Drug Development

At Last, Help for Advanced Alzheimer's Symptoms

Picture a 76-year-old woman in the more advanced stages of Alzheimer's disease. She looks okay, she can walk (with difficulty), and she's even able to communicate somewhat. Of course, her memory is weak, and the simple mechanics of everyday life—dressing, bathing, eating—are beyond her ability. What can modern medicine do for this woman? What hope can it offer to those who love her, take care of her, and don't want to lose her?

To date, very little. Existing treatments such as donepezil (Aricept) and tacrine (Cognex) target only mild to moderate Alzheimer's, while most experimental drugs are aimed at preventing the early stages of the disease from advancing. There is currently no approved medication for moderate to severe Alzheimer's, but that could change very soon, thanks to the promising performance of a new drug called memantine.

In a study published in an April 2003 issue of the *New England Journal of Medicine*, the 97 volunteers with moderate to severe Alzheimer's who took memantine daily for 28 weeks scored better in tests of mental and physical function than the 84 who took placebos (dummy pills). More important, the researchers noted marked improvement in the behavior of those taking memantine. Generally, they showed less agitation, their reasoning abilities increased, and their memories improved. Many were better able to dress, bathe, and feed themselves and tend to bathroom needs. Caretakers were able to spend fewer hours with them. While none of this means a cure is at hand, the drug's ability to offer these improvements answers many prayers from Alzheimer's patients and their loved ones.

How it works. Memantine is being hailed as a breakthrough for two reasons. One is its application for people in more advanced stages of Alzheimer's. But the drug also works in an unprecedented way. Typical drugs for mild Alzheimer's increase the supply of a memory-aiding brain chemical called acetylcholine by limiting the enzymes that break it down. Memantine, on the other hand, quells the action of another brain chemical called glutamate, which is so overproduced in people with Alzheimer's that it damages nerve cells (neurons). Less neuron damage means milder symptoms.

Availability. Memantine is already available in Europe and is under FDA review in the United States. If the approval process goes well, the manufacturers expect the drug to be available to Americans in mid-2004. By that time, a treatment that combines memantine with one of the existing medications now used for milder Alzheimer's symptoms may be available for late-stage patients. Results of a newer study announced in April 2003 indicated that advanced Alzheimer's patients who took both memantine and Aricept showed marked improvement in cognitive (mental) functioning. ■

Drug Development

New Approach to an Alzheimer's Vaccine

Back in February 2002, a promising vaccine for Alzheimer's disease had to be abandoned abruptly when test subjects started showing signs of nervous system damage. Fortunately for Alzheimer's patients, science seldom gives up.

Fast-forward to January 2003, when researchers sponsored by the National Institutes of Health and the Alzheimer's Association unveiled a potential new way to achieve the same positive results as the ill-fated vaccine without the dangerous consequences.

The hoped-for Alzheimer's vaccine is not what we think of as a typical vaccine, such as a flu shot, which is intended to prevent an ailment. Rather, it's meant to treat existing Alzheimer's. It's called a vaccine because it uses the vaccine-like strategy of triggering an immune system response to activate defender cells known as antibodies. The failed vaccine worked from within the brain to help these cells escort out proteins called beta amyloids, which form the clumps, or plaques, in the brain that are associated with Alzheimer's. Researchers now think it was that in-the-brain activity that caused the negative reactions—and they may have found a way around the problem.

How it works. Working with mice, the researchers found that two compounds, known as gelsolin and GM1 (substances extracted from cow brains), can reduce amyloid buildup by attaching to the proteins and ushering them away from the brain before they can enter. By working in the area surrounding the brain, gelsolin and GM1 act like doormen outside a trendy nightclub, keeping the riffraff—the amyloids—from entering the premises. That's safer than trying to kick out the troublemakers after they're already inside, which was the old vaccine's approach.

The researchers injected gelsolin, GM1, or a placebo (dummy drug) into mice with Alzheimer's disease every other day for three weeks. The ones who got the gelsolin or GM1 had less beta-amyloid in their brains than the others, as well as fewer brain plaques.

Availability. No one is suggesting that either gelsolin or GM1 be tested in humans based solely on the findings of the mouse experiments. But the authors of the study, published in January 2003 in the *Journal of Neuroscience*, say their results clearly show that beta-amyloids in the brain and the plaques they form can indeed be reduced by drug compounds that work safely outside the brain.

Such a "proof of concept," as it's known in scientific circles, brings us one step closer to the day when a new Alzheimer's treatment or even a preventive drug will be available. ■

ALSO in the NEWS

Strong Bones for a Strong Mind

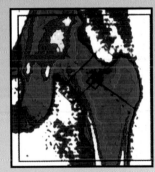

If you're a woman concerned about age-related mental decline, pay attention to how fast you lose bone density after menopause. Researchers studying more than 4,000 women over age 70 in Baltimore, Minneapolis, Pittsburgh, and Portland, Oregon, have found that those who experience rapid bone loss in the hip area are more likely to lose some mental function than those who lose bone more slowly. Previous studies indicated a link between bone loss and mental capacity. But the new study (published in the January 2003 issue of the *Journal of American Geriatrics*) went a step further, finding that the connection exists regardless of whether a woman carries the ApoE gene, the so-called Alzheimer's gene. Ruling out the gene as a factor more firmly establishes the correlation between bone loss and memory loss.

The study authors don't consider bone loss a likely cause of mental decline, nor do they foresee using bone-strengthening treatments to prevent it. But bone loss, they say, may eventually serve as a warning of accelerated aging processes or problems, such as inflammation, that promote mental decline. The National Osteoporosis Foundation recommends a bone mineral density test for all women over 65 and postmenopausal women who are at risk for osteoporosis. The test is quick, painless, and sometimes covered by Medicare and private insurance. ■

Drug Development

Growth Hormone Debate Grows Larger

A new study confirms that injections of human growth hormone (HGH) increase muscle mass as they reduce body fat in older people. Those results caused a big buzz among the growing legions dedicated to fighting the aging process by taking supplements. But more cautious experts in the medical establishment are citing the same study, warning that the supposed anti-aging benefits of the hormone are unproven and its potential risks unknown.

Who's right? The study, published in the *Journal of the American Medical Association* (*JAMA*) in November 2002, offers something for both sides. After injecting 27 women and 34 men ages 68 to 88 with either HGH or a placebo (dummy drug) for 6 1/2 months, the researchers confirmed what was first revealed in a study published in 1990—that HGH treatment does indeed firm up older bodies, adding muscle mass and noticeably reducing body fat.

When potbellies shrink without diet or exercise, the world takes notice, and this study has no doubt fueled what was already a growing demand for HGH treatment. HGH therapy is FDA-approved for younger people who are deficient in naturally occurring growth hormone, but physicians can (and some do) prescribe it for anti-aging purposes.

Others are raising a warning flag, including the editors of *JAMA* and the *New England Journal of Medicine*, where the 1990 HGH study was published. They point out that the improvements in body composition caused by HGH treatment didn't translate into better aerobic fitness or muscle strength. The people in the study got the packaging without the contents, so to speak. More important, the risks of cancer and other possible complications of HGH treatment in the elderly won't be known until larger, long-term safety studies are carried out.

A risky proposition. The authors of the new study were worried by higher incidences of diabetes and glucose intolerance among the people who got HGH. They explicitly recommend against HGH use for anti-aging purposes except by elderly people participating in approved clinical studies. And finally, both medical journals scolded Internet-based purveyors of so-called HGH supplements for claiming that the medical literature supports their use for anti-aging purposes, which it doesn't. Most of those products are oral forms of HGH, which are useless, since growth hormone that's swallowed is broken down by stomach acid before it can have any effect. Other popular supplements aren't HGH at all but rather substances that supposedly encourage the body to use more of its own HGH. There's no evidence that these "HGH releasers" work.

Awaiting answers. The medical establishment's consensus is that more studies are needed to look at HGH treatment in the long term. But the pro-HGH camp points out that baby boomers pushing 60 aren't inclined to wait. The question then becomes, Is it worth it to spend as much as $10,000 a year for a treatment that may not work and may have side effects? Judging by the recent increase in the number of physicians prescribing HGH, plenty of hopeful people are saying yes. But countless studies, including one in the same issue of *JAMA* in which the HGH study was published, point to a better anti-aging strategy: exercise. ∎

ALSO in the NEWS

Male Hormones for Memory?

It's no secret that aging men experience a decline in two things they'd just as soon hang onto—the male hormone testosterone and cognitive ability, including memory, reasoning, and learning. Now, a study of men between ages 51 and 91 has confirmed a long-suspected connection between the two.

Scientists working with a research program known as the Baltimore Longitudinal Study of Aging followed some 400 men for 10 years, analyzing their blood levels of testosterone and their scores on a series of cognition tests. The results were clear: More testosterone in the blood meant better mental function. The researchers say the study shows a "beneficial relationship" between testosterone and mental performance in older men. Larger studies are needed to show whether testosterone replacement actually protects mental function. Testosterone replacement therapy, like estrogen replacement therapy for women, poses serious safety concerns. ∎

Key Discovery
One Key to Longevity Revealed

Tiny bits of genetic material found in all our cells may reveal our chances of surviving well into old age. These "telomeres," which cap the strands of gene-bearing chromosomes like the plastic tips at the ends of your shoelaces, have recently intrigued longevity researchers, and there appears to be a connection between their length and the risk of premature death.

Until a recent study by researchers at the University of Utah, no one had actually compared the survival rates of older men and women with varying telomere lengths. The study results, published in a February 2003 issue of the British medical journal *Lancet*, are exactly what anyone interested in a long, healthy life wants to hear. The researchers found that people over 60 with longer telomeres are much less likely to die from age-related killers such as heart disease and infectious diseases than people the same age who have shorter telomeres. Why is that a welcome finding? Because it points to a potential way to delay death. If shorter telomeres mean a shorter life span, why not make them longer? The researchers think this is a real possibility. "Medical interventions that lengthen telomeres may help people stay healthy longer and live longer," says lead study author Richard Cawthon, M.D.

Exactly what interventions may successfully elongate the tips of trillions of chromosomes will have to be revealed by future research. Gene therapy? Hormones? Perhaps—but the answer may even be found in something as simple as diet or exercise, Dr. Cawthon suggests.

A shortcut to long life. Telomeres shorten naturally with age, losing a bit of length each time a cell divides, but they shrink at different rates in different people. Knowing that, the researchers measured telomere lengths from blood samples given in the 1980s by 143 people over age 60. Analysis of the donors' subsequent medical records revealed that those whose telomeres measured among the longest were three times less likely to die from heart disease and eight times less likely to die from infectious diseases. On average, they lived four to five years longer than those in the bottom half of rankings of telomere length.

The link between shorter telomeres and increased risk of age-related disease may have something to do with the telomeres' effect on overall cell health. It's possible that once a telomere shortens to a certain point, the cell that encases it essentially commits suicide. When that happens often enough, a cell-depleted body lacks the resources to fight off disease and eventually even to stay alive.

It's also possible, however, that shortened telomeres only predict a shorter life span rather than cause it. Even if that's the case, the new study results suggest a line of research that could help fend off age-related disease and death. Since the difference in telomere length between age-matched people is largely hereditary, researchers could try to identify the genes that influence it. There's a good possibility that some of those genes are "longevity genes" that influence the rate of aging. Such a discovery would bring us closer to finding life-extending treatments. ■

A computer illustration of a human X chromosome shows the telomeres at the ends in green.

Key Discovery

Absent-Minded? Blood Sugar May Be to Blame

Can't recall the name of the book you read last week? Forget what you needed at the grocery store? For some people, noticeable memory lapses are the bane of middle age. While they're less serious than true dementia, they're certainly annoying. Medical researchers have been searching hard for causes of age-related memory loss, and new research from the New York University School of Medicine has uncovered a likely suspect: high blood sugar. The discovery may mean that the key to a lifelong sharp memory is as simple as watching your diet, keeping your weight down, and exercising regularly—all proven ways to avoid blood sugar complications, including diabetes.

The problem of glucose intolerance. Food converted by the digestive system to glucose (blood sugar) is the main fuel that powers the cells of all organs in the body, including the brain. But many people, especially those past their youth, have poor glucose tolerance, meaning they have trouble processing glucose out of the bloodstream and into their cells. People who have diabetes have seriously impaired glucose tolerance—and as a result, high blood sugar—and studies show that at any age, they often experience some degree of memory impairment.

What the latest research found, however, is that even mild, nondiabetic glucose intolerance appears to reduce short-term memory in middle age and beyond—and that presents a hopeful possibility. By

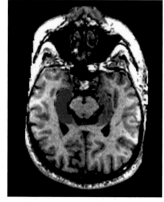

An MRI of a 63-year-old man with normal glucose tolerance. Notice the hippocampus, in red.

taking steps to keep your blood sugar metabolism healthy, you'll not only reduce your risk of diabetes but also protect your memory.

How they found out. The researchers gathered 30 healthy men and women between ages 53 and 89 and measured their blood sugar metabolism by injecting glucose into their blood and measuring how long it took to reach their organs. They also gauged the subjects' short-term memory with a series of recall tests and by measuring a brain structure called the hippocampus, which is responsible for short-term memory. The results, published in the *Proceedings of the National Academy of Sciences* in February 2003, showed a clear connection between blood sugar and memory loss. The people with the poorest glucose tolerance scored worse on the memory tests and had smaller hippocampuses.

What it means. Does glucose intolerance literally starve the brain into memory impairment

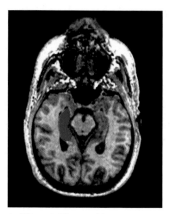

A different 63-year-old man—one with impaired glucose tolerance—has a smaller hippocampus.

by depriving it of the glucose it needs? One 30-person study isn't enough to provide a definitive answer, so the same research team is conducting further tests. In the meantime, the finding is good news if you want to protect your memory, because the best ways to maintain proper blood sugar metabolism are already well known. The top priorities are to get your weight down to where it should be (and keep it there) and to exercise regularly, whether you're overweight or not. Also, eat reasonably sized meals at regular intervals, emphasizing fiber-rich whole grains and vegetables over "white" carbohydrates such as pasta, white bread, potatoes, and white rice. Finally, choose the good fats—the kind found in vegetable oils, nuts, seeds, avocados, and fish—over the bad saturated fats in meat and whole-fat dairy products and the even worse hydrogenated fats in margarine, packaged baked goods, snack foods, and many other processed foods. ■

Key Discovery

Exercise Your Body to Preserve Your Mind

For years now, "use it or lose it" has been sage advice for older men and women hoping to keep memory sharp. But while you're challenging your intellect by solving crossword puzzles or mastering a foreign language, set aside some time for another mind-preserving activity: exercise. A six-year study of 349 adults age 55 and over has provided solid new evidence that staying physically fit as you age keeps your brain as well as your body in shape.

The new findings should be enough to get just about anyone off the couch and onto the walking path or exercise bike. Simply put, the people in the study who were most physically fit maintained more of their mental acuity over the course of the study than those who were less fit. The most fit had the best scores on mental function tests (such as word recall), while the least fit scored the worst.

Previous evidence had already linked poor physical fitness with poor mental fitness, but the latest study, published in April 2003 in the *Journal of the American Geriatrics Society*, gives the body-mind connection a big boost for two reasons, according to the authors.

One is that it's the first well-designed study that looked exclusively at older people (age 55 and up). The other is that instead of relying on the subjects' own reports of their fitness activity (in other words, taking their word for how much they exercised), the researchers measured their fitness levels by putting them through treadmill tests—which never lie. For healthy people, the more cardiorespiratory exercise (meaning endurance-type activities such as swimming, jogging, biking, and stair climbing) they get, the better they'll do on the treadmill test.

An old way to kick health problems is exercise. Now it seems that staying physically active may help keep your brain as well as your body in shape.

How it works. The researchers aren't yet sure why regular exercise keeps the old gray matter performing above par. One possibility is that many of the conditions that exercise guards against—such as high blood pressure, heart disease, and diabetes—may themselves impair mental function with age. Blood-pumping exercise also increases the amount of oxygen-rich blood that reaches the brain. So if an old friend pokes fun at you for hitting the jogging trail every morning "at your age," challenge her to a race—and then to a game of "Jeopardy." Chances are, you'll come out ahead in both. ■

CHILDREN'S
HEALTH

TALK ABOUT TURNING CONVENTIONAL WISDOM ON ITS HEAD.

This is the year we learned that divorce doesn't have to mean damaged children (just a few hours of parental training can make a huge difference), that household pets can actually *prevent* allergies, and that soccer helmets really don't work, at least if your child "heads" the ball. On the drug front, parents now have a nonstimulant alternative to Ritalin for treating attention deficit hyperactivity disorder in their kids, and a large study found that one cholesterol-lowering drug, Zocor, appears to be safe for the young set—a timely discovery, given the growing epidemic of obesity in American children. That epidemic also prompted the leading professional heart association to issue its first-ever guidelines for preventing heart disease in kids.

Finally, in "hot" news, if you've ever despaired of getting an accurate temperature reading when your little one is sick, you'll be happy to know about a clever new thermometer that even kids will be able to keep in their mouths.

Drug Development

Nonstimulant ADHD Drug Excites Parents

Few parents want people to know that their children take methylphenidate (Ritalin), the most commonly prescribed drug for one of the most commonly diagnosed behavioral disorders in children— attention deficit hyperactivity disorder, or ADHD. That's because the stimulant, classified as a controlled substance just like narcotics, has gotten a bad rap in recent years: reports about the large number of children taking the medication, concern about possible long-term effects, and stories of adolescents selling their medications to others who want the speed-like "high" they could provide. But for 30 years, parents haven't had a choice. Stimulants—Ritalin and amphetamines such as Dexedrine—were the only FDA-approved drugs for ADHD.

That changed in December 2002, when the FDA approved the nonstimulant drug atomoxetine (Strattera) for the treatment of ADHD in kids and adults. Doctors are thrilled to have another option, says Daniel L. Coury, M.D., professor of clinical pediatrics and director of behavioral-developmental pediatrics at Columbus Children's Hospital in Ohio.

How it works. Researchers don't know exactly how Strattera improves ADHD symptoms, but they theorize that it prevents certain receptors in the brain from soaking up the brain chemical epinephrine, which is believed to play a role in ADHD. Stimulant medications also work on epinephrine receptors, as well as on receptors for another brain chemical, dopamine.

While it's not yet known if the new drug works better than stimulants, it does offer several advantages. "First, it doesn't have the stigma of the stimulants," says Dr. Coury. "Often we see kids whose

parents say, 'Do anything, but please don't put him on Ritalin.'" Strattera is also easier to prescribe because it isn't a controlled substance. With stimulant drugs, patients have to see their doctors each month for a new prescription, an inconvenience that causes some children to stop taking the medication. Doctors can write prescriptions for Strattera for months at a time, and they can be refilled by telephone. There's also no opportunity for abuse with Strattera, says Dr. Coury, who led some of the clinical trials on the drug. This makes it particularly effective for adolescents who may be experimenting with drugs, or for those who live with a family member who has a substance abuse problem.

Another advantage: One dose is effective for 24 hours. Even long-acting forms of methylphenidate and amphetamine work for only 8 to 12 hours.

Side effects. Strattera can cause nausea, weight loss, and dizziness, all of which usually disappear after a couple of months of taking the medication. ◾

TOP Trends

AND BABY MAKES THREE— IN THE BED

After years of putting baby in her own room to sleep (and getting out of bed to feed her in the middle of the night) because experts said it was safer and healthier for children to sleep in their own beds, more and more parents are saying "Enough."

A large study published in the January 2003 issue of the *Archives of Pediatric Adolescent Medicine* found that in 2000, almost 13 percent of babies throughout the country slept with a parent or other caregiver—nearly a 7 percent increase since 1993. Another study found that about half the babies in Washington, D.C., shared a bed with an adult, suggesting a link with culture as well as economic status.

To exhausted nursing mothers, the idea makes sense. What could be easier than rolling over, letting the baby latch on, and dozing back off to sleep? But some experts are concerned that parents could unwittingly roll over on a baby. They also point out that sleeping with an adult is a major risk factor for sudden infant death syndrome, or SIDS. Still, as researchers conclude, "given that this practice seems to be widespread and strongly influenced by cultural factors, more studies of the consequences of bed sharing are needed to inform health care providers and parents on the risks and benefits." ◾

Alternative Answers
Biofeedback Helps Kids Focus

Psychologist Vince Monastra, Ph.D., gives new meaning to the words "out of pocket," since he paid some of his patients to undergo biofeedback training in his upstate New York clinic as part of a major study on the use of the therapy in kids with ADHD.

The results were published in the December 2002 issue of *Applied Psychophysiology and Biofeedback*. Dr. Monastra found that while a year's worth of counseling and medication relieved some ADHD symptoms among a group of children, only those kids receiving biofeedback therapy managed to hold onto those gains after going off the medication.

How it works. Dr. Monastra, clinical director of the FPI Attention Disorders Clinic in Endicott, New York, studied 100 kids between the ages of 6 and 19 who had ADHD. They were all treated identically in terms of medication, counseling, and even training for their parents. But half also had weekly EEG biofeedback sessions in which they learned to modify their brain activity through a kind of "physical therapy" for the brain.

With leads placed on their heads to measure the electrical activity of their brains, the kids spent a half-hour per week in front of a computer using only their brain waves to "play" a video game, then spent another half-hour doing homework. When they "turned on" the front part of the brain, which is responsible for sustaining attention, focus, concentration, and problem-solving, they were rewarded

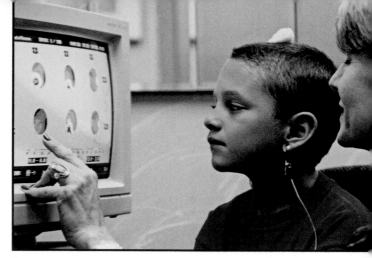

By measuring brain wave patterns, EEG biofeedback helps kids use their brains in ways associated with sustained attention and focus.

either with points that later entitled them to money or with a movement on the video screen.

When the study ended, Dr. Monastra took all 100 children off their medication for a week, then retested them. The children who had not participated in the biofeedback training had all relapsed, with no sustained improvement as gauged by either observational or computerized tests. Those who did receive the training continued to show enough improvement to reduce their medication by at least half, and 40 percent were able to stop taking it altogether.

Dr. Monastra is adamant that biofeedback is not a substitute for medication. It may, however, prove an important adjunct and, in some instances, may bring on the kind of permanent changes in the brain that may eventually enable some children (and adults) to forgo some or all of their medication.

Availability. Each biofeedback treatment, available at biofeedback centers around the United States, costs between $60 and $150, and 30 to 40 treatments are necessary. Check with your insurance carrier to see if they are covered. ■

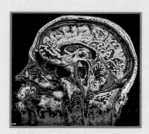

Key Discovery

Is Autism on the Rise?

In the late 1990s, the Centers for Disease Control and Prevention (CDC) began getting calls from health professionals, educators, and parents in the Atlanta area. The callers were concerned about what they saw as an unprecedented rise in the incidence of autism, a condition involving severely impaired development of communication and social skills. So the CDC did what any self-respecting public health agency would do—it launched a study.

The results, published in a January 2003 issue of the *Journal of the American Medical Association*, show that the public concern was justified. The study focused on autism rates for children living in five counties around Atlanta in 1996. Researchers found a rate of autism 10 times higher than those found in studies conducted in the 1980s. Although study author Marshalyn Yeargin-Allsopp, M.D., warns that direct comparisons between the two studies are difficult because they were conducted on different populations using different methods, the results do suggest a significant increase in the prevalence of the condition.

"Autism is not a rare condition," says Dr. Yeargin-Allsopp. "It's certainly as common as cerebral palsy and other developmental disabilities in children, and it is a very important public health problem today."

The CDC has launched several studies to investigate the reasons for the increase. Suspects include a broadening of the definition of the disorder in the mid-1990s and the fact that federal law now requires schools to provide special services for children with autism, which could lead to more children being diagnosed. But another study presented in October 2002 found that the increase couldn't be blamed on loosening the diagnostic criteria, immigration, changes in the number of parents reporting problems, or misclassification. That study, by University of California, Davis, epidemiologist Robert S. Byrd, M.D., was conducted in response to a 1999 report that found a whopping 273 percent increase in the condition among California children.

Dr. Byrd's study "is an important study in that it also brings attention to the fact that this is a huge problem and a very important problem, and that the magnitude is larger than previously recognized," says Dr. Yeargin-Allsopp.

One possible culprit can probably be ruled out: the childhood vaccine against measles, mumps, and rubella (MMR), a prior suspect in the rising number of autism cases in the United States and other countries. Researchers evaluated records of 537,000 Danish children, 80 percent of whom had received the MMR vaccine, and found that those who had been vaccinated were no more likely to develop autism than those who hadn't. The results were published in the *New England Journal of Medicine.* ∎

Bobbie Gallagher, above, contacted federal authorities after she learned that both her children, as well as numerous other kids in her New Jersey township, were autistic. The government is now studying an apparent and as yet unexplained rise in the disorder.

Key Discovery

Spare the Rod, Improve the Parent

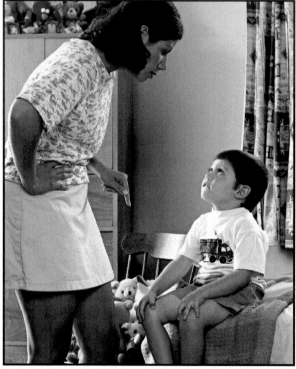

Not sure how to discipline your child? Programs that teach parents to better manage their kids result in far fewer behavior problems.

You need a license to cut hair, groom animals, and drive a car. But no instruction is required for the most difficult job of all: raising children. Maybe it should be. A study published in the December 2002 issue of *Archives of Disease in Childhood* found that parents who undergo 20 hours of specialized training cope better with their children, improving their kids' behavior as well as their own quality of life.

Although numerous studies have shown that counseling and training can improve parenting skills for at-risk parents and parents of children already identified with behavior or mental health problems, this was one of the first to evaluate the effect of training on parents who weren't significantly concerned about their kids' behavior.

The parents, whose children ranged in age from

3 to 10, were chosen from a general medical practice and asked to complete a questionnaire. Researchers selected 116 parents who, based on their answers, had the greatest disciplinary problems with their kids.

"They were the sort of problems all parents have and express," says study author Sarah Stewart-Brown, Ph.D., BM BCh (the British equivalent of M.D.), professor of public health at Warwick University in Coventry, England. "There were times they didn't feel in control, they didn't know how to handle certain problems, their children were throwing temper tantrums." In the United Kingdom, where the study was conducted, 60 percent of children under 1 and 90 percent of those under 4 are spanked, she says. "Most parents aren't happy about that. They say they lose their temper and would rather have other strategies, but they don't know what else to do. These positive discipline strategies are good to learn."

How it works. Half of the parents received weekly two-hour group counseling sessions for 10 weeks, and half did not. The sessions followed the Webster-Stratton parenting program, which teaches parents how to manage their children's behavior with positive reinforcement, limit setting, nonphysical discipline alternatives (such as time-outs), and effective communication skills, among other approaches. Six months after the sessions, researchers retested both sets of parents and found that there were far fewer behavior problems reported by the group that received the training than by the control group.

Interestingly, a year after the training, that difference had diminished—not because parents in the counseling group reported more problems with their children, but because those in the control group, some of whom had gone on their own to get counseling, reported fewer problems with *their* children. Filling out the questionnaire and talking to the researchers, some parents said, made them realize that they needed some help with their kids.

What it means. Programs using the Webster-Stratton approach are offered throughout the United States and in other countries. The fact that a 10-week program made such a difference in a "typical" group of parents means that "there are things that parents can do that really make a difference to their children's health and well-being, and to their own family life," says Dr. Stewart-Brown. "The vast majority of parents who go through the training say, 'Why didn't someone tell me this a long time ago?'" ■

Key Discovery

Helping Kids through Divorce

Divorce itself is painful enough, but you're also worried about how it's affecting the kids, who are acting out. Take heart: The results of a long-term study on the children of divorced parents show that a short intervention program designed to improve communication skills and support healthy parenting can make a significant difference in kids' behavior and overall mental well-being.

The authors of the study, published in the *Journal of the American Medical Association* in October 2002, spent six years tracking 218 families in the midst of divorce. At the start of the study, the children were between 9 and 12 years old, all lived primarily with their mothers, and none were receiving treatment for psychological problems. The families were then randomly assigned to either an intervention program for the mothers, a program for both mothers and children, or a control group that was simply given three books about adjusting to divorce.

The programs focused on helping the mothers increase the positive quality of their relationships with their children, using more effective discipline, increasing the fathers' access to the children, and reducing conflict between the parents. The mothers were taught how to provide "sensitive parenting," which included:

- Spending more positive time with their children on a regular basis
- Listening to their concerns and worries
- Noticing their good behaviors
- Providing clear, consistent discipline

Families were interviewed immediately after completing the program, three months later, six months later, and six years later.

The results. After six years, the researchers found that both the mother-only program and the mother-plus-child program had positive long-term effects. Teens who had entered the program with significant behavior problems and whose mothers had participated in the mother-only program were less aggressive; used less marijuana, alcohol, and other drugs; and had fewer symptoms of mental disorders than those in the control group. Teens in the mother-plus-child program were also less aggres-

sive, were 50 percent less likely to be diagnosed with a mental disorder than those in the control group, and reported having fewer sexual partners. The study found that children who had been having the most problems when they entered the program benefited the most.

What it means. Not all children have adjustment problems after divorce. "No child will happily accept a divorce, but most adjust fine with time and some sensitive parenting," says study author Sharlene Wolchik, Ph.D., a clinical psychologist at Arizona State University in Tempe. But for the 20 to 30 percent who show more serious problems, "these findings provide strong evidence that the problems children experience after parental divorce are preventable." The bottom line: Keep the focus on the children, not the spouse you're divorcing. In the long run, that will be the most important factor in how your kids turn out, says Dr. Wolchik. ■

ALSO in the NEWS

Want to Fend Off Allergies? Get the Kid a Dog

Along with the crib and car seat, you might consider getting a dog before you bring that new baby home from the hospital. In one of the best designed, most reliable studies ever conducted on the issue, researchers found that owning dogs and cats during a child's early years may actually reduce the overall risk of allergies.

Michigan researchers tracked 835 children from birth, checking in on them once a year until they turned 7 (by that time, 474 of the children remained in the study). Using blood and skin tests, they tested the children for reactions to a wide range of common allergens, then compared the results with information on whether there was a pet in the household and how long it had lived there. They found that chil-dren who had been exposed to two or more cats or dogs in their first year of life had half the rate of allergies of those who had less or no exposure. ■

ALSO in the NEWS

A New Weapon Against Kids' Diarrhea

A new drug approved by the FDA in December 2002 promises the first effective treatment for diarrhea caused by two common waterborne parasites. The liquid medication, called nitazoxinide (Alinia), can be used for children ages 1 to 11 who are infected with Cryptosporidium or Giardia.

Cryptosporidium is largely responsible for a near doubling of outbreaks of waterborne illnesses in the United States between 1997 and 2000. An estimated 20 percent of U.S. children are exposed to it by age 7. Outbreaks have been associated with day care centers, swimming pools, water park wave pools, and public water supplies. Most kids experience little more than a bout of diarrhea and fever that's often mistaken for stomach flu, but this parasite as well as Giardia can cause illnesses that last for several weeks and may be fatal for the very young or people with weakened immune systems.

Until now, there was no effective drug for cryptosporidiosis, while drugs for giardiasis either weren't available for children, tasted bad, or had to be taken for 10 days. Approval for a tablet form of Alinia for adolescents and adults was expected sometime in late 2003. ■

Don't Blame the OB for Cerebral Palsy

Obstetricians have been among the hardest hit during the ongoing malpractice insurance crisis, with some ob-gyns facing annual insurance premiums of more than $100,000. One reason for this is the long-held belief that one of the more common birth defects, cerebral palsy, stems from problems encountered during labor and delivery—problems that are often blamed on the doctor.

Now, a landmark scientific report published by the American College of Obstetricians and Gynecologists and the American Academy of Pediatrics reveals that nearly all brain damage in newborns occurs as a result of developmental or metabolic abnormalities, autoimmune and blood defects, infection, trauma, or combinations of these factors that occur during conception or pregnancy, not during labor or delivery. The findings could open new avenues of research into the causes of these conditions, say experts, potentially leading to earlier interventions. ■

Key Discovery

Tomboys Are Born, Not Made

Give a little boy a doll, and chances are he'll beat something with it. Give a little girl a tool belt, and see if she doesn't decorate it with sequins and pink Magic Marker. Anyone who has tried to raise a child in a gender-neutral environment can tell you: Kids are hardwired to behave in certain gender-specific ways. There are exceptions, of course, such as the tomboyish girl who'd rather climb a tree than dress a Barbie. But are the exceptions the result of upbringing or biology? A surprising new study points to biology.

British researchers, who published the results of their study in the journal *Child Development* in November 2002, evaluated data on 679 children and their mothers. They took blood samples during the women's pregnancy. Then, when the children were 3 1/2 years old, they gave the primary caregivers a survey designed to assess certain gender-specific behaviors in the children, such as which toys, games, and other activities they preferred. It turns out that high testosterone levels in mothers during pregnancy corresponded with high masculinity scores in preschool girls.

The correlation remained even after taking into account such variables as the presence of older siblings and/or a male adult in the home and parental adherence to traditional sex roles. But the researchers didn't find any relationship between testosterone levels and boys' gender-role behavior. The reason for that discrepancy, they suggest, is that boys are not only exposed to more prenatal testosterone in the first place, they are also discouraged more strongly from engaging in "girlish" activities than girls are dissuaded from "acting like boys." ■

Diagnostic Advance
Throwing Thermometers a Curve

Getting a child to keep a thermometer under his tongue until it beeps is about as easy as getting him to eat liver and onions. Parents thought they had the problem licked with the introduction of the infrared thermometer, a device you stick in your kid's ear for a second and click—until an article published in the August 2002 issue of the British medical journal *Lancet* found that such devices don't give very accurate readings.

It may look like a wristwatch, but it tells your temperature, not the time.

Then, in February 2003, a new thermometer from Timex (yes, the watch people, albeit their health care division) hit drugstores, providing new hope of getting an accurate temperature reading from even the squirmiest 4-year-old. Not only does the AccuCurve 30-Second Digital Thermometer sit sweetly in the "hot spot" under the tongue, but one version even talks to you: "Your current temperature is . . ."

The plastic device resembles a hook more than a thermometer. The curved end, which contains the temperature-sensing tip, rests comfortably in the mouth. As advertised, the thermometer provides a temperature reading in about 30 seconds. It comes in two sizes: regular for older children and adults and small for little ones.

"It's one of those ideas you look at and think, 'Why didn't someone come up with this before?'" says Stephen Fanning, M.D., a family practitioner in Greenville, Rhode Island. Eighteen years of treating young children has taught him the facts of temperature taking: It's hard to keep that thing under a kid's tongue. Why? "That's the million-dollar question," he says. "Even adults have a hard time keeping them under their tongues and keeping their mouths closed. It's just a fact of life." ∎

BEHIND THE BREAKTHROUGHS

Three Moms Rethink the Thermometer

The Rhode Island–based Lindon Group, which designs medical devices, has just three employees: Mindy Penney, Sherry Lussier, and Dalita Tomellini. Between them, the women have eight kids ranging in age from 1 to 9, and they know firsthand the challenges of temperature taking. So when they were asked to redesign the traditional thermometer, they turned to the experts they knew: 20 neighborhood moms, who said they were frustrated with trying to get their kids to keep thermometers in their mouths long enough to get accurate readings.

The Lindon executives returned to their corporate offices (a.k.a. the Penney basement) and brainstormed. One of them (no one recalls who) put her finger in her mouth and curved it down along her chin. "We should do it like this," she said. So they molded aluminum foil into the appropriate shape and corralled their children, husbands, and friends for product testing, finding that regardless of the size or shape of the tester's mouth, the curved shape fit the "hot spot" for everyone. *Voilà!* The AccuCurve was born. ∎

The inventors of AccuCurve (from left, Mindy Penney, Dalita Tomellini, and Sherry Lussier, with Jeff Jacober of Medport, the manufacturer) used common sense as their guide.

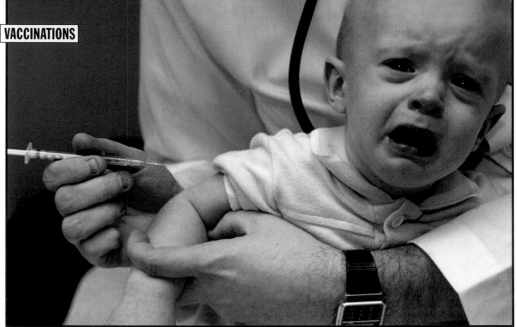

A new 5-in-1 vaccine means fewer needle sticks for wee ones—and fewer trips to the doctor for Mom and Dad.

Drug Development
Fewer Shots for Baby

It's easy to see how an infant might feel like a human pincushion these days. After all, a baby who receives all her recommended immunizations on time could be stuck with a needle 15 to 20 times in her first year of life alone. That's why pediatricians (and the nurses who usually have to give those shots) welcome a new vaccine that includes five childhood immunizations in one. The FDA approved the vaccine, Pediarix, in December 2002. It combines the diphtheria, tetanus, pertussis, hepatitis B, and polio vaccines and could result in up to six fewer shots for infants by the time they are six months old.

That's assuming that infants get their vaccines on time, but most don't. A study published in the November 2002 issue of *Pediatrics* found that more than half of American children don't receive all of their early childhood vaccines by the time they reach 2, and just 9 percent of children receive all of their infant vaccines during the recommended time period. Kids with younger mothers and several siblings are least likely to be vaccinated on time. The most common reason for missing a scheduled shot? A fever. Although fevers don't disqualify kids from immunization, many parents and health professionals are often reluctant to vaccinate feverish children.

With more than 300 vaccines currently under development, some of which will eventually be recommended as part of routine childhood vaccinations, parents may find it even more difficult to track the schedule and make the doctor's appointments. Next up: A 20-in-1 vaccine? ■

RESEARCH ROUNDUP

Nursing: A Baby's Painkiller

The next time you take your baby in for his shots, consider feeding him while the needle goes in. According to a study published in a January 2003 issue of *BMJ*, it may ease the pain.

Researchers evaluated 180 newborns during routine heel sticks. They split the babies into four groups: Some were breastfed, some were held in their mothers' arms, some received a sugar solution on a pacifier, and some received sterile water. Researchers evaluated the babies' pain based on facial expressions, movement of their arms and legs, the cries they made, their heart rates, and the amount of oxygen in their blood (when you're in a lot of pain, your breathing is shallower, so you take in less oxygen). They found no difference between the babies who were held in their mothers' arms and those who received sterile water, but of the 44 babies who were breastfed, all had scores reflecting minimal or no pain, similar to the results of those who sucked on a pacifier with a sweet solution on it. ■

Progress in Prevention

For Chickenpox Vaccine, Is Once Enough?

Millions of parents breathed a sigh of relief back in 1995, when the FDA approved the first varicella (chickenpox) vaccine. No more oatmeal baths. No more crusty red pustules, scarring, and repeated admonitions to "Stop scratching!" And, best of all, no more days lost from school or work. Finally, we all thought, one of the true scourges of childhood had been vanquished.

Not so fast. As it turns out, even kids who've been vaccinated against chickenpox are susceptible to the

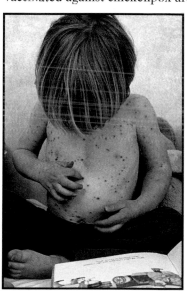

virus. A study published in a December 2002 issue of the *New England Journal of Medicine* found that the varicella vaccine protected children against mild and uncomplicated forms of chickenpox—the most common forms—less than half of the time. It performed better against moderate and severe forms of the disease, providing protection 86 percent of the time.

The researchers evaluated an outbreak at a day care center in New Hampshire. When they examined the timing of the children's vaccinations and compared it with their risk of contracting the virus during the outbreak, they found that those who had been vaccinated more than three years beforehand were more than twice as likely to get sick as those who'd been vaccinated later.

Anne Gershon, M.D., of Columbia University in New York City, an international expert on chickenpox, wrote in an accompanying editorial that the

study is a warning signal to doctors. "The time for exploring the possibility of routinely administering two doses of varicella vaccine to children seems to have arrived," she says. Current recommendations call for just one vaccination between 12 and 18 months of age. Dr. Gershon points out that it eventually took two doses of vaccine to control the measles virus in the United States. ■

ALSO in the NEWS

Babies Take Cues from TV

If you thought you didn't have to worry about "inappropriate" television content until your kids could talk, think again. New research finds that yes, babies really do watch TV.

At Tufts University in Boston, psychology professor Donna Mumme, Ph.D., and her colleagues already knew that infants watch the emotional reactions of other people and take cues from them. That's why if you're upset, your baby may become upset. But in this study, published in the January/ February 2003 issue of *Child Development*, the researchers learned that infants as young as 1 year can pick up such cues from television characters.

First, babies watched a video in which an actress looked at and responded to an object (a red spiral letter holder, a bumpy blue ball, or a yellow garden hose attachment). Then researchers gave identical items to the babies. They found that the babies reacted the same way the actress had. For instance, after watching the actress respond negatively to an object, the babies avoided that object and played with another one instead. "This means that adults might want to think twice before they speak in a harsh or surprising tone or let an infant see television programs meant for an older person," says Dr. Mumme. ■

WELLNESS

THE BIG NEWS THIS YEAR WAS ABOUT THE **FOOD ON OUR PLATES.**

We learned that fish isn't quite the health food we thought it was, thanks to a common modern-day problem: mercury contamination. New research shows that people who eat fish tainted with mercury actually raise their risk of heart disease. Swordfish and tuna steak are among the worst offenders; safer choices are salmon, sole, and shrimp.

Meanwhile, in other nutrition news, one study vindicated the Atkins Diet by finding that the low-carb, high-fat regimen actually lowers cholesterol—the opposite of what many doctors expected, including those who conducted the study. And beer drinkers can rejoice: It turns out that all types of alcohol are as good as wine at guarding against heart disease.

If a sweet tooth is your Achilles' heel, take heed: The World Health Organization issued a strong statement against sugar, calling on everyone to drastically limit their consumption of the sweet stuff to just 10 percent of daily calories.

Progress in Prevention
Beer Drinkers Have Their Day

For years, one of Ken Mukamal, M.D.'s colleagues forced himself to drink red wine on a regular basis for his heart. "He didn't like it at all," says Dr. Mukamal with a chuckle. Today, the friend has switched to beer and other alcoholic drinks that he prefers, thanks in part to a new study on the effects of alcohol on heart health conducted by Dr. Mukamal, an internist at Beth Israel Deaconess Medical Center in Boston.

In the largest and best designed study on alcohol and heart health to date, researchers analyzed data from more than 38,000 men ages 40 to 75, looking at their consumption of beer, red wine, white wine, and liquor individually by amount and frequency over 12 years. The results showed that men who consumed alcohol three to seven days a week had a much lower risk of heart disease than those who drank less often. Those with the lowest risk drank five to seven days a week. And here's

TOP Trends

EXERCISERS GET ON THE BALL

Power yoga was the exercise of choice in the late 1990s. Pilates became the rage of the early millennium. The new trend is balance training with the help of large, air-filled fitness balls (sometimes called Swiss balls). Exercisers sit on the balls as they perform traditional strength-training moves such as abdominal crunches and bicep curls. Research at the University of Waterloo in Ontario, Canada, shows that the instability of the ball causes people to use more muscles in order to stay balanced than they'd use without the ball. ■

BARCODES HIT HOSPITALS

Thanks to the development of hand-held computers, handwritten hospital charts are quickly becoming passé. More and more hospitals are going high-tech—and the FDA may soon require all to do so. At issue is the number of medical errors made at hospitals, particularly mistakes in dispensing drugs. An estimated 7,000 patients die each year because of such drug errors.

The solution: barcodes, just like the ones used at supermarket checkout counters. Before dispensing medication, a nurse scans the code on the drug bottle and one on the patient's bracelet to be sure they match. If they don't, an alarm beeps. "Requiring barcodes for medications and blood products may be the single most powerful FDA action to help reduce medication errors in hospitals," says pharmacist Diane D. Cousins, R.Ph., vice president of the U.S. Pharmacopeia's Center for the Advancement of Patient Safety. ■

SMOKERS' RIGHTS EXTINGUISHED

Once considered a symbol of sex appeal, cigarettes are now as untrendy as legwarmers. Only 25 percent of the U.S. population smoked in 1995, down from 42 percent in 1965. As the number of smokers has decreased, the number of smoking bans in cities and states has grown. Since the fall of 2002, Delaware, Florida, Hawaii, and New York have put such laws into effect, making a total of 47 states with some sort of restriction on smoking in public places. ■

FAST-FOOD SALADS DROWN IN CONTROVERSY

Several fast-food joints have beefed up their menus with upscale new salads, hoping to lure health-conscious consumers. But should you pat yourself on the back for eating one? Maybe not. According to the Physicians Committee for Responsible Medicine, which released a report rating 34 salads from seven restaurants ranging from Wendy's to Subway, some of the salads are no better for you than a burger, thanks largely to cheese toppings, fried croutons, and high-fat dressings. According to the analysis, the Crispy Chicken Bacon Ranch Salad at McDonald's packs more fat and calories than a Big Mac.

Critics of the report note that salad oils contain "good" fats that are far healthier for your heart than the saturated fat found in meat, and any salad made with vegetables offers fiber and vitamins that a burger-and-fries meal can't match. ■

why Dr. Mukamal's friend stopped drinking wine: Despite the widespread belief that red wine is better for your heart than other types of alcohol, the study found that all varieties—beer, wine, and hard liquor—lowered heart disease risk similarly. The results were published in the January 2003 issue of the *New England Journal of Medicine.*

How it works. Many people believe that red wine has special powers because it contains antioxidant plant substances called flavonoids. While flavonoids may be good for your health in other ways, they don't seem to offer additional protection against heart disease, says Dr. Mukamal. Some other component of alcohol seems to do the trick, possibly by raising levels of "good" (HDL) cholesterol and making blood platelets less likely to clump together and cause potentially dangerous clots.

"All types of alcohol are good for your heart," says Dr. Mukamal. "Red wine is probably still more beneficial than other types of alcohol for other diseases, but for heart disease, it looks like it's the alcohol per se, and in fact the frequency with which people drink alcohol, that make the most difference," he says.

Dr. Mukamal stresses that the study results aren't a green light to drink as much as you want. In fact, if you drink about nine drinks at once one or two days a week, you may *raise* your risk of heart disease. And overconsumption of alcohol can also increase the risk of other health problems, such as breast cancer and liver disease, he says. The study shows that you need to con-sume only one alcoholic drink (12 ounces of beer, 5 ounces of wine, or 1.5 ounces of 80-proof liquor) most days of the week to see an effect. ■

Key Discovery
Low Estrogen Linked to Heart Attack Risk

Women who haven't yet gone through menopause benefit from natural protection against heart attacks because of their high levels of estrogen. But if they have lower-than-normal estrogen levels—possibly because of stress or depression—their risk could be higher than normal.

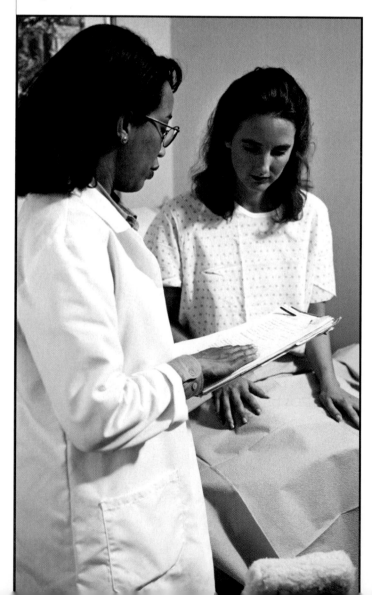

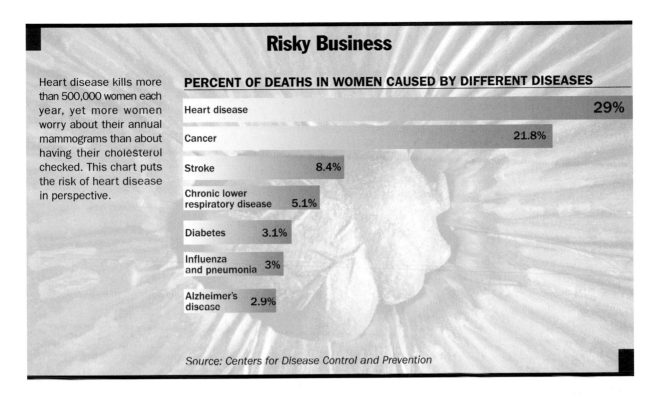

Risky Business

Heart disease kills more than 500,000 women each year, yet more women worry about their annual mammograms than about having their cholesterol checked. This chart puts the risk of heart disease in perspective.

PERCENT OF DEATHS IN WOMEN CAUSED BY DIFFERENT DISEASES

Disease	Percent
Heart disease	29%
Cancer	21.8%
Stroke	8.4%
Chronic lower respiratory disease	5.1%
Diabetes	3.1%
Influenza and pneumonia	3%
Alzheimer's disease	2.9%

Source: Centers for Disease Control and Prevention

In a study published in the February 2003 issue of the *Journal of the American College of Cardiology,* researchers tested estrogen levels and heart disease prevalence in 95 premenopausal women who were enrolled in a much larger study about women and heart disease. They found that women in their forties with chronically low estrogen levels were more likely to have advanced heart disease than women with normal levels. They also found that women who were taking prescription anti-anxiety or anti-depressant medication were more likely to be low in estrogen, suggesting that emotional problems may lower estrogen levels and contribute to heart disease.

Estrogen and your arteries. "When you don't have enough estrogen, particularly as a younger woman, your arteries are more likely to misbehave by constricting and dilating inappropriately," says C. Noel Bairey Merz, M.D., endowed chair and director of the Preventive and Rehabilitative Cardiac Center and the Women's Health Program at Cedars-Sinai Medical Center in Los Angeles. "That's what hot flashes are all about. In general,

this usually doesn't get you into trouble unless you have other problems like coronary blockages."

Although researchers aren't sure exactly how emotional stress factors into the low estrogen equation, they know from animal studies that emotional and environmental stress can lower estrogen levels and lead to disrupted menstrual cycles, even stopping ovulation.

"We don't know yet if low estrogen levels are causing anxiety and depression, if heart disease is causing low estrogen levels and anxiety and depression, or if the anxiety and depression are causing the low estrogen and the heart disease," says Dr. Merz. "While we have a good hypothesis based on animal studies, we still need to do more work."

Know your risk. Researchers are a long way from recommending estrogen screening for pre-menopausal women, and they're even further from recommending supplemental estrogen. However, they do recommend that all women talk to their doctors about their heart disease risk factors. (Remember that heart disease is the number one killer of both men and women in the United States.) Finally, if you're premenopausal and don't menstruate regularly, consult a doctor to find out why. ■

Factors that lower your estrogen levels—including menopause and possibly stress or depression—may contribute to heart disease. Talk to your doctor about how to lower your risk.

Progress in Prevention

A New Spin on Toothbrush Choice

Picking out a toothbrush these days isn't an easy task. Should you go with a big head or a small one, soft bristles or hard, manual or powered? Even among powered brushes, there's more selection than any consumer knows how to deal with, with some offering side-to-side brushing action, others a vibrating action, and still others a circular motion. It's enough to make your head spin.

Recent research could help get you out of the drugstore faster. The results were released in January 2003 by the Cochrane Collaboration, an international nonprofit organization that reviews existing studies in order to help health consumers make better decisions. They found that electric toothbrushes that provide "rotation oscillation"—in which the toothbrush spins in one direction and then reverses—removed more plaque and more effectively prevented gum disease than manual and other types of electric toothbrushes. "Other powered brushes were as

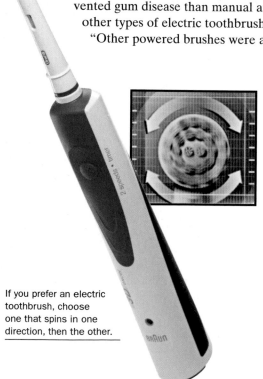

If you prefer an electric toothbrush, choose one that spins in one direction, then the other.

good as manual brushes. Only rotation oscillation brushes were better," says William Shaw, Ph.D., study coordinator and professor of orthodontics at the University of Manchester in England.

Types of rotation oscillation brushes include numerous Braun Oral B models and the Phillips Jordan HP 735. Use of such brushes resulted in a 7 percent reduction in plaque and a 17 percent reduction in gum disease compared with manual brushing and outperformed other powered brushes such as Interplak and Philips Sonicare as well.

Don't rush for a new brush. One drawback of the study is that it compared existing studies—many of them carried out by the manufacturers of the toothbrushes that were evaluated. Even the researchers who conducted the review concede that many of the studies were not as well designed as they would have liked. "Despite this being a multibillion-dollar industry, no single trial was of sufficient duration to allow the long-term value of powered toothbrushes to be assessed," says Dr. Shaw.

In fact, it may be the toothpaste and not the brush that makes the most difference in whether or not you develop cavities or gum disease. In past research, fluoride seemed most important in helping to prevent cavities—so whatever toothbrush you choose, pair it with a fluoride toothpaste, advises Dr. Shaw, and brush well. "The most important tip in brushing is that each time you do it, it should not be for less than 2 minutes." ◼

Key Discovery

Cell Phones: Not So Mobile After All

When Frank Drews, Ph.D., sees a driver talking on a cell phone—hand-held or hands-free—he either slows down to put more distance between himself and the other car, or he passes.

Dr. Drews has reason to be wary. As assistant professor of psychology at the University of Utah in Salt Lake City, he has been studying the effects of cell phone use on driving behavior. His most recent results, published in the March 2003 issue of the *Journal of Experimental Psychology*, may make you wary, too. According to his research, even people who use hands-free cell phones exhibit slowed reaction times and poorer driving behavior. That's bad news, since about 85 percent of cell phone owners talk on their phones while driving.

For the study, Dr. Drews and his colleagues asked 110 participants to drive inside a driver training simulator while talking either on a hands-free cell phone or to a passenger. When the participants conversed on the cell phone, they braked more slowly in response to traffic; some of them even rear-ended the simulated cars ahead of them.

How it works. It seems counterintuitive that you can drive effectively while talking to a passenger but not while talking on a hands-free phone. That's why Dr. Drews and his colleagues are now studying precisely why cell phone users get into accidents. Their preliminary data suggest that passengers converse with drivers differently than people on the other end of a cell phone conversation.

"Car passengers modulate their conversation depending on traffic density," says Dr. Drews. "When a driver approaches a traffic jam, the passenger actually slows down or stops talking completely." On the other hand, a person speaking to a driver on a cell phone has no idea about traffic density and continues to talk and question the driver in all driving conditions.

Dr. Drews is skeptical that any new cell phone technology could make talking while driving safer, because the human brain is simply incapable of doing two complex tasks—tasks that require the brain to think, process, and react—at once. In fact, he suspects that some newer technologies, such as navigational systems that spit out directions for motorists to look at while driving, may also contribute to inattention, and he hopes to study those soon. In the meantime, he suggests driving as he does: Keep your cell phone in your car, but use it only in case of an emergency and after you've pulled to a stop on the side of the road. ■

Call it an accident waiting to happen: New research shows that using a cell phone while driving makes for slow reactions and bad driving.

Set the table and gather 'round. Research shows that routines such as eating dinner together help families thrive, both emotionally and physically.

Key Discovery

Family Dinner: A Big Helping of Therapy

As her son grew from a toddler to a child, then to a teen, and finally to a young adult, Barbara Fiese, Ph.D., made dinnertime a family priority. She held firm to the routine even during her son's high school years, when extracurricular activities sometimes made it tough for the family to find a common eating time any earlier than 8 P.M.

She did so in part because of a growing body of research linking family routines such as dinner to the physical and emotional well-being of families. Dr. Fiese and her colleagues at Syracuse University in New York, where she is professor and chair of psychology, recently examined 50 years' worth of studies on routines and rituals. Overall, families who practiced routines and rituals such as eating dinner together reported greater marital satisfaction, better children's health and academic achievement, and

stronger family relationships. Children in these families experienced shorter bouts of respiratory infections, and predictable bedtime routines allowed youngsters to fall asleep sooner and wake less frequently during the night.

A security blanket. Routines, such as reading your child a story at bedtime every night, and rituals, such as birthday and holiday celebrations, may boost family health by organizing family life, creating a sense of security, and making family members feel that they're part of a special group. Such routines can be especially important during tough times. "We know that all families go through transitions and changes, and it's during these transitions that individuals are the most vulnerable in terms of their physical or mental health," says Dr. Fiese. "The studies that have been done during these transitions—such as becoming a parent for the first time or going through a divorce—show that the predictability of these routines tends to provide a buffer. In the case of divorced families, it provides parents and particularly kids with a feeling that some things in life are going to stay the same."

Keep it simple. You may already have established routines and rituals that you're not even aware of. They can be as simple as a comment you make every night to your spouse or child or how you greet your spouse or children when they arrive home. As for dinner, don't stress yourself by trying to force a long, elaborate family dinner every day. "Most of the mealtimes [in the studies] lasted only 20 minutes and took place about four days a week," says Dr. Fiese. "We're not talking about long, drawn-out, hour-and-a-half meals." ■

Progress in Prevention
Thwarting Hospital-Acquired Infections

Hospitals can be dangerous places—ask anyone who's gotten a sickness from one. It's not entirely surprising, considering how many germs other ailing people bring with them when they check in. One bug that poses a serious threat is the dreaded staph bacteria *(Staphylococcus aureus)*. If sanitation is inadequate, staph lingers on hospital equipment and countertops for weeks and can quickly spread from one patient to another. And antibiotics can't always help once you've been infected. In fact, today, more than 50 percent of staph infections are resistant to at least one drug.

You see, bacteria are the Borg of the germ universe. Just as those *Star Trek* aliens can quickly adapt to and overcome threats to their health, so can bacteria—which is why, almost as soon as scientists developed antibiotics, strains of bacteria resistant to the drugs began to emerge on the scene.

According to the Centers for Disease Control and Prevention (CDC), two million patients are infected with drug-resistant bacteria each year in U.S. hospitals, and 10 to 25 percent of those infections prove fatal. People with compromised immune systems—such as patients in intensive care units—are especially susceptible. "These people are already frail. The last thing they need is an antibiotic-resistant infection," says Mark E. Rupp, M.D., associate professor of infectious diseases and medical director of the department of health care epidemiology at the Nebraska Medical Center in Omaha.

There is a solution. Research published in the January 2003 issue of *Archives of Internal Medicine* shows that hospitals could gain the upper hand by adopting a simple procedure: screening incoming patients for drug-resistant infections and then isolating those who test positive to prevent the spread of infection to others. The researchers tracked drug-resistant staph infections at 14 intensive care units for six months. They screened all 2,347 patients entering the ICU, identified 96 who carried the infections, and took steps to isolate them. Those steps helped to prevent the spread of the diseases to other patients.

Some hospitals already aggressively screen for drug-resistant staph infections, but many don't. Should all hospitals screen all patients? Dr. Rupp says no. It may make sense for some hospitals to screen everyone, while for others, it may be enough to screen only high-risk patients, such as elderly people, patients coming from nursing homes, and those who have a history of surgery or hospitalization, he says. "I think it has to be left up to each institution. If the [drug-resistant infection] rate is high in the surrounding community, then it makes sense to try to screen patients and prevent the spread to others."

In addition, health care workers should wear gowns and gloves and wash their hands after treating infected patients, and health care

Staph bacteria can ride on instruments like this one, traveling from one patient to another. A new study advocates screening patients for staph and isolating those who test positive.

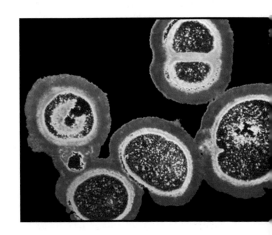

ALSO in the NEWS

Too Much Tylenol Linked to Liver Failure

Most cases of acute liver failure in the United States are caused not by alcohol but by unintentional overdoses of acetaminophen, the painkiller used in Tylenol and other products. A December 2002 study at the University of Texas Southwestern Medical Center in Dallas found that 39 percent of cases of acute liver failure were caused by acetaminophen.

"The bulk of the people who suffer from acute liver failure at the hands of acetaminophen inadvertently exceed the package labeling by a lot, say, 13 grams a day instead of the recommended 4 grams," says William Lee, M.D., professor of liver disease at the medical center. In most cases, the patients took acetaminophen along with cold medicine or some other drug that also contains acetaminophen. The FDA is working on guidelines that would require manufacturers to more prominently feature acetaminophen on labels of all combination medications, such as Tylenol PM and Theraflu. ■

Cruise Ships Clean Up Their Act

Epidemics of stomach flu swept through cruise ships in the fall of 2002 and winter of 2003, causing 23 outbreaks on 19 ships and grounding the *Disney Magic*

and the Holland America *Amsterdam*. The bug quickly became known as the cruise ship virus, although experts at the Centers for Disease Control and Prevention (CDC) say the same flu affected more people on land than on the water. Also, a report released by the Vessel Sanitation Program, the National Center for Environmental Health, and the CDC found that as cruise ships improved their sanitation practices in the 1990s in response to mandatory sanitation inspections, stomach flu rates dropped. Ships that scored better on inspections tended to report the fewest flu outbreaks. If you're considering going on a cruise, check out the ship's inspection score at http://www2.cdc.gov/nceh/vsp/vspmain.asp. ■

equipment, such as blood pressure cuffs and stethoscopes, should be disinfected after each use.

Speak up for yourself. At least two groups, the Society for Healthcare Epidemiology of America and the CDC, are drafting screening guidelines for hospitals, which should be available by 2004. In the meantime, if you or a loved one is admitted to a hospital, watch health care workers and make sure they wash their hands before giving treatment. Ask politely whether items such as stethoscopes have been disinfected before use. "Having a caring, observant, questioning loved one by the bedside is the best guarantee of getting good care," says Dr. Rupp. ■

[THE LONG AND SHORT OF ANTIBIOTICS]

The next time you fill a prescription for antibiotics, you may find so few pills—just enough to last a day or two—that you may wonder where the rest went. Chances are, however, that it's not a mistake, says Mark E. Rupp, M.D., associate professor of infectious diseases and medical director of the department of health care epidemiology at the Nebraska Medical Center in Omaha.

To help stem the growth of antibiotic-resistant bacteria, doctors and researchers are promoting the use of higher doses of antibiotics for shorter periods of time. For example, urinary tract infections are now treated for 3 days rather than 7, and sinus infections for 7 days instead of 10. Childhood ear infections can be treated in 1 to 3 days.

Higher doses kill more bacteria and do it faster, making it easier for the immune system to take over and destroy any stragglers, some of which may be naturally drug resistant. If allowed to linger, these bugs could multiply into an entire drug-resistant colony, contributing to a growing problem. Certain bacteria strains—particularly sexually transmitted bacteria and those that cause urinary tract infections—are now completely resistant to nearly all available drug treatments.

Researchers are still unraveling exactly how short a course of antibiotics is needed for certain infections. Meanwhile, always finish the course of antibiotics you're prescribed, even if you start to feel better before you've taken all the pills, since a few germs may linger. ■

Progress in Prevention

Another Fat Lip for Saturated Fat

You may already know that saturated fat is bad for your heart. But here's something that you probably didn't know: It may also be bad for your blood sugar levels. Intriguing new findings, published in the April 2003 issue of the *Journal of Biological Chemistry*, explain why—and present the tantalizing prospect of a brand new way to treat, and perhaps prevent, diabetes.

People with type 2 diabetes are resistant to the hormone insulin, which normally helps blood sugar enter cells, including muscle cells, which use it for energy. When the body doesn't respond to insulin as it should, blood sugar is "locked out" of the cell and accumulates in the bloodstream. High blood sugar levels wreak havoc throughout the body and contribute to serious health problems, up to and including kidney failure and blindness.

Previous research has shown that eating too much saturated fat is linked to insulin resistance. In fact, scientists have known for some time that the accumulation of fat inside muscle tissue—much like the marbling you see on a piece of prime steak—seems to contribute to the condition. But no one was sure why, until now. The culprit, as it turns out, is a chemical called ceramide, a by-product of the breakdown of saturated fat.

The ceramide connection. When people with diabetes eat foods that are high in saturated fats, their bodies convert too much of the fat into ceramide. Ceramide then accumulates inside the muscles, inhibiting the entry of blood sugar. The implications are significant. According to the researchers, "These findings suggest that medication aimed to prevent ceramide accumulation in the body tissue might lessen or even prevent insulin resistance and lead to breakthroughs in the treatment of type 2 diabetes." In their laboratory study (think petri dishes, not humans), the researchers used drugs to block the conversion of the fats into ceramide—and this prevented insulin resistance.

There's another reason to go easy on saturated fat: Some research shows that ceramide accumulation may destroy insulin-producing beta cells in the pancreas. There's also more reason than ever to get your exercise. According to Scott Summers, Ph.D., assistant professor of biochemistry and molecular biology at Colorado State University in Fort Collins, "We know that exercise improves insulin's ability to shuttle sugar into cells while simultaneously lowering ceramide levels."

Words to the wise. In the hierarchy of research, test tube studies fall near the bottom. Before drugs can be developed to block the conversion of saturated fat to ceramide, studies must be done on animals and then on humans. Current drugs that block ceramide have been linked to cancer, so new drugs must be developed before human trials can be done.

Dr. Summers is planning a series of animal studies to see if the existing drugs that block ceramide improve the body's response to insulin. In the mean time, if you have diabetes, it seems wise to cut back on your consumption of saturated fats from animal products such as full-fat dairy foods, meat, and eggs. ■

That juicy burger could do more than pack on the pounds; it could also raise your risk of diabetes.

113

Key Discovery
Fish's Healthy Reputation Flounders

A couple of years ago, Jane H. Hightower, M.D., an internist in San Francisco, followed a gut instinct that has sent health experts fishing for answers. A number of her patients were complaining of a strange set of symptoms: hair loss, moodiness, and fatigue. Some had gone from doctor to doctor and

been tested for multiple sclerosis, chronic fatigue syndrome, and other ailments.

But Dr. Hightower noticed something the other doctors had not. Such patients seemed to have one thing in common: They all ate a lot of fish, as often as every day.

She suspected that eating fish contaminated with mercury caused their symptoms, so she followed her hunch and tested 113 of her fish-eating patients for their blood levels of mercury. A startling 89 percent of them tested higher than the National Academy of Science's recommended limit of 5 micrograms per liter of blood.

Dr. Hightower's research, published in April 2003, heightened concerns about fish, once considered an ideal, heart-healthy food. Several months earlier, a study of more than 1,400 men published in the November 2002 issue of the *New England Journal of Medicine* had found that those with the highest mercury levels had double the risk of heart attack compared with those who had the lowest levels. "I was very concerned that

TYPES OF FISH	MERCURY LEVEL	HOW MUCH YOU CAN SAFELY EAT
Golden bass, golden snapper, swordfish, shark, king mackerel	high	none
Tuna steak, red snapper, orange roughy, pollack, halibut, northern lobster, marlin, moon fish, saltwater bass, wild trout, bluefish, grouper, croaker, sablefish	medium	1 meal per month
Canned tuna, crab, cod, mahi mahi, haddock, whitefish, herring, spiny lobster	low	1 meal per week
Salmon, oysters, shrimp, farm-raised channel catfish, farm-raised rainbow trout, flounder, sole, perch, tilapia, clams, scallops, red swamp crayfish	lowest	more than 1 meal per week (if pregnant or nursing, limit to 12 ounces per week)

Source: Purdue University

Dr. Hightower's study was able to demonstrate that people who had a high intake of these predatory fish [such as shark and swordfish] could suffer from toxic symptoms," says Charles Santerre, Ph.D., associate professor of foods and nutrition at Purdue University in West Lafayette, Indiana. "This is the first time I have heard of the exposure level being great enough to cause symptoms."

Mercury on your plate? Fish has long been promoted as a health food because species that live in cold water contain important types of insulating fat called omega-3 fatty acids. Omega-3s are known not only to reduce heart disease risk but also to help lift depression, ease joint pain related to inflammation, and possibly even promote weight loss. However, the addition of mercury may nullify those benefits.

Fish become tainted with mercury in polluted waterways. Power plants, waste facilities, and incinerators release mercury into the air. It eventually settles into nearby waterways, where bacteria absorb it. Small fish then eat the bacteria, and larger fish eat the small fish. Neither fish nor humans can eliminate mercury easily once they ingest it, so mercury contamination becomes increasingly concentrated as it travels up the food chain.

Mercury poses the biggest threat to children, nursing infants, and developing fetuses. Children often consume mercury from tuna sandwiches, infants get it through their mothers' milk, and fetuses get it through their mothers' blood. Mercury poisoning in children can cause nerve and brain damage. In adults, it may lower immunity, impair reproduction, and raise heart disease risk.

What should you do? Salmon and rainbow trout—both of which are loaded with omega-3 fatty acids—tend to be lowest in mercury and can be safely eaten twice a week by pregnant women, says Dr. Santerre. That's good news because omega-3s in fish are important for a baby's brain development as well as for preventing postpartum depression in women. "One 8-ounce meal of farmed or wild salmon or farmed or wild rainbow trout per week provides as much omega-3 fatty acids as a pregnant or nursing mother needs," he says. ▪

How Mercury Gets to Your Dinner Table

Man-made pollution has increased the amount of mercury in the fish supply to sometimes harmful levels, especially for unborn children.

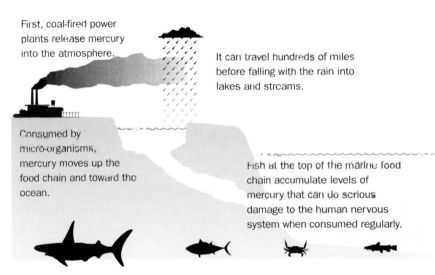

First, coal-fired power plants release mercury into the atmosphere.

It can travel hundreds of miles before falling with the rain into lakes and streams.

Consumed by micro-organisms, mercury moves up the food chain and toward the ocean.

Fish at the top of the marine food chain accumulate levels of mercury that can do serious damage to the human nervous system when consumed regularly.

Large predatory fish
At the top of the food chain, these fish acquire mercury levels above 1 part per million. The FDA recommends that pregnant women avoid swordfish, tilefish, king mackerel and shark altogether, or risk nervous system damage to an unborn child.

Smaller saltwater fish
These fish such as cod and tuna can have levels between .17 and .60 ppm. The FDA recommends pregnant women not consume more than 12 ounces per week.

Shellfish
These can contain harmful levels of mercury with lobster leading the FDA list at .31 ppm.

Freshwater fish
Mercury levels vary according to the concentration in the water. Local officials should be contacted to assess mercury risk.

Sources: Food and Drug Administration, Environmental Protection Agency

Progress in Prevention

Sugar's Reputation Sours

During the 1990s, health experts told us that fat was the archenemy of good health. Now, another villain has taken its place: sugar.

Not only does sugar contribute to tooth decay, it has also been implicated as one of the main causes of high blood pressure, heart disease, obesity, and syndrome X, a cluster of symptoms that include high blood pressure, high triglycerides (an artery-clogging type of fat in the blood), low levels of heart-healthy HDL cholesterol, and excess abdominal fat.

In response to a growing body of research detailing sugar's dirty work in the body, the World Health Organization (WHO) and the Food and Agriculture Organization (FAO)—the United Nations agencies in charge of health and nutrition—recommended in March 2003 that we hold our sugar consumption to just 10 percent of daily calories. For most people, that's the amount of sugar in a single can of soda. That suggested limit, which is much lower than the Institute of Medicine's September 2002 recommendation of 25 percent or less of daily calories, received applause from health experts.

"It's about time somebody took a stand against the sugar industry—eating too much sugar is the dietary equivalent of standing in oncoming traffic," says Susan Kleiner, R.D., Ph.D., author of *High Performance Nutrition*.

Marie Spano, M.S., R.D., a health scientist at the Centers for Disease Control and Prevention, adds, "I don't know of one dietitian who disagrees with this recommendation."

What's wrong with sugar? Most of the problems stem from sugar's effects on blood sugar (glucose) levels. Your body digests sugar—particularly white table sugar or the type listed on labels as high-fructose corn syrup—very quickly, dramatically raising blood sugar levels. Your pancreas responds by overproducing insulin, the hormone that's needed to shuttle glucose into cells. Too much insulin, however, lowers blood sugar too quickly. An hour after you eat a candy bar, for example, your blood sugar levels are lower than before you ate, and you feel fatigued and hungry. So you eat again, even though you don't need the calories. Over time, this piles on the pounds. Chronic blood sugar problems can lead to yeast and fungal infections, low immunity, and type 2 diabetes.

What should you do? Some sugars—such as fructose in fruit, lactose in milk, and maltosein in legumes—exist in wholesome plant foods, along with important vitamins, minerals, and other nutrients that help keep you healthy. You don't have to cut back on those types of sugar. High-fructose corn syrup and white (refined) table sugar, on the other hand, contain nothing but empty calories, and those are the forms you should restrict to less than 10 percent of your total calories.

To get your sugar consumption under control, read product labels. Choose packaged foods that contain fewer than 2 grams of sugar (it's listed on the food label under "carbohydrates") per 100 calories. Aim for fewer than 40 grams of sugar a day, advises Spano.

"And cut out sugary drinks—they're the greatest contributor to sugar intake," Dr. Kleiner says.

Is it okay to get the sweetness you crave from a sugar substitute? In moderation, yes, says Spano. "But 'sugar-free' does not mean a food is healthy or even low-calorie," she notes. She also cautions against the sugar alcohols (such as sorbitol and mannitol) found in many sugar-free confections, chewing gum, and desserts. Many people don't tolerate sugar alcohols very well and experience bloating, cramps, and diarrhea. ■

radiation (sometimes called irradiation) has been used to kill harmful bacteria that can sometimes grow on certain foods

# of Regulations
Foods

-growing segment of U.S. agriculture, doubling in size over
on industry. Until recently, however, organic foods weren't
icides and other chemicals. You never knew if the "organic"
own with the same stringent standards (no pesticides,

Organic Food Gets Official Seal

All foods labeled *organic* must now meet USDA standards, and they bear a USDA seal. Organic food is created without conventional pesticides or synthetic fertilizers, and the animal products are free of antibiotics and growth hormones.

Top 10 organic packaged products
1. Non-dairy beverages
2. Milk, half & half, cream
3. Packaged fresh produce
4. Frozen entrees
5. Yogurt & kefir
6. Cold cereals
7. Chips, pretzels, snacks
8. Bread and baked goods
9. Cheese and cheese alternatives
10. Tofu

Number of certified organic growers

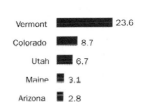
'92 '93 '94 '95 '96 '97

States with the highest percentage of acres used for organic vegetable farming

State	Percentage
Vermont	23.6
Colorado	8.7
Utah	6.7
Maine	3.1
Arizona	2.8

Total organic food/beverage sales for 2001

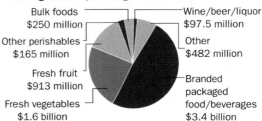

Bulk foods $250 million
Other perishables $165 million
Fresh fruit $913 million
Fresh vegetables $1.6 billion
Wine/beer/liquor $97.5 million
Other $482 million
Branded packaged food/beverages $3.4 billion

*No data available; data taken from most recent U.S. Agricultural Census

Sources: USDA, Natural Marketing Institute, SPINS

Organic foods also must be grown with environmentally friendly farming methods such as crop rotation, and government officials inspect each farm before certifying it as organic. They also inspect processing plants and stores that handle organic food. That way, at every step—from the farm to the store—the organic integrity of the product is maintained, says Shaffer. If at least 95 percent of the ingredients are organic, the packaging will display a seal that reads "USDA Organic." Any manufacturer who makes false claims on a label now faces a $10,000 fine for each offense. ■

[WHAT THE NEW LABELS MEAN]

Under new USDA guidelines, product labels may make four different organic claims:

100 percent organic. Every ingredient, including the oil used to cook the foods, is organic. The labels read "Certified 100 Percent Organic" and carry the "USDA Organic" seal.

Organic. At least 95 percent of the ingredients are organic. Often, the nonorganic ingredients (such as baking soda) aren't readily available in organic form. These foods also display the "USDA Organic" seal.

Made with organic ingredients. At least 70 percent of the ingredients are organic. Check the ingredients list. These foods don't carry the USDA seal, but they may list the name and address of the government-approved certifier who inspected the organic ingredients in the product.

Contains some organic ingredients. Less than 70 percent of the ingredients are organic. These products may not use the word *organic* on their packaging, but they may specify which ingredients are organic in their ingredients lists. They may not display the USDA seal or list the name of a government organic certifier. ■

Key Discovery

Study Finds No Beef with High-Protein Diets

As soon as high-protein diet books such as *Protein Power, Dr. Atkins' New Diet Revolution,* and *Sugar Busters* hit the bestseller lists, most cardiologists and nutritionists began warning their patients to avoid them. Eating so much meat and saturated fat, they argued, had to boost cholesterol levels.

Eric Westman, M.D., associate professor of medicine at Duke University in Durham, North Carolina, was one of those doctors. But a few years ago, while he was an internist at the Veterans Affairs Medical Center in Durham, something changed his mind. "A couple of my patients did the diet after I told them not to. One fellow told me all he did was eat steak and eggs. He had lost all of this weight, but I told him his cholesterol must have gone up. We checked it, and it hadn't. It actually had improved. So I started to explore this further."

Dr. Westman's most recent study, presented in November 2002 at the annual meeting of the American Heart Association, followed 60 people on the low-carbohydrate Atkins Diet as well as 60 people who went on a low-fat diet for six months. Those on the Atkins Diet consumed less than 25 grams of carbohydrate a day but otherwise ate as much as they wanted. They also took supplements of fish oil, borage oil, and flaxseed oil as recommended in the Atkins program.

After six months, all had lost weight, and the Atkins Diet hadn't increased their cholesterol.

In fact, those on the Atkins Diet saw their "bad" LDL cholesterol drop by 10 points and their "good" HDL cholesterol increase by 10 points. (Those on the low-fat diet experienced a similar reduction in total cholesterol, but some of it came from a drop in healthy HDL cholesterol. They also experienced a much smaller drop in triglycerides.) A few other studies, presented at meetings of other organizations, such as the North American Association for the Study of Obesity, have arrived at similar results.

How it works. Robert C. Atkins, M.D., who died in April 2003, developed the Atkins Diet in the 1970s. Precisely how it reduces blood cholesterol levels is not well understood. Dr. Atkins's theory was that the body doesn't metabolize fat and carbohydrate well at the same time. When you cut carbohydrate out of your diet, your body starts to burn the fat that you eat to create energy, rather than storing it. This means that there's less excess fat floating around in your bloodstream and therefore less need for cholesterol to transport it to your fat cells.

Because of its effect on blood sugar, the Atkins Diet may hold the line on heart disease as well: A growing number of researchers suspect that high blood sugar damages the lining of artery walls, encouraging the buildup of cholesterol and plaque. High insulin levels also signal the liver to convert excess blood sugar to fat, which raises blood cholesterol levels as the newly created fat makes its way through the bloodstream in search of a fat cell to call home.

> **Those on the Atkins Diet saw their "bad" cholesterol drop by 10 points and their "good" cholesterol increase by 10 points.**

But even Dr. Westman says that more research must be conducted before the medical community will give low-carbohydrate diets a green light. His studies lasted only six months, which may not be long enough to gauge the true health impact of these diets. Because the study subjects were still losing weight, the weight loss in itself could have affected their cholesterol levels favorably. "We don't know everything about these diets, but at least we've opened the door to more research being done," he says.

Dr. Westman cautions that cholesterol levels jump in 1 out of 60 people who switch to a low-carb diet. These people may have a genetic predisposition to a rise in cholesterol levels with that kind of diet.

Should you try it? The National Institutes of Health has funded a longer study to examine the health effects of low-carb versus low-fat diets over one year. Stay tuned: The results may be available sometime in 2004. In the meantime, if you decide to try a low-carb diet, tell your doctor about it. "Ninety percent of the time, your doctor will tell you not to do it, but if you go on the diet anyway, your doctor should monitor your cholesterol levels," says Dr. Westman. ■

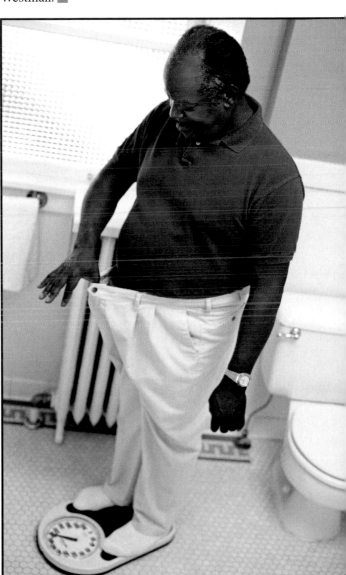

Besides helping you lose weight, the Atkins Diet may actually lower your risk of heart disease.

Key Discovery

Diet Books Worth Their Weight

Nutritionists have always known that the key to dieting is really quite simple: Just eat less. That's why just about any diet you may have tried has probably worked—at least for the short term. Most require you to give up certain foods. As soon as you do, the weight comes off because your overall calorie consumption goes down. But designing a weight-loss program that not only helps you lose weight but also helps you keep it off and improve your health in the process is a much bigger challenge.

To help make sure that your diet meets that challenge, the Physicians Committee for Responsible Medicine now offers some guidance. In January 2003, the nonprofit health organization analyzed more than a dozen top-selling diet books for nutritional soundness and safety. Their standards included diets that promoted a daily intake of 25 grams of fiber and five servings of fruits and vegetables, plus no more than 50 milligrams of cholesterol, 30 percent of calories from fat, and 10 percent of calories from saturated fat.

The recommendations mirror those from the American Heart Association and other health organizations that place a heavy emphasis on fiber and plant foods to lower cholesterol, guard against cancer, and promote bowel health. Most of the books that received low marks failed to meet the fruit, vegetable, and fiber recommendations.

"These are basic health recommendations, and I was very surprised at how few books earned four or five stars. A lot of these diets didn't even offer the basic five servings a day of fruits and vegetables or meet a minimum amount of fiber," says Brie Turner-McGrievy, R.D., clinical research coordinator for the committee.

The committee used a starring system, with 5 stars meaning "outstanding" and 0 stars "unsafe." Few books earned more than 3 stars. Although some people have accused the committee's 5-star winner, *Eat More, Weigh Less,* of being too strict for a normal, time-deprived, food-loving person to follow, Turner-McGrievy counters that increasing your fiber intake is as simple as opening a can of beans and mixing them into some brown rice. Increasing your vegetable consumption, she says, is as easy as ordering a takeout salad at Wendy's rather than a burger.

Winners and losers. Here are the ratings for some popular diet books. Five stars indicate "outstanding," 4 stars "good," 3 stars "marginal," 2 stars "unsatisfactory," 1 star "poor," and 0 stars "unsafe." Despite their increasing popularity—and the mounting evidence that they don't increase cholesterol levels—high-protein diets such as the Atkins Diet and Protein Power rated no stars because they fall short on fiber, fruit, and vegetables.

EAT MORE, WEIGH LESS, ★★★★★
   by Dean Ornish, M.D.

GET WITH THE PROGRAM, ★★★★
   by Bob Greene

THE PH MIRACLE, ★★★★
   by Robert O. Young, Ph.D.

EAT RIGHT FOR YOUR TYPE (TYPE A), ★★★
   by Dr. Peter D'Adamo

8 MINUTES IN THE MORNING, ★★★
   by Jorge Cruise

THE PEANUT BUTTER DIET, ★★★
   by Holly McCord, R.D.

THE ZONE, ★★★
   by Barry Sears

BODY FOR LIFE, ★★
   by Bill Phillips

EAT RIGHT FOR YOUR TYPE (TYPE O), ★★
   by Dr. Peter D'Adamo

THE FAT FLUSH PLAN, ★★
   by Ann Louise Gittleman

THE INSULIN RESISTANCE DIET, ★★
   by Cheryl Hart, M.D.

THE OMEGA DIET, ★★
   by Artemis P. Simopoulos, M.D.

SUGAR BUSTERS! ★★
   by Sam Andrews, M.D., et al.

EAT RIGHT FOR YOUR TYPE (TYPE AB), ★
   by Dr. Peter D'Adamo

EAT RIGHT FOR YOUR TYPE (TYPE B), ★
   by Dr. Peter D'Adamo

THE SCHWARZBEIN PRINCIPLE II, ★
   by Diane Schwarzbein, M.D.

DR. ATKINS' NEW DIET REVOLUTION,
   by Robert Atkins, M.D.

PROTEIN POWER, *by Michael Eades, M.D., and Mary Eades, M.D.* ■

ALSO in the NEWS

New Weight-Loss Secret: Get a Skinny Doctor

If you want more motivation to lose weight, choose a lean family physician. A January 2003 study of 226 patients at five physicians' offices found that patients who saw leaner physicians felt more confident about the weight and fitness counseling they received than those who visited obese physicians.

"It takes a good example to motivate people to accept a change in behavior," says Larrian Gillespie, M.D., of Los Angeles, author of *The Menopause Diet*, *The Goddess Diet*, and *The Gladiator Diet*. A physician who is overweight, smokes, and otherwise displays behaviors known to increase disease does not provide a good example, she says. ■

Stubborn Wound? Give It Oxygen

In the past, if you had a wound that wouldn't heal, doctors placed you in a pressurized chamber filled with 100 percent pure oxygen. The treatment was cumbersome, to say the least. Now, a January 2003 study shows that simply placing a bag filled with oxygen over a wound can equally speed healing time.

"We know that oxygen works to decrease the incidence of infection, enhance the creation of collagen [a component of skin], and stimulate new blood cell formation," says study coauthor Gayle Gordillo, M.D., a plastic surgeon and assistant professor at the Ohio State University College of Medicine and Public Health in Columbus.

The study paves the way for widespread use of bagged oxygen rather than the traditional oxygen chambers to treat hospital patients with slowed wound healing due to age, diabetes, cancer, or some other ailment. "We hope the results of our study will make oxygen therapy accessible to more patients, especially those suffering from chronic wounds," Dr. Gordillo says. ■

BRAIN
AND NERVOUS SYSTEM

IF THE SLIGHTEST BUMP, SCRAPE, CUT, OR NEEDLE STICK MAKES YOU HOWL WITH PAIN, **BLAME YOUR GENES.**

Researchers have identified a genetic blip that helps decide whether you're a wimp or a stoic. And if you're a woman, how much it hurts depends not only on your genes but also on the time of the month.

Do you know the saying "Everything old is new again"? Indeed. A century-old surgery is gaining new favor for treating epilepsy, while researchers have concluded that electroshock therapy—immortalized in *One Flew Over the Cuckoo's Nest* but far more benign today—works better than drugs to alleviate depression.

One approach that's decidedly new is a virtual-reality therapy to desensitize people who are afraid to fly. There's no more need to go to an airport or get on a plane to confront your aviation demons.

A very different demon, homocysteine (an amino acid), isn't just a heart disease risk anymore; now it's implicated in strokes and Alzheimer's disease. Fortunately, there's a simple way to lower your levels. See page 137 to learn what it is. Finally, there's more reason than ever to have your child tested for levels of lead.

High-Tech Help

Fear of Flying: A Virtual Cure

Fear of flying isn't uncommon these days. What with the terrorist attacks of 9/11, would-be shoe bombers, and souped-up airport security, it's no wonder some of us would rather have a root canal than get on an airplane. About 20 percent of people, though, have bona fide phobias that make them either extremely anxious while flying or unable to fly at all, even to the point of putting their careers at risk.

For decades, behavioral therapists have known that the best way to treat such anxiety is through a process known as desensitization, in which the frightened person is gradually exposed to the very thing that causes the fear. For instance, someone who is scared of flying might first visit an airport with the support of a therapist. Once he felt comfortable enough, he might sit in the waiting area by the gate, then sit in a stationary plane, and so forth.

In real life, this method can be quite time-consuming and expensive, particularly for people who don't live near commercial airports, so therapists have begun taking advantage of a technology more commonly associated with video games. They're using virtual reality, in which people are desensitized with computer simulations of airports and airplane flights. A study published in the October 2002 issue of the *Journal of Consulting and Clinical Psychology* found that virtual reality therapy is just as successful as standard exposure therapy in treating fear of flying.

How it works. The subject sits in an airline seat wearing a goggle-like device that fits over the head and eyes and transmits images. The images are extremely realistic, says researcher Nicholas Maltby, Ph.D., of the Anxiety Disorders Center in Hartford, Connecticut. He remembers one person who stared straight ahead, gripping the arms of the chair so hard her knuckles turned white. When Dr. Maltby suggested that she turn her

To us it looks like this woman is sitting in an office, but to her eyes and brain, she's sitting in an airplane. Sensors track her body's responses.

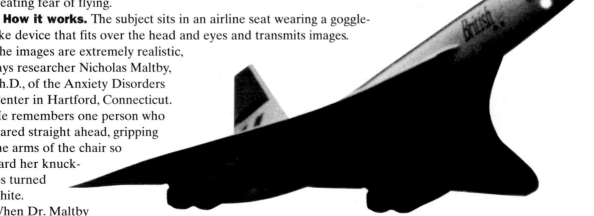

head left and look out the window, she replied, "No way. We're up too high."

Dr. Maltby and his colleagues are now working to integrate artificial intelligence with the virtual reality device. The idea is for sensors that measure anxiety levels (through heart and respiratory rates) to provide "real time" feedback, enabling a computer to automatically adjust the scenario. For instance, if the computer is simulating a smooth takeoff and the person remains relatively calm, it could add some turbulence.

Availability. For a list of centers where the technology is available, go to www.virtuallybetter.com. Check with your insurance provider to see if the therapy is covered. ■

With virtual reality therapy, you can enter the airport, pass through security, and board a plane without ever leaving your chair.

A Glowing Report for Shock Therapy

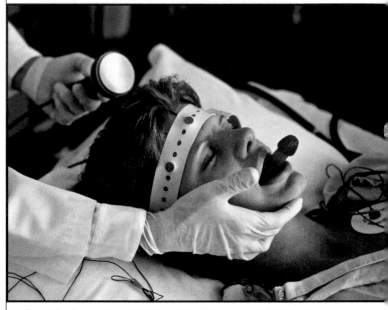

For major depression, electroconvulsive therapy is regaining favor. According to a new study, it works better than drugs.

Despite the dozens of new medications approved to treat severe depression in the past 20 years, a large study has found that the most effective treatment for the often crippling mental condition remains electroconvulsive therapy (ECT), or "shock therapy." But instead of being the medieval-like torture depicted in the film classic *One Flew Over the Cuckoo's Nest,* today's shock therapy is more benign than having your tonsils out. During the treatment, electrodes placed on the patient's head deliver a brief, controlled series of electrical pulses, creating seizures within the brain that last for about a minute.

The study, published in March 2003 in the British medical journal *Lancet,* reviewed 73 trials on the procedure. The results showed not only that ECT was more effective than drugs in treating depression but also that high-dose ECT was better than low dose and that delivering ECT to both sides of the brain (bilateral) was better than delivering it to just one side (unilateral).

Depression Linked to Earlier Menopause

Many women complain of depression and other mood changes as they move through menopause, leading many experts to suggest that dropping estrogen levels may be to blame. Now, a study published in the January 2003 issue of *Archives of General Psychiatry* adds credence to the idea that low estrogen and depression are linked. The study looked at women ages 36 to 45 with and without histories of depression. It followed them for three years to see how many of them entered perimenopause, when the body's production of reproductive hormones begins to decline.

The researchers, from Harvard's Brigham and Women's Hospital in Boston, found that women who had histories of depression were 20 percent more likely to experience menopausal symptoms, such as skipped periods, changes in menstrual cycles, or hot flashes, earlier than women who hadn't experienced prior depression. Women who scored high on a scale of depression during the study were twice as likely to enter perimenopause early; those currently using antidepressants were three times as likely. What the study doesn't answer is whether depression lowers estrogen levels, leading to menopause, or whether low levels of estrogen result in depression. ■

Researchers Find Depression Gene

How do you make a cool million? If you are Salt Lake City–based Myriad Genetics, you discover a gene linked to depression. Pharmaceutical giant Abbott Laboratories, which paid out the million dollars, expects the discovery of the gene, dubbed DEP1, to trigger an entirely new class of drugs to treat depression. Current antidepressants aim to increase the levels of brain chemicals such as serotonin and nor-epinephrine, but the identification of DEP1 suggests that there may be other brain chemicals involved—and opens the door to brand new ways to target the disease.

To identify the gene, researchers at Myriad Genetics, which also isolated the two major genes linked to breast cancer, analyzed the DNA of more than 400 Utah families with strong histories of depression. Three of the largest families included more than 50 people with depression, all of whom participated in the study. ■

An increasingly popular option. The findings come as no surprise to Richard Weiner, M.D., a psychiatrist at Duke University in Durham, North Carolina, who heads the American Psychiatric Association's task force on ECT. Although there are no good figures on the use of ECT in the United States, many in the field say it has been quietly inching upward, with about 100,000 Americans receiving the treatment annually—up from 33,000 in 1980.

Not only is ECT more likely to work than drugs, says Dr. Weiner, it also works faster than drugs, which may take four to six weeks to reach full effect. People with the kind of deep, intractable depression that ECT is most commonly used to treat are at high risk of dying from suicide or other medical conditions exacerbated by their depression. They need help fast.

Today's ECT. People undergoing ECT are put to sleep using general anesthesia and are carefully monitored during the procedure. The "shock," when it's given, results in slight twitching, so mild that the journalists Dr. Weiner allows to observe ECT are often disappointed, he says. Patients typically have treatments three times a week for 6 to 12 weeks and begin to improve after the first couple of sessions. Each treatment takes about a minute.

Still, as with any medical procedure, there are risks as well as benefits. The most common side effects are nausea, headache, and muscle pain that last for a couple of hours after the patient wakes up, says Dr. Weiner. More severe but less likely side effects include some memory problems, although many people report that their memory improves, he says. ECT doesn't help prevent episodes of depression, as medication can. It's also a bigger hassle, since it requires hospitalization. ■

High-Tech Help

Mini-Brain Offers New Avenues for Drug Testing

It sounds like the premise for a horror movie: Scientists keep slivers of brain tissue alive for weeks on a 1-inch-square silicon microchip while testing dozens of compounds on it, looking for the next Prozac or Valium. But it's not fiction. A small biotechnology company based in Irvine, California, working in conjunction with researchers at the University of California, is marketing just such a device. The "Brain on a Chip," as it's known, may one day revolutionize the development of new medications for disorders of the central nervous system, including Alzheimer's disease.

How it works. The Brain on a Chip consists of a glass chip that contains tens of thousands of interconnected living brain cells taken from rats or mice. The cells are kept alive in a solution of artificial cerebrospinal fluid, the liquid that surrounds the brain and spinal cord. An array of 64 electrodes on

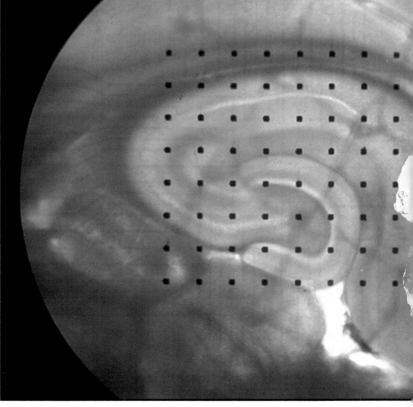

The Brain on a Chip is a glass chip that contains living brain tissue slices. On the chip's surface, 64 tiny electrodes record the activity of the "mini-brain."

the chip's surface monitors the electrical activity of the brain tissue just like an electroencephalograph (EEG), which monitors brain waves through the skull. The electrodes then feed the information to a computer. Researchers are using the technology to test chemical compounds for their effect on brain cell activity, a critical step in determining which compounds should undergo further testing.

ARTIFICIAL SPARE PARTS FOR THE BRAIN

While Tensor Bioscience's Brain on a Chip is designed to be primarily a drug development tool, similar technology developed by scientists at the University of Southern California in Los Angeles may one day be able to replace parts of the brain that no longer work. Dubbed "the world's first brain prosthesis" in a March 2003 issue of *New Scientist* magazine, the new device is designed to mimic the activities of the hippocampus, the area of the brain responsible for mood, memory, awareness, and consciousness.

It took scientists 10 years to develop the prototype of the artificial hippocampus. Using complex mathematical

models, the researchers subjected slices of rat hippocampus to millions of electrical signals, then processed and recorded the slices' responses to those signals before programming them onto a chip, thus creating an artificial hippocampus that acts like a real one. In theory, the chip would be attached to the outside of a human skull and communicate with the brain through electrodes.

The team behind the invention, led by neuroscientist Theodore Berger, Ph.D., announced in March 2003 that they were ready to begin testing the chip, first on slices of rat brain, then on live rats, and then on monkeys trained to carry out memory tasks. ■

The technology is a major advance from current drug testing, which uses EEGs of the entire brain to see the effects of a drug. This is a crude method, says Miro Pastrnak, Ph.D., director of business development for Tensor Biosciences, the company marketing Brain on a Chip. There are various types of circuits in the brain, he notes, and when scientists research a new drug, they need to examine its effects on a particular circuit. Brain on a Chip enables them to study the EEGs of specific parts of the brain and allows them to "disturb" an individual circuit to learn more about how the compound affects it. It's akin to following the path of one thread through a sweater rather than examining the sweater as a whole. "This would be very difficult to do in a whole brain," Dr. Pastrnak says, "where many interacting circuits are present."

Early forms of the mini-brain enabled scientists to test just three or four compounds a day, but in the past three years, Tensor has improved the technology to allow testing on up to 16 slices of tissue at once, using 16 interconnected chips. This means researchers can scan 40 to 50 compounds a day. Another benefit: Testing brain slices in a petri dish, where the slices exhibit no electrical activity of their own, requires many times the ideal dose of a drug to get an effect. Brain on a Chip enables the recording of natural, rhythmic, electrical brain activity, which previously could be measured only in live animals, says Dr. Pastrnak.

Because the brain tissue lives for several weeks, researchers can monitor the effects of drugs such as antidepressants, which don't become fully effective right away. Other potential uses for the chip include screening drugs that target other parts of the body to determine if they affect the brain, notes Dr. Pastrnak. For instance, a drug meant to treat the heart could be tested on brain tissue to see if it has any negative effects. ■

ALSO in the NEWS

Changing the Brain through Meditation

Scientists have known for some time that when people meditate, their brain waves change, differing from those typical of sleep, wakefulness, and dreaming. Now, a study has found that long-time practitioners of transcendental meditation (TM) have brain waves typical of a meditative state even when they're not meditating.

Study author Frederick Travis, Ph.D., director of the EEG, Consciousness, and Cognition lab at Maharishi University of Management in Fairfield, Iowa, discovered this by comparing electroencephalograms (EEGs) of the brain wave patterns of 17 people who had been meditating for 24 years with those of people who had meditated for 7 years and others who didn't meditate at all. The results were published in the November 2002 issue of *Biological Psychology*.

"This research suggests that the human brain has an innate capacity to function at much higher levels, where mental processes become very calm, precise, and efficient," explains Dr. Travis. "In practical terms, this means you can continue to deal with the day-to-day details, but you never get lost in them because you have this expanded sense of self." ■

Help for Your Short Game

It's something all golfers dread—the "yips," that slight twitch in the hands that makes accurate putting nearly impossible. The yips can short-circuit a pro golfer's career faster than a 30 handicap and make weekend duffers wish for snow. Now comes research suggesting that the yips aren't all in the mind.

What the experts found. Researchers from the Mayo Clinic in Rochester, Minnesota, asked 72 good golfers (with an average handicap of 6.7) to complete a survey describing the yips. It was the first time researchers had ever asked golfers to describe the affliction, says lead researcher Aynsley M. Smith, Ph.D., who directs sports psychology and sports medicine research at the clinic. Typically, doctors and researchers are the ones who do the describing.

The results were surprising. More than half of the golfers (55 percent) described the yips in physical terms, such as "involuntary jerking of the hands during putting," while just 22 percent gave more psychological descriptions, such as "nervousness and a tight feeling in the body prior to and during the putt." The remainder gave definitions that didn't fit either category.

"We've always known that people with the yips experience a jerk or tremor or freezing made worse by anxiety, but until this study, we didn't see quite as clearly that perhaps there really are two very different groups of golfers who have the yips," says Dr. Smith. One type suffers from a neurological prob-

[WHICH YIPS DO YOU HAVE?]

Aynsley Smith, Ph.D., who conducted the yips research at the Mayo Clinic in Rochester, Minnesota, says the condition may eventually be categorized into type 1 yips and type 2 yips. Below are some ways golfers describe the yips. Which category do you fall into?

TYPE 1: DYSTONIA	TYPE 2: PSYCHOLOGICAL
Jerky, uncontrollable swing with the putter	Can't start the golf swing
Flinching on impact	Adrenaline surges and nervousness sets in at certain times
Failure to control the club facet at contact	Inability to consistently make a 3- to 4-foot putt while putting under pressure
Twitch of the hands at a putt	Your mind tells you that you can't make short putts, thus you either push or pull the putt
When putting, just before contacting the ball, having a spasm that causes the player to miss the putt	Nervousness and a tight feeling in the body prior to and during the putt

lem and the other from extremely high anxiety. That neurological problem is called dystonia, a movement disorder characterized by involuntary muscle contractions that force certain parts of the body into abnormal, sometimes painful, movements or postures.

Get a grip—a new one. So what does it mean for the poor golfers? Well, says Dr. Smith, if the findings hold true in future studies, dystonia-affected golfers should make immediate changes in their putting patterns—whether a different grip, a different kind of putter, or a different stance—before the yip becomes ingrained in their brain circuits.

"It's our belief that when you move your hand position or change the grip or start to putt left-handed, you've broken yourself out of this template that had the 'hiccup' in it," says Dr. Smith. "You're firing different motor pathways in the brain."

To test this theory, she held a putting tournament in July 2003 with 16 "yippers," half of whom fell into the dystonia category and half into the psychological category. The golfers were so desperate for help that they paid their own travel and lodging expenses. One man flew all the way to Minnesota from Scotland.

While they putted, researchers monitored their heart rate, stress hormones, grip tension, and even their brain waves in some cases. Dr. Smith says she hopes the results, which had not been published as of press time, will point to new information about the yips and suggest potential treatments. "They just want help so badly," she says of the yippers. ■

Tournament participant Russ Burkoben is hooked up to monitors that measure his brain waves while he putts. The aim of the study is to get to the bottom of the twitches known as the "yips."

ALSO in the NEWS   HRT Increases Dementia Risk

In recent years, tantalizing evidence that estrogen may protect against or even reverse dementia had proponents of hormone replacement therapy (HRT) curling their toes in excitement. But in May 2003, the data came in, and the excitement fizzled faster than a dot-com IPO. New results from the ongoing, federally funded Women's Health Initiative found that the most popular hormone combination, Prempro, doubled the risk of dementia in women over 65. The study is the same one that in the summer of 2002 found that Prempro increased women's risk of heart disease, stroke, and breast cancer. ■

Surgical Solution

Surgery Gains Favor for Curbing Seizures

Imagine that you have a debilitating illness that leaves you unable to work or lead a normal life. Then imagine that for 18 years, your doctors tried one medication after another before finally recommending the surgery that eventually cured you. By then, however, you had missed out on your youth, your education, and many of life's joys.

That's the reality for people with the most common form of epilepsy, called mesial temporal lobe epilepsy (MTLE). Most don't respond to drugs, and their seizures severely disable them. Although there is a brain surgery that's been in use for more than a century and relieves seizures in 60 to 90 percent of people for whom drugs don't work, with few risks, it's recommended to less than 1 percent of these patients.

That could change. In February 2003, the American Academy of Neurology, the American Epilepsy Society, and the American Association of Neurological Surgeons released the first set of guidelines for MTLE surgery, calling on doctors to

Surgery can help epileptics lead normal lives. The earlier it's done, the less likely it is that recurrent seizures will cause permanent brain damage.

recommend the surgery for *all* MTLE patients who have disabling seizures and don't respond to antiepileptic drugs. Although surgery is one of the least used options for treating intractable seizures, the panel found that it's the most effective, says Jerome Engel, M.D., Ph.D., professor of neurology and neurobiology at the UCLA School of Medicine. Dr. Engel headed the committee that developed the parameters, which were published in *Neurology*.

Support for the surgery. The guidelines rely heavily on one of the best studies ever conducted comparing surgery with drugs. The study, published in the *New England Journal of Medicine* in 2001, followed 40 patients who received drug treatment for a year and 40 who received immediate surgery. One year after the procedure, 64 percent of those who had the surgery remained seizure-free, while just 8 percent of those on medication had stopped having seizures. None of the surgical patients died, while one patient on drug therapy did.

The procedure, in which surgeons identify and remove the area of the brain from which the seizures emanate, has been around for more than a century, notes Dr. Engel. Ironically, he says, back in

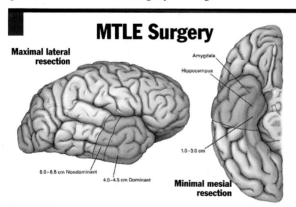

MTLE Surgery

Maximal lateral resection

Amygdala

Hippocampus

1.0–3.0 cm

6.0–6.5 cm Nondominant

4.0–4.5 cm Dominant

Minimal mesial resection

In surgery for epilepsy, doctors remove a portion of the brain responsible for the seizures—in this case, part of the temporal lobe.

Source: New England Journal of Medicine

the 1960s, when technology was light years behind where it is today, patients were referred for surgery sooner than they are now. "Doctors tend to drag their feet and keep trying new drugs instead of referring for surgery," he says, perhaps because there are more drugs available than there once were.

Getting the word out. Now, the challenge is getting the message about surgery out to people with epilepsy and their doctors. The earlier the surgery is done, Dr. Engel says, the less likely it is that recurrent seizures will cause permanent brain damage. Because the guidelines don't address when surgery should first be considered, the National Institutes of Health is conducting a large trial to determine if it might be regarded as more effective than medications when only two drugs have failed. To learn more about the trial, log on to www.erset.net.

Because the surgery could help people with other forms of epilepsy, says Dr. Engel, "as many as 200,000 patients nationwide who are treating disabling seizures with anti-epileptic drugs potentially could lead happier, more productive lives with surgical intervention." ■

RESEARCH ROUNDUP

Gene Variation Tied to Drug Resistance

Researchers have long known that one-third of people who have epilepsy don't respond to medication, putting them at greater risk of death or other complications from the disease. Now, British researchers from the University College London have identified a gene variation that they suspect may be responsible.

Among the study participants with drug-resistant epilepsy, the researchers found that about one-third had a variation in a gene that results in high levels of a certain protein. That protein seems to put up a kind of wall around cells, which in turn causes the active ingredients in anti-epileptic drugs to "bounce" against it. Among study subjects who were not drug resistant, just 16 percent had the gene variation. Being able to predict which people will probably be drug resistant could save valuable time in treating them, leading doctors to try other approaches, such as surgery, earlier. The study results were published in an April 2003 issue of the *New England Journal of Medicine*. ■

Key Discovery

Even "Safe" Doses of Lead May Affect Kids' IQ

You bought that beautiful, if run-down, Victorian, and now you're sanding and scraping like mad. Well, if you have kids, beware. A major study published in an April 2003 issue of the *New England Journal of Medicine* found that even blood levels of lead currently considered safe in children can significantly impair their intellectual development. And that paint you're scraping? It probably contains lead.

The five-year-long study found that blood lead concentrations lower than 10 micrograms per deciliter (mcg/dl)—which the Centers for Disease Control and Prevention (CDC) define as safe—result in a decline in IQ that's actually greater than the decline in children with higher levels of lead in their blood.

Testing, testing, testing. Currently, the American Academy of Pediatrics recommends blood testing for lead at age 9 to 12 months and again at 24 months for children who live in areas in which about a third of the housing was built before 1950 or in which 12 percent or more of 1- and 2-year-olds have elevated lead levels (above 10 mcg/dl). But that may not be enough.

"Parents should consider having their children

tested even if they don't meet all the qualifications of a child at risk for lead exposure," says the study's lead author, Richard L. Canfield, Ph.D., senior research associate in the division of nutritional sciences at Cornell University in Ithaca, New York. Parents who have their children tested for lead also should ask to see the exact test results, he says. Dr. Canfield can't say precisely what number might be considered safe. He does say, however, "If it were my child, and he had a lead level of 5 or greater, I would work very hard to find out where that lead might be coming from." Nearly 1 in 10 young children have levels above 5 mcg/dl, according to CDC figures.

Dr. Canfield doesn't know why lower levels of lead had a greater effect on intelligence than higher levels. An increase from 1 mcg/dl to 10 mcg/dl resulted in a 7.4-point drop in IQ, compared with a 4.6-point drop for each 10 mcg/dl increase *over* 10 mcg/dl. One theory is that once lead levels hit 10 mcg/dl, some mechanism within the body kicks in to protect the brain.

Redefining "safe." The study highlights the ongoing controversy over just where safe levels of lead in the blood should be set. Before 1970, child-

PROTECTING YOUR
FAMILY FROM LEAD

Children are most commonly exposed to lead by inhaling lead-paint dust or eating paint flakes, even though such paint was banned in 1978. Still, according to the Centers for Disease Control and Prevention (CDC), about 40 percent of U.S. homes still contain some lead-based paint. Many playgrounds also have lead paint. A 1996 study of paint from 26 playgrounds in 13 cities found that 16 had levels of lead high enough to be recognized as a federal priority for lead hazard control measures.

Other sources of environmental and household lead include lead wicks in candles (now banned, but millions are still in use in the United States), drinking water contaminated by old lead pipes or lead-soldered joints in newer plumbing, vinyl miniblinds (some contain lead as a stabilizer, and exposure to sunlight and heat makes the plastic deteriorate, forming dust that's high in lead), pottery and other food and drink containers, some home or folk remedies and cosmetics, and some fertilizers.

To lead-proof your environment, the CDC recommends that you:
- Ask your state or local health officials about testing paint and dust from your home for lead if it was built before 1978, especially if you have young children in the house. Don't try to remove the lead yourself. Check the Yellow Pages for a professional skilled in working with lead paint.
- Wash your child's hands, toys, and pacifiers frequently. Damp-mop the floors and damp-wipe other surfaces.
- Consume only cold water from the tap. Hot water is more likely to contain lead from plumbing.
- Avoid home remedies (such as arzacon and greta, Latino cures for stomachache) and cosmetics (such as kohl, a Middle Eastern eyeliner) that contain lead.
- Take steps to decrease your exposure to lead if you remodel buildings built before 1978 or if you regularly work with lead-based products. For example, shower and change clothes after finishing tasks.

hood lead poisoning was defined as a blood lead concentration greater than 60 mcg/dl. Since then, the threshold declined several times before reaching the current value of 10 mcg/dl in 1991. A CDC advisory committee is now reevaluating those levels. ■

Key Discovery

The Next Time It Hurts, Blame Your Genes

We all know people who can't tolerate the pain of a paper cut and others who sail through a root canal with nary a drop of Novocaine. Likewise, some women make it through childbirth without drugs, while others plead for medication as soon as the first contraction hits. Are some people simply less brave than others, or is there more to it than that? Researchers at the University of Michigan in Ann Arbor and the National Institute of Alcohol and Alcoholism have uncovered a clue to the answer, and it lies in our genes.

Nature's painkillers. Everyone's brain has receptors that natural painkilling chemicals (enkephalins and endorphins) "dock" onto. Called µ-opioid receptors, they are the same ones to which narcotics such as morphine attach in order to block pain. Not everyone has the same number of them, though. And not everyone's natural painkilling system kicks in as readily in response to pain.

To "watch" the µ-opioid receptors in action, researchers injected minute quantities of saline solution into participants' jaw muscles to simulate a painful condition called temporomandibular disorder (TMD). Then they examined the subjects' brains using a PET scan, which revealed the µ-opioid

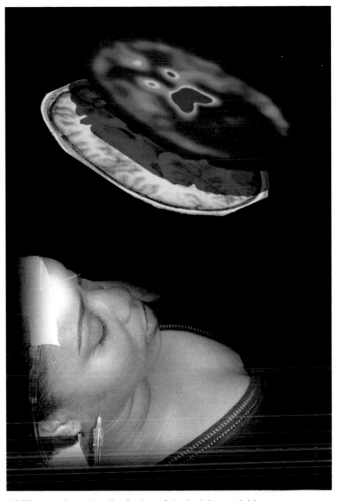

A PET scan shows the distribution of the brain's µ-opioid receptors, to which natural painkillers "dock." Warm colors (red) indicate high concentrations, and cool colors (blue) are low concentrations. The receptors are activated by the body's response to pain, triggered here by a salt solution infused into the jaw.

RESEARCH ROUNDUP

Pain Tolerance Linked to Estrogen Levels

If you're a woman, your hormones may influence your pain tolerance, according to University of Michigan pain researcher Jon-Kar Zubieta, M.D., Ph.D. He and his team exposed women to mildly painful stimuli, then used PET scans to examine their brains. First, they tested women early in their menstrual cycles, when estrogen levels are at their lowest. Later, they gave the women estrogen patches for a week to raise their levels to those normally seen during the later stages of the cycle.

The results showed that the higher the levels of estrogen, the better the women were at activating their internal anti-pain mechanisms. The lower the estrogen levels, the more sensitive women were to the identical type of pain. The researchers presented their findings at the February 2003 meeting of the American Association for the Advancement of Science.

"This makes some evolutionary sense," says Dr. Zubieta. "During pregnancy [when estrogen levels are high], you need to be able to withstand pain. At other times, particularly prior to ovulation, women may need to be protected against injury so they can continue having and raising children. The higher pain sensitivity serves as a warning signal that they're in danger." It's just one more way that Mother Nature knows best. ■

ALSO in the NEWS

New Hope for Cluster Headaches

Cluster headaches hurt so much they can make a migraine seem like a paper cut. Until now, there have been few ways for patients (mostly men) to find relief. Options included gulping pure oxygen or taking major pain medication just as the headaches began. Now researchers think that deep brain stimulation, in which a wire implanted in the brain emits small electrical shocks, may be a cure.

Italian researchers tried the approach with eight people who had suffered severe, disabling headaches for years. They implanted nine electrodes in the patients' brains, with a wire running under the skin of the scalp to a small electrical stimulator implanted under the collarbone. After about four weeks, the men's headaches completely disappeared; 26 months after the procedure, three of the eight remained pain-free without any medication, and the remaining five required low doses of medication. None experienced any side effects from the electrical stimulation. The researchers presented the results of their work at the April 2003 meeting of the American Association of Neurological Surgeons. ■

Headache? Try Rolling Over

The next time you find yourself reaching for yet another aspirin for your throbbing head, consider changing your sleeping position instead. A study published in the April 2003 issue of the journal Neurology found that people who had chronic head-aches (at least 15 a month) were more than two times more likely to be snorers than those who had occasional headaches, even considering other factors related to snoring, such as weight and alcohol intake. Researchers don't know yet whether the headaches cause the snoring or the snoring causes the headaches, but they say that finding out could lead to new treatments for both. ■

receptors and showed whether they became activated by the pain. "We had seen that some subjects had more μ-opioid receptors and some less, and that some subjects were more efficient at activating them in response to pain," says Jon-Kar Zubieta, M.D., Ph.D., the study's lead researcher. "But we never knew why."

Enzyme answer. To find out, they looked more closely at the brains of their study subjects. Specifically, they looked at the ways in which common variations in an enzyme called catechol-O-methyl transferase, or COMT, affected the response to pain. This enzyme is important for "mopping up" dopamine and norepinephrine, brain chemicals that contribute to pain sensations. The less dopamine and norepinephrine in the brain, the less pain.

The researchers found that people who experienced the greatest pain had weak forms of COMT. Conversely, those with the strongest form of the enzyme were the least affected by pain. The differences in COMT strengths are genetically linked. Dr. Zubieta estimates that one-fourth of the population have the weaker forms, another quarter have the stronger forms, and half have a mixture, putting them in between pain stoics and pain wimps.

What it means. The discovery paves the way for better understanding of why pain medications sometimes have different effects in different people. It may also help explain why some people are more prone to chronic pain or other problems associated with pain, such as depression, says Dr. Zubieta. "Forty percent of people with chronic pain develop depression," he notes. "Why does this happen with some and not others? This is hinting that some people may have more vulnerability to depression or other stress-related conditions." ■

Key Discovery
A New Culprit in Stroke and Alzheimer's

In recent years, a growing body of evidence has thrown suspicion on the naturally occurring amino acid homocysteine as a contributing factor to heart disease, including heart attacks. Now, it appears that it's also a culprit in stroke and Alzheimer's disease.

Homocysteine is formed when the body breaks down protein, especially protein from animal sources, such as meat and poultry. Then B vitamins, particularly folate and vitamins B_6 and B_{12}, break down homocysteine so cells can use it for energy before disposing of any excess. If this breakdown phase fails to occur—say, if you don't get enough B vitamins—homocysteine builds up to an unhealthy level, damaging the cells lining the arteries in your heart. It may also make blood cells stickier, encouraging the formation of potentially dangerous blood clots.

Now, a study published in the October 2002 issue of the journal *Stroke* has found that even a moderate elevation in homocysteine levels is associated with a more than fivefold increase in the risk of stroke and almost triple the risk of Alzheimer's disease.

What the study shows. Researchers from Queens University in Belfast, Ireland, studied 83 people with Alzheimer's, 78 with other forms of dementia caused by poor blood flow to the brain (called vascular dementia), 64 stroke patients, and 71 healthy volunteers. The researchers took into account differences in other risk factors (including diet, smoking, and blood pressure and cholesterol levels) and screened for a genetic defect that causes problems with the metabolism of folate. When they looked at homocysteine levels, they found that subjects with moderately elevated levels (13.3 micromoles per liter or higher) had a nearly 3 times greater risk of Alzheimer's than those with lower levels, their risk of stroke was $5\frac{1}{2}$ times higher, and their risk of vascular dementia was nearly 5 times greater.

What it means. Reducing homocysteine levels is pretty simple: Just get enough folate, vitamin B_{12}, and/or vitamin B_6 in your diet (good sources include meats, fortified cereals and breads, potatoes, fish, eggs, bananas, nuts, and seeds) or from supplements. If other researchers arrive at the same results when they repeat the study, the next step may be to test B vitamin supplements and their ability to reduce the chances of stroke and dementia in people who are at increased risk for them. But you don't have to wait. Older people in general may want to talk to their doctors about supplementing with these vitamins now, since studies find that 6 out of 10 older Americans don't get enough folate in their diets to prevent high levels of homocysteine. Additionally, with age, the body has a more difficult time absorbing B_{12} from food. ■

RESEARCH ROUNDUP

Blood Pressure Drug Cuts Risk of Stroke and Heart Attack

If you have high blood pressure and are taking the beta-blocker atenolol (Tenormin), you may want to ask your doctor about the benefits of a newer medication, losartan (Cozaar). A large study published in a September 2002 issue of the *Journal of the American Medical Association* found that while both drugs worked equally well at reducing blood pressure, people taking Cozaar had a 46 percent lower death rate from heart attacks, a 40 percent lower rate of stroke, and an overall death rate 28 percent lower than that of people taking Tenormin. They also had a lower rate of diabetes.

The study evaluated 1,326 people ages 55 to 80 with isolated systolic hypertension, the most common form of high blood pressure, in which the top number (systolic pressure) is too high, but the bottom number (diastolic) is normal. With this form of hypertension, the pumping chambers of the heart are also enlarged, because the heart works harder to pump blood out. The study was funded by Merck, which makes Cozaar. ■

CANCER

IN SEEKING CURES FOR THE DISEASE, CANCER RESEARCHERS ARE GETTING AS AGGRESSIVE AS CANCER ITSELF.

This year brought further progress. For instance, one of the first trials using gene therapy to treat cancer had spectacular results in several patients with late-stage pancreatic cancer. And a genetically modified version of the infamous anthrax toxin has treated and even eliminated certain cancers in mice. No stone is being left unturned: Even the firefly has been tapped as a way to destroy cancer cells.

For women, there's a new—and perfectly painless—imaging technique in the works that can actually tell whether a breast cyst is benign or cancerous. And for men, new microsurgery eliminates suspicious testicular lumps without removing the testes.

Scientists are also making progress in pinpointing the causes of certain cancers. They now think that a common virus may be responsible for some colon cancers, perhaps paving the way for a preventive vaccine. More certain is the link between obesity and cancer. Figuring out a preventive strategy for that is fairly easy. Getting people to follow it is nearly impossible.

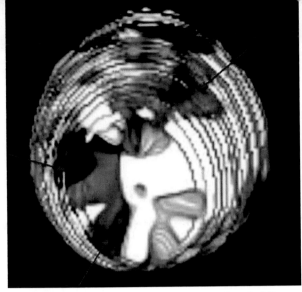

CTLM takes a series of images and reconstructs them in 3-D to clearly show the shape and extent of breast cysts.

Diagnostic Advance

Shining a Light on Breast Cancer

Don't use the word *mammogram* to describe the new breast diagnostic test that radiologist Eric Milne, M.D., is pioneering. That word carries with it images of radiation and painful breast compression. But CT laser mammography (CTLM) involves neither.

Dr. Milne is professor emeritus of radiology at the University of California-Irvine, and chief radiologist at Florida-based Imaging Diagnostic Systems, the company that invented CTLM. Not only is the test more comfortable for women, it also has the potential to significantly slash the number of invasive biopsies performed to check suspicious tissue that may turn out to be benign, and it can clearly image any breast, no matter how dense the breast tissue — all of which are significant improvements over existing technology.

In one preliminary study, 120 women underwent both conventional mammography and CTLM. Had radiologists relied on just the CTLM scans, says Dr. Milne, the number of biopsies ultimately performed would have plummeted from 80 to 40. Typically, 80 percent of biopsies performed after conventional mammography turn out to be negative, resulting in unnecessary stress and medical procedures for thousands of women. Dr. Milne presented these results at

the European Congress of Radiology in Vienna in early March 2003.

How it works. Instead of standing while her breast is compressed between two x-ray plates, a woman lies on a table on her stomach with her breast placed through a hole. "It looks perfectly comfortable, and nothing touches the breast at all," says Dr. Milne. Instead of the x-rays used in conventional mammography or even conventional CT scans, CTLM uses a laser beam not much bigger than a pencil to peer through tissue as if it were glass.

The test relies on the theory that in order to grow and spread, malignant tumors require a blood supply. Toward that end, they send out signals that spur the growth of new blood vessels, which often are visible long before the tumor is large enough to be seen. Hemoglobin in the blood absorbs the CTLM laser light more than surrounding tissue, making blood vessels emerge as bright, white images so that any new growth is obvious.

The laser circles the breast, then drops down

RESEARCH ROUNDUP

Improving on the Radiologist's Eye

One of the hottest areas in mammography is computer-assisted diagnosis (CAD), which helps remove some of the human error and guesswork involved in reading mammography x-ray films. Now, a physicist at the Moffitt Cancer Center at the University of South Florida in Tampa is looking to patent a software program that, in clinical studies on 350 women, pinpointed tumors with 100 percent accuracy and determined which were malignant with 80 percent accuracy. Human evaluation of mammograms, on the other hand, leads to biopsies of all suspicious areas, or calcifications, only 20 percent of which turn out to be cancerous.

"If we can bring it down from 100 women having a biopsy to 50 having a biopsy, that's a big improvement already," says Maria Kallergi, Ph.D., associate professor and director of the imaging science research department at Moffitt. The software program, called computer-aided diagnosis for breast calcifications, examines calcium deposits and, using an algorithm that includes information on the patient's medical and family history, determines whether the deposits are most likely benign or suspicious. ■

slightly and makes another circle, collecting a series of images in "slices," or tomograms, from the chest wall to the nipple. Those images are reconstructed in real time into one colorful (read: green and white), three-dimensional computer image that a radiologist can immediately read. Dr. Milne compares it to a goldfish bowl, in which the weeds in the bowl represent the globular, or fatty, structure of the breast, and the large fish hiding in the corner represents the cancer. "The 'fish,' or cancer, stays in position as you rotate

One day soon, getting screened for breast cancer could look like this—no more compressing the breast between metal plates.

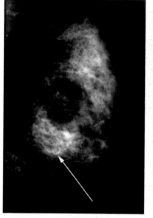

An X-ray does not show whether a lump is malignant or benign.

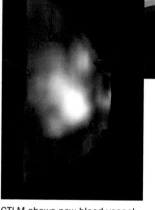

CTLM shows new blood vessel growth, which indicates cancer.

the goldfish bowl around to see it best," he explains. The entire scanning process takes about 15 minutes.

The image is so clear, says Dr. Milne, that radiologists can also tell whether a lesion is a harmless cyst or a tumor—something that's very difficult with mammograms. And unlike breast MRIs, which also provide very clear, detailed pictures but which cost

up to $1,000, CTLM is not expected to cost any more than a typical mammogram. In fact, it may cost less, because the machine used for the procedure is less expensive than today's digital mammography units, he says.

Availability. In late February 2003, the company that invented CTLM submitted results from 700 procedures conducted at five centers in the United States and Mexico to the FDA as part of its application for approval to market the device in the United States as an adjunct to mammography. Eventually, says Dr. Milne, CTLM may replace mammography altogether. The FDA was expected to rule on the application in the fall of 2003. ■

Dense Breasts Likely a Genetic Trait

About 40 percent of women have very dense breasts—defined as breasts with significant amounts of connective tissue and blood vessels (not fat)—that make it nearly impossible to locate potential cancers with mammography. Researchers have long known that these women also have a risk of breast cancer 1.8 to 6 times higher than that of similar women without dense breasts.

Now, a study published in a September 2002 issue of the *New England Journal of Medicine* finds that having

dense breasts is probably genetic. Australian and Canadian researchers evaluated 962 pairs of twins and found that identical twins, who share exactly the same genes, had similar breast densities, while fraternal twins, who share half their genes, had similar breast densities about half the time. The next step: locating the specific gene or genes responsible, which could help identify more women who are at risk and potentially point the way to treatments. ■

Key Discovery
A Sinister Role for the "Obesity Hormone"

Researchers have known for years that overweight women have an increased risk of breast cancer and that women who are obese when diagnosed with breast cancer tend to have a more aggressive disease with a poorer prognosis. They blame fat cells in older women, which convert androgens (male hormones) to estrogen, the female reproductive hormone that plays a major role in breast cancer. Estrogen induces breast cells to divide, and the more often they divide, the more likely it is that something will go wrong, making them unable to stop dividing, and resulting in cancer. Now, new research led by University of Minnesota researcher Margot P. Cleary, Ph.D., points to another possible culprit: leptin, the so-called obesity hormone.

Researchers discovered several years ago that as body weight increased, so did levels of leptin, which is secreted by fat cells. Dr. Cleary became intrigued with the possible connection between leptin and breast cancer after reading several papers suggesting the hormone might be involved in other types of cancer, such as adrenal, stomach, and lung cancer. Researchers had identified leptin receptors—"docking ports" for the hormone—on some cancer cells and found that adding leptin to these cancer cells resulted in increased proliferation, or division.

How it works. Dr. Cleary and her team, collaborating with researchers at the Mayo Clinic, tested the effects of leptin on human breast cancer cells in the lab. In the presence of leptin, the number of cancerous cells increased by 150 percent. Without exposure to leptin, the number increased by just 50 percent. The researchers also identified leptin receptors on the breast cancer cells. Further evidence of leptin's influence on breast cancer: The researchers bred several groups of mice, some of which were genetically programmed to develop breast cancer but were deficient in leptin. The mice that should

RESEARCH ROUNDUP

Fat Consumption Linked to Leptin Levels

More body fat means higher levels of leptin—the so-called obesity hormone, recently linked to an increased risk of breast cancer. But according to a small study at the University of Texas M.D. Anderson Cancer Center in Houston, women who switch to a low-fat, high-fiber diet can lower their leptin levels regardless of their weight. Measuring blood leptin levels could provide an additional marker for measuring breast cancer risk, along with body fat composition, estrogen levels, and other factors such as family history, number of pregnancies, and age at first menstruation, say the researchers. ■

have developed breast cancer did not. The study results were published in a November 2002 issue of the *Journal of the National Cancer Institute.*

These findings add new weight to the admonition that women should work to remain at a healthy weight, particularly as they age and their risk of breast cancer increases, notes Dr. Cleary. In fact, the findings served as an incentive for the doctor herself. "I lost a few pounds," she admits. ■

Key Discovery

Common Virus: The Colon Cancer Culprit?

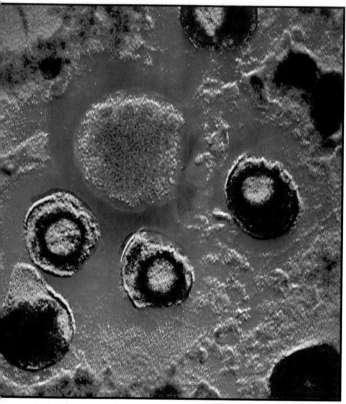

Many people are infected with the human cytomegalovirus, one of the herpes viruses, without knowing it. Now scientists are wondering whether the virus may increase the risk of colon cancer.

Charles S. Cobbs, M.D., is a neurosurgeon, so you wouldn't think he'd have much to do with colon cancer. Yet in one of those strange-but-true serendipitous discoveries that make science the fascinating field it is, he's found that a common virus that infects 50 to 80 percent of American adults may be linked to colon cancer. This paves the way for potential new treatments or even a vaccine.

Dr. Cobbs, associate professor in the departments of surgery and cell biology at the University of Alabama at Birmingham Medical Center, researches the role of chronic inflammation in brain cancer.

The more he studied the topic, however, the more convinced he became that there must be some persistent virus contributing to brain cancer. There was: the human cytomegalovirus (CMV), which causes severe infections in people with compromised immune systems and can lead to mental retardation in babies of infected mothers. The virus had been strongly linked to malignant glioma, the most prevalent and malignant type of brain tumor. Once Dr. Cobbs began studying it a bit more, he realized that CMV may also be linked to colon cancer.

How it works. It turns out that CMV is ideal for causing cancer, says Dr. Cobbs. Once it infects you, it never goes away, lying dormant until something—such as stress or reduced immunity—reactivates it. It also causes DNA mutations (a key step in turning a normal cell into a rapidly dividing cancer cell) and enables cells to move around (critical to cancer cells, which metastasize, or spread). Most important: Once CMV infects a cell, it produces a kind of protein-based "invisibility cloak" that keeps that cell hidden from immune system cells that could destroy it.

During his research, Dr. Cobbs dug up journal articles from the 1970s hinting at the possibility that CMV might play a role in colon cancer. To explore that theory further using 21st-century research techniques, he obtained specimens of colorectal polyps (precancerous cells), colorectal tumor cells, and normal cells from 28 people with the disease and tested them for CMV. He found two specific CMV proteins in about 80 percent of the polyps and about 85 percent of the cancer samples. The results of that study were published in a November 2002 issue of the journal *Lancet*.

The theory is that the virus may infect cells that already have a slight DNA injury. Infection with CMV is like adding insult to injury, turning what may have been a slow-growing mutation into a fast-growing cancer. "If we show that's the case, then it would raise a lot of questions," Dr. Cobbs says. For instance, should people with a high risk of colon cancer be treated with existing drugs that block CMV infection? Or should a vaccine be developed to prevent CMV infection, much like the vaccine currently under development to prevent infection with human papillomavirus, which causes cervical cancer? Those are all questions, notes Dr. Cobbs, that future research will help answer. ■

Progress in Prevention

A New Phrase for Oncologists: "Take Two Aspirin"

The mundane aspirin has been getting quite the wonder drug reputation lately. Research has found that it helps prevent not only heart attacks, strokes, and possibly Alzheimer's disease, but lung, prostate, and colon cancer as well. And that's not all. Now it appears the bitter white tablets may have some effect against breast and ovarian cancer.

Breast cancer. A study that followed 27,616 women over six years found that those who took aspirin six or more times a week cut their relative risk of breast cancer by nearly a third. The results were published in the journal *Cancer Epidemiology Biomarkers and Prevention* in December 2002.

Ovarian cancer. Another study, published in the October 2002 issue of *Obstetrics and Gynecology*, found that regular aspirin alone prevented the growth of ovarian tumor cells—at least in the laboratory—by as much as 68 percent. Combined with a drug that blocks the action of certain proteins that encourage cancer cell growth, it decreased ovarian cancer cell growth by 84 percent. Of course, test tube studies don't show what would happen in real women with cancer. Much more study is needed before anyone could point to aspirin as part of ovarian cancer treatment.

Colorectal cancer. The evidence that aspirin may prevent colorectal cancer is mounting as well. A large study published in a March 2003 issue of the *New England Journal of Medicine* followed more than 1,000 people who had previously been diagnosed with colorectal adenomas—early signs of colorectal cancer. The study participants took either 81 milligrams of aspirin (equivalent to a baby aspirin), 325 milligrams of aspirin, or a placebo (dummy pill) every day. A follow-up colonoscopy three years later revealed that those taking the low-dose aspirin were 19 percent less likely to have their adenomas recur than those taking placebos. Participants taking the higher dose of aspirin saw their risk drop 4 percent compared with the placebo group. Even more significant, researchers found, was that the relative risk of advanced adenomas, which are more likely to be precursors of cancer, dropped 41 percent in those taking the low-dose aspirin. ■

Way beyond headache medicine: The millions of people who now take aspirin to help stave off a heart attack or stroke may be doing themselves an extra favor by lowering their risk of certain cancers.

Key Discovery
A Cancer Danger in Your Food?

To toast or not to toast? Believe it or not, how you eat your bread may have an effect on your risk of cancer.

Scientists have known for some time that a white, odorless substance called acrylamide causes cancer, at least in mice. The substance is used to make poly-acrylamide, a chemical found in everything from cosmetics to plastics. It's also used to treat sewer and wastewater and to purify drinking water.

In 2002, Swedish researchers made a disturbing discovery: Even people who had no known acrylamide exposure showed signs of the substance in their blood. After further investigation, the researchers concluded that the source of the toxin was food.

Suspect foods. It seems that acrylamide is formed as a result of the chemical changes that occur when foods are baked, fried, or roasted. Many foods with the greatest amounts of acrylamide are also those that are the worst for you, such as French fries, potato chips, and baked sweets. A December 2002 study published in the journal *Chemotherapy* found that the substance passes through the placenta in pregnant women and through breast milk, prompting the scientists to recommend that pregnant and nursing women avoid foods high in acrylamide.

In October 2002, the FDA launched its own investigation, testing for acrylamide in a variety of foods. In February 2003, the agency announced preliminary results of some of that research, noting that acrylamide appeared not only in greasy fried foods but even in coffee and Cheerios. Most interesting: Acrylamide levels varied widely not only among types of food but also among different *brands* of the same type. For instance, Schmidt Old Tyme Split-Top Wheat Bread had 130 parts per billion, while Home Pride Butter Top Wheat Bread had 52 parts per billion. Acrylamide levels also differed depending on how the food was prepared. Plain slices of bread contained very little, but toasted slices had quadruple the amount.

No final answers yet. Not everyone agrees that acrylamide in food is a cancer threat. In January 2003, a study by the Harvard School of Public Health that evaluated the diets of 987 cancer patients and 538 healthy people in Sweden found no association between eating foods high in acrylamide (primarily crispbreads and pan-fried potatoes) and increased risk of bladder, bowel, or kidney cancer. Another study published in July 2003 found similar results for additional cancers (oral, pharyngeal, esophageal, laryngeal, breast, and ovarian).

In Europe, publication of the Harvard study reversed months of declining sales in foods high in acrylamide. But Michael Jacobson, Ph.D., executive director of the Center for Science in the Public Interest (CSPI), thinks the danger still exists. In late spring 2003, the CSPI petitioned the FDA to set limits on the amount of acrylamide foods can contain. ◼

Baked, fried, and toasted foods are often high in acrylamide, a known carcinogen.

Debating the Safety of Our Food

Point / Counterpoint

The acrylamide question is far from settled. On one side of the issue are consumer activists concerned that our food supply poses a serious cancer threat. On the other side are researchers who are finding little risk when they compare the amount of acrylamide some populations consume with their overall cancer risk.

Point

Lorelei Mucci, Ph.D., is a researcher in the department of epidemiology at the Harvard School of Public Health. She is lead author of the study published in January 2003 that found no link between acrylamide in food and an increased risk of bladder, large bowel, and kidney cancer in humans.

Q: It seems that your study disputes what the animal studies found. How is that possible?

A: Animal studies are based on amounts [of the toxin] several hundredfold higher than what humans are exposed to. Also, the way animals are exposed is different than humans. Animals are injected with the chemical or they inhale it, as opposed to consuming it in their food supply. It's a little tricky to extrapolate those very high dosages to what we're seeing consumed through the diet of the average person.

Q: So are you saying that acrylamide is not dangerous in the food supply?

A: A lot of additional research needs to be done to confirm our findings, but it seems that we can tone down some of the high levels of concern that were raised. It's probably not responsible for the thousands of cancer cases that people said it was.

Q: Are you still conducting research on this?

A: Yes. We are correlating data examining the use of coffee and examining the risk to additional cancer sites [other parts of the body where the cancers are found].

Counterpoint

Michael F. Jacobson, Ph.D., is executive director of the nutrition advocacy organization Center for Science in the Public Interest, based in Washington, D.C.

Q: The Harvard study and an Italian study found no cancer risk from acrylamide. Does this make it a non-issue?

A: The study provides no reassurance whatsoever that acrylamide is safe for humans. The researchers considered three cancers—bladder, colon, and kidney—but those are not the ones that acrylamide causes in animals. Moreover, the researchers' estimates of acrylamide exposure are flawed because they were based on a limited number of foods. We get acrylamide from a wide range of foods, and someone who eats a lot of fried potatoes may eat less bread, which is also a source of acrylamide. You have to look at things a lot more closely. Also, acrylamide *doesn't cause that many cancers* (fewer than 1 percent of all cancers). To detect something in an epidemiological study [like the Harvard and Italian studies], you need a blockbuster carcinogen like tobacco.

Q: So how great a threat is acrylamide?

A: The risk is significant, but it's not like smoking cigarettes or eating hot dogs or some of the other foods that have been linked with cancer. I've been looking at different ways to estimate risk, and the number varies between about 1,000 cancers per year and 25,000 per year. So it's not an enormous risk, and it's hard to expect that people are going to avoid all French fries just because of that.

Q: So what should consumers do?

A: Our general advice has been to eat less of the least nutritious, most contaminated foods, things like French fries, potato chips, corn chips, and coffee. Other foods, like Cheerios or bread, that have some acrylamide, I wouldn't say to cut out, because they have other nutritional benefits. The ultimate answer will be for scientists to figure out how to prevent or minimize its formation.

Key Discovery

To Cut Your Risk of Cancer, Drop a Few Pounds

The list of health problems linked with being overweight is long and getting longer: heart disease, high blood pressure, diabetes, insulin resistance, arthritis, depression. Now we can add cancer to that roster, based on the findings of a seminal study of more than 900,000 American adults. The results, published in an April 2003 issue of the *New England Journal of Medicine,* can be summed up in one sentence: The more you weigh, the more likely you are to die from cancer—*any* cancer.

How they did it. Researchers from the American Cancer Society used data from the Cancer Prevention Study II, which has tracked more than 1 million people since 1982. The study looked at factors such as the subjects' health and various lifestyle and physical characteristics, including weight. First, the researchers chose participants who were cancer-free and not underweight when they enrolled in the study. Then they took into account other factors related to cancer, such as smoking, alcohol intake, and diet as well as race, educational status, and physical activity. They used the body mass index (BMI), which considers weight and height, to evaluate weight status. A BMI between 18.5 and 24.9 is considered normal, while one between 25.0 and 29.9 indicates overweight, and 30.0 or more is considered obese.

What they found. Men with a BMI over 40 were 52 percent more likely to die from cancer, while women whose BMI was more than 40 were 62 percent more likely to die from

the disease. Overall, the authors estimated, as many as 14 percent of all cancer deaths in men over 50 and 20 percent in women over 50 are attributable to being overweight. Specific risks varied according to the cancers, but being overweight could increase the risk of some cancers by between 34 and 50 percent.

Although the study didn't examine the reasons for the link between weight and cancer, researchers believe an explanation may lie in hormonal changes that result from being overweight, along with some mechanical changes that occur. For instance, heavy people are more susceptible to acid reflux, or heartburn, which is a risk factor for esophageal cancer.

The findings garnered great attention in the United States, where 64 percent of Americans are overweight or obese. Lead study author Eugenia E. Calle, Ph.D., director of analytic epidemiology at the American Cancer Society, doesn't view the findings as a reason for dismay. Rather, she hopes they will serve as another wake-up call to health providers, health policy experts, and the public about the enormity of the weight problem facing this country. Combating it, she says, will take a tremendous shift in cultural norms, as happened with cigarette smoking. "And the very first thing you need for that shift is awareness of the issue," she says. The level of interest she's received from the media and public on the study, she says, has made her realize that "no, everyone didn't have the message. We weren't just telling a story that everyone had heard." ∎

AS WAISTLINES GROW, SO DOES CANCER RISK

This table shows by what percentage your risk for various cancers increases if you're overweight. A body mass index (BMI) between 18.5 and 24.9 is considered normal. A BMI between 25.0 and 29.9 indicates overweight, and 30.0 or more is obese.

CANCER	BODY MASS INDEX					
	25.0–29.9		30.0–34.9		35.0–39.9	
	Men (%)	Women (%)	Men (%)	Women (%)	Men (%)	Women (%)
Colorectal cancer	20	10	47	33	84	36
Liver cancer	13	—	90	40	352	68
Pancreatic cancer	—	11	—	28	—	41
Prostate cancer	0.8	—	20	—	34	—
Kidney cancer	18	33	36	66	70	70
Breast cancer	—	34	—	63	—	70
Non-Hodgkins' lymphoma	0.8	22	56	20	49	95

Source: New England Journal of Medicine

High-Tech Help
Fireflies Light the Way in Cancer Treatment

The firefly, that staple of childhood summer nights, may have a role to play in cancer treatment.

The goal of most cancer treatments today is to kill cancer cells or, more accurately, to make the cells commit suicide. But it's nearly impossible to know if such treatments work until weeks or months after they're used. Researchers from the University of Michigan Health System may have found a way around that problem with the help of the gene responsible for a firefly's glow.

The researchers inserted the gene into mice with cancer, but first, they manipulated the gene so that it was turned "off" until cancer cells began to die. The cancer cells' death turned the glow gene "on," causing the mice to emit faint traces of firefly light. Once perfected, the technique could be used to determine if cancer treatments are working days or weeks after they're administered, rather than months. The researchers' work was published in the December 2002 issue of the journal *Proceedings of the National Academy of Science.*

In Britain, researchers are using the firefly light gene to actually kill cancer cells. They first inserted the gene into cancer cells, which made them glow.

Then they added a chemical called a photosensitizing agent. When it's exposed to the firefly light, it makes the cells produce a toxin that kills them. The technique is similar to an existing treatment called photodynamic therapy (PDT), in which the photosensitizing chemical is injected into the bloodstream. It's absorbed by cells all over the body—both cancer cells and healthy ones—but it lingers longer in cancer cells. When the cells are exposed to laser light, the photosensitizing agent absorbs the light, producing a form of oxygen that acts like an explosive, bursting the cells.

> The cancer cells' death turned the glow gene "on," causing the mice to emit faint traces of firefly light.

One problem with PDT is that the light source can pass through only a very thin layer of cells, so it's been used primarily to treat tumors just below the skin or on the outer parts of organs. With the firefly gene, the light source is implanted directly into the tumor cell, so even tumors deep within the body can be targeted. ∎

Key Discovery

Rewriting the Script: Anthrax to Be a Hero

The same deadly toxin that terrified a nation back in the fall of 2001 may one day turn out to be an effective cancer treatment. Researchers at the National Institutes of Health (NIH) found in tests on hundreds of mice that a genetically modified version of the anthrax toxin dramatically reduced and even eliminated certain cancers, without harming the mice. The study results were published in the January 2003 issue of *Proceedings of the National Academy of Sciences*, and leading cancer-toxin biologist Arthur Frankel, M.D., told the *Philadelphia Inquirer*, "It's the most important breakthrough in our field in the last 20 years."

How it works. Researchers have been investigating the use of biological poisons, including diphtheria toxin and ricin (a poisonous protein in the castor bean) for cancer treatment for decades. It's not as crazy as it sounds. After all, what are chemotherapy drugs if not poisons? The idea to try anthrax came from a chance conversation between NIH scientists Stephen Leppla, Ph.D., and Thomas Bugge, Ph.D., over lunch one day when Dr. Leppla was temporarily assigned to the NIH's Institute of Dental and Craniofacial Research.

Dr. Bugge was telling Dr. Leppla about his work with plasminogen activator systems, which are enzymes found only on cancer cells. These enzymes cut apart other proteins, clearing a path so cancer cells have room to spread. Because they're found only on cancer cells, they make good targets for drugs and other cancer treatments. The two men wondered if plasminogen activators could somehow be used in conjunction with anthrax, which Dr. Leppla had been studying for years.

The idea to bring anthrax into the picture was inspired by way the toxin works. In order for it to do its damage, it has to hook up with an enzyme called furin, found on the surface of nearly all cells. Without this enzyme, anthrax is basically harmless. Pairing it with furin, though, is the equivalent of pulling the pin in a hand grenade.

What would happen if the anthrax toxin were modified to hook up only with a plasminogen enzyme? To find out, the two scientists "rewrote" a sequence of amino acids in one anthrax protein (the bacterium itself is made up of hundreds of these proteins). The new sequence amounted to a change in instruction for the protein, telling it to combine only with the plasminogen activator found on tumor cells.

The results were tremendous. In trials in mice, a single injection of the modified anthrax toxin shrank lung tumors by an average of 65 percent and reduced soft-tissue tumors such as melanoma and fibrosarcoma, two forms of skin cancer, by 92 percent. The tumors shrank even more after two treatments. In effect, the anthrax was doing what it was designed to do—destroy cells—only in this case, they were all cancer cells. It had no effect on normal cells.

Availability. The Danish biotechnology company OncoTac has licensed the technology, which may move into human clinical trials sometime in 2004. ◼

Anthrax killed five people when it was sent through the mail in the United States. Now the deadly toxin is being unleashed on cancer.

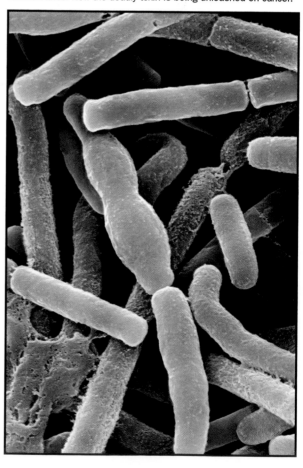

Surgical Solution
First, Remove the Liver. . .

A team of Italian surgeons and researchers has given new meaning to the term "out-of-body experience." In what must surely be one of the most unique cancer treatments in history (successful ones, at least), they removed a patient's liver, transported it via a police-escorted ambulance to a nuclear reactor 1/3 mile away, and blasted it with radiation. Then they returned it to the operating room and reimplanted it in the 48-year-old patient. Doctors performed the 21-hour operation in December 2001, and the man was still cancer-free as of his quarterly checkup in April 2003. "The result is beyond our hope," says physicist Tazio Pinelli, Ph.D., of the National Institute of Nuclear Physics in Italy.

The patient had colon cancer that had spread to his liver. The liver cancer hadn't responded to chemotherapy, and the cancer was so pervasive that conventional radiation would have destroyed the liver entirely. So Dr. Pinelli and his team decided to try a procedure they'd been working on for more than 13 years, called boron neutron capture therapy, or BNCT. It's been tried in brain cancer patients in several countries (without removing the brain, of course) including the United States, with poor results.

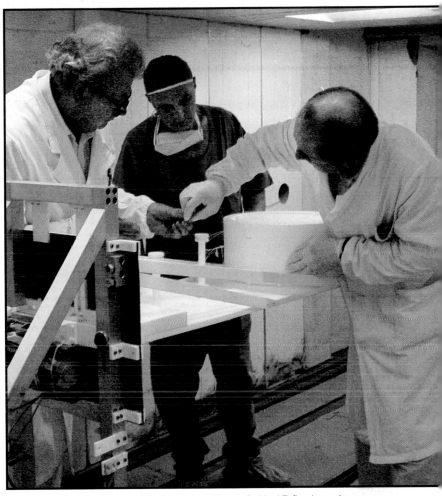

A cancerous liver has been removed and placed in a cylindrical Teflon bag, above. Soon the organ will be irradiated and returned to the patient.

How it works. Key to the procedure is infusing the organ—in this case, the liver—with boron, an element that has both metallic and non-metallic properties. Cancer cells, which grow faster than normal cells, take up more boron atoms. When the neutron beam, or radiation, is turned on, the beam splits the boron atoms into destructive high-energy particles, which then kill the cancer cells. It would be difficult to provide this level of radiation while the organ is in the body, because healthy tissue would also be damaged, says Dr. Pinelli.

The patient's liver was placed in a Teflon bag for its trip to the reactor. Meanwhile, the patient was kept alive by extracorporeal circulation, or an artificial liver, just as he would have been during a traditional liver transplant. The liver was out of his body for about two hours.

Availability. Dr. Pinelli and his team are preparing to conduct additional "out-of-body" surgeries at another facility elsewhere in Europe in 2004. "A large field of research is opening for extending the cancer treatment to progressively larger parts of the human body," he says. ■

Drug Development
New Target for Old Breast Cancer Drug

Randolph Urmston, here with his family, was lucky to survive lung cancer.

Seattle lawyer Randolph Urmston never smoked and had no family history of lung cancer. So when he was diagnosed with the disease in 1997, it was an immense shock, particularly when he learned the cancer had already spread to his brain. Standard chemotherapy and radiation treatment did little to stem its progression. Then his doctor started him on the chemotherapy drug docetaxel (Taxotere), used to treat breast cancer. After four months of drug treatment, along with additional radiation therapy, the cancer disappeared. And it has stayed gone, a miracle that Urmston, now 58, attributes in part to the docetaxel.

Now, more lung cancer patients should benefit from the drug. The FDA approved docetaxel for use in the primary treatment of lung cancer (in combination with the chemotherapy drug cisplatin) in December 2002. It's the first new medication approved for the disease in more than four years.

How it works. Docetaxel belongs to the taxoid class of chemotherapy drugs, which also includes the breast cancer drug paclitaxel (Taxol). These drugs prevent cancer cells from dividing by "freezing" the cell's internal skeleton, which is made up of structures called microtubules. Microtubules assemble and disassemble as the cell divides. Docetaxel encourages their assembly but blocks their disassembly, thereby preventing cancer cells from dividing.

The FDA based its approval on a clinical trial of 1,218 patients that compared the effect of docetaxel plus cisplatin or docetaxel plus carboplatin (another chemotherapy drug) to the standard chemo combination of vinorelbine plus cisplatin. Patients in the docetaxel/cisplatin group had a median survival time of 10.9 months vs. 10.0 months for patients treated with the standard regimen. Overall, 31.6 percent of the patients responded to docetaxel plus cisplatin, compared with 24.4 percent of those treated with vinorelbine plus cisplatin.

"It's not the home run we'd all like," admits Mark R. Green, M.D., Gilbreth Professor of Clinical Oncology at the Medical University of South Carolina in Charleston, who participated in the clinical trials. "But we're talking about taking another step forward."

When it comes to lung cancer, every little step makes a difference. The disease is the second most common cancer in the United States. It's also the number one cause of cancer deaths among men and women and has surpassed breast cancer as the number one cancer killer of women, claiming approximately 155,000 lives each year and accounting for 28 percent of all cancer deaths. ▪

High-Tech Help
Erasing and Replacing the Immune System to Combat Cancer

Groundbreaking new research suggests a "scorched earth" approach may be the best way to help patients with the deadliest form of skin cancer, melanoma. Replacing a patient's entire immune system with specially targeted killer cells developed to attack the cancer has been shown to either stop the cancer cells from growing or destroy them altogether.

How it works. Researchers from the National Cancer Institute, led by Steven A. Rosenberg, M.D., Ph.D., took immune system cells called T cells that were already attacking patients' tumors and grew massive numbers of them in the laboratory. While the cells were growing, the researchers used chemotherapy to destroy the patients' existing immune systems to make room for the new immune cells. Then, in the space of about 20 minutes, they infused more than 70 billion of these new tumor-attacking cells into the patients. (The new cells also defend the body against viruses and bacteria.)

Researchers also gave the patients high doses of a protein called interleukin-2 (IL-2), which stimulates T cell growth.

Dr. Rosenberg performed the procedure on 13 patients with metastatic melanoma, some of whom had only months to live despite previous highly aggressive treatment. The results, published in the online version of the journal *Science* in September 2002, were astounding. One 16-year-old boy, who'd been given just two months to live, was still free of disease two years after the procedure. Overall, the treatment shrank the tumors by half in six of the patients, with no growth or appearance of new tumors, while four patients saw some of their tumors disappear entirely. Three of the original patients have since died, however. Side effects included relatively mild autoimmune disorders, with some patients developing white patches on their skin where the T cells destroyed the pigmentation, and one patient experiencing an inflammation of the iris.

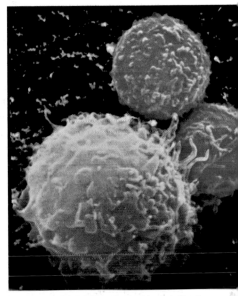

A cancer cell (pink) is attacked by two T cells (orange). Doctors have tried replacing cancer patients' entire immune systems with T cells.

Availability. The therapy is still highly experimental, says Dr. Rosenberg, and at least two years away from widespread use in cancer patients. Meanwhile, he and his team are testing it against breast, prostate, and ovarian cancers. It may also eventually be used to treat some infectious diseases, such as AIDS. ■

ALSO in the NEWS

Relief from Bone Cancer Pain

Once cancer gets into the bone, it results in excruciating pain that even morphine and other strong narcotics often can't touch. Now, bone cancer patients have another option for pain relief: radiofrequency ablation, which uses intense heat transmitted through the tip of a needle to kill nerve endings and much of the cancer tissue in the bone, alleviating pain. In October 2002, the FDA approved the marketing of the technology for cancer patients whose disease had spread to the bone.

A clinical study of 43 patients conducted at nine medical centers throughout the United States and Europe that found that 95 percent of the patients treated with the procedure experienced significant pain reduction. Before the treatment, patients' pain averaged 7.5 on a scale of 1 to 10, with 10 being unbearable pain. After the procedure, pain scores dropped by half, and by eight weeks following the procedure, the average score was 1. ■

High-Tech Help

Conquering Pancreatic Cancer with a Trojan Horse

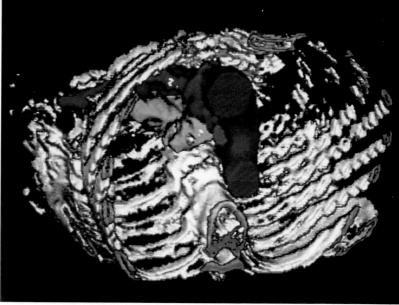

Pancreatic cancer (green) is notoriously difficult to treat. A new type of gene therapy makes the tumors more susceptible to cancer drugs.

Pancreatic cancer is one of the most frustrating cancers to treat. The disease, which strikes more than 30,000 Americans a year, is almost always fatal because it is often found so late and because it seems to be so resistant to traditional chemotherapy and radiation. So researchers are looking for novel ways to destroy these cancers. Results from the first phase of a gene therapy trial suggest they may have found one.

While most gene therapy trials in cancer have focused on the use of genetically modified vaccines to bolster the immune system, this method, developed by Ralph Weichselbaum, M.D., and his research team at the University of Chicago, is designed to make the tumor cells more susceptible to chemotherapy and radiation.

How it works. Certain white blood cells secrete a protein called tumor necrosis factor (TNF), which binds to areas on cancer cells aptly described as "death receptors," spurring those cells to commit suicide. These proteins also make tumor cells more receptive to chemotherapy and radiation. More recent research suggests that TNF also blocks the blood supply to tumors.

In the gene therapy process, a genetically engineered virus containing the TNF gene (called TNFerade) is injected into the tumor once a week for five weeks. The virus is designed to have an "on-off" switch, and it remains turned off until it receives a signal from a dose of radiation, delivered four hours after each injection. Once that signal is given, the virus spreads out into the tumor cells and infects them, dropping off its "package"—the TNF gene—like a biological Trojan horse.

Results from a pilot study of 24 late-stage cancer patients (4 of whom had pancreatic cancer) were presented at the November 2002 meeting of the American Society of Clinical Oncology. Of the patients with pancreatic cancer, three had significant improvements in their tumors and were still alive and doing well a year or more after treatment. The fourth died before completing the treatment.

In spring of 2003, another study had 22 patients enrolled at eight centers. Five were being treated at Virginia Commonwealth University's Massey Cancer Center in Richmond by radiation oncologist Theodore Chung, M.D. All were in the final stages of pancreatic cancer, with little or no hope of recovery. Four months after treatment, "we're seeing responses that are quite dramatic," Dr. Chung says. One patient was "doing marvelously." A second, whose tumor was too large to be removed surgically before the treatment, had it removed three months after the gene therapy. And an autopsy on the one patient who died showed that nearly all of the tumor had been destroyed. The patient was simply too sick to survive even after the treatment.

> **"We're seeing responses that are quite dramatic,"** Dr. Chung says.

Ironically, such success may make it difficult to recruit patients for future randomized trials in which some would receive the therapy and others standard treatment. That could be a problem, since the initial study was designed primarily to test safety, not effectiveness. "Objectively, we cannot make any claims about how much better, if any, this treatment is compared with standard treatment" until more studies are completed, says Dr. Chung. But hopes are high. "I think it presents a unique, novel approach," he says.

Availability. As of fall 2003, TNFerade was in Phase II clinical trials. ■

Surgical Solution
Preserving Male Fertility with Micro-surgery

When bicyclist Lance Armstrong learned he had testicular cancer in 1996, he banked his sperm before having one of his testicles removed and later was able to father three healthy children. But thousands of other men with testicular cancer aren't as lucky.

Generally, the testes are removed along with the tumor even before it's confirmed that the tumor is cancerous. In many such cases, the tumor isn't malignant, but the man's fertility is already compromised by the surgery. Now, a New York reproductive specialist has pioneered a new microsurgery technique that allows the removal of tumors while preserving the testes in some men.

How it works. With the advent of high-resolution scrotal ultrasound, testicular tumors can be identified even before they're felt, notes Marc Goldstein, M.D., professor of reproductive medicine and urology at Weill Medical College of Cornell University in New York City. Because the incidence of these tumors is 38 times higher in infertile men than in men without fertility problems, Dr. Goldstein began doing ultrasounds on every infertile man he saw. "I was picking up small tumors, but I didn't want to remove the testicles before I was sure they were cancer," he says.

To find out if the tumors were cancerous, he borrowed a trick from breast cancer surgeons, who

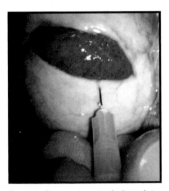

A new microsurgery technique lets doctors biopsy suspicious lumps—and even remove tumors—without removing the testicle.

use an ultrasound-guided needle to biopsy suspicious breast lumps. He combined the needle with the operating microscope and microsurgical tools he uses for reversing vasectomies and found that the three together enabled him to find and remove these tiny tumors—some no bigger than a grain of rice—without removing the testes.

Of the 65 men who underwent fertility evaluation in his study, 5 percent had testicular tumors, half of which were benign. The study was published in the *Journal of Urology* in September 2002.

Availability. Dr. Goldstein is now teaching the technique to other surgeons. Once more doctors learn how to do the surgery, he says, "It will change the way we approach testicular tumors." He compares it to the situation with breast lumps: Formerly, women who had lumps were automatically given mastectomies, but today, biopsies and lumpectomies are the norm. ∎

ALSO in the NEWS

Rescuing Gleevec from Failure

The magic bullet wasn't so magic. Soon after headlines touted the success of Gleevec (imatinib) against chronic myelogenous leukemia (CML) three years ago, there were reports that some patients became resistant to the drug, then eventually relapsed and died. The reason may be that molecular mutations either impair the "fit" between the enzyme Gleevec targets and the drug molecule itself—creating a sort of broken zipper track—or weaken Gleevec's bond with the enzyme.

Now, researchers at the Howard Hughes Medical Institute and Oregon Health Sciences University Cancer Institute have found a compound, called PD180970, that overcomes the problem and could help Gleevec keep working longer. Ideally, the compound could be developed into a drug that would be given with Gleevec to prevent resistance. The results of the research were published in the December issue of the journal *Cancer Research*. ∎

DIGESTION
AND METABOLISM

IF YOU HAVE TYPE 2 DIABETES, RESEARCHERS FROM AROUND THE WORLD HAVE IMPORTANT NEWS TO SHARE **WITH YOU.**

A Danish study has demonstrated for the first time that exercising faithfully, eating right, and aggressively treating health threats such as high cholesterol with medication can slash your risk of diabetes-related problems (such as heart disease and eye, kidney, and nerve damage) by a whopping 50 percent. And if your spouse has diabetes, British research warns that you should be extra aware of your own health, since you're twice as likely to develop it, too.

In other news, more people have celiac disease than was previously thought. If you have abdominal pain and your symptoms worsen when you eat wheat products, you just may be one of them. Also, a new type of drug that knocks out Crohn's disease is in the final stage of testing, and a vaccine that targets the bacteria that cause most stomach ulcers is in the works.

Finally, if your nights are sleepless due to a combination of acid reflux and a common breathing condition, new research shows that one treatment can fix them both.

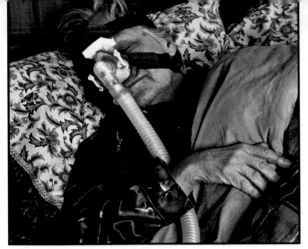

It's not pretty, but it works: Wearing a sleep mask like this one to bed can alleviate both sleep apnea and nighttime heartburn.

High-Tech Help
Breathing Mask Foils Two Sleep Thieves

Barking dogs, car alarms, and telephone callers with the wrong number may top your list of most aggravating sleep disturbances, but they're mere nuisances compared to sleep apnea and nighttime heartburn. Either condition can make you toss and turn at night, leaving you groggy during the day—but when they strike as a team, they can make a good night's sleep doubly difficult to come by.

A recent study found that one remedy can reduce the symptoms of both of these sleep robbers. The solution is a treatment called continuous positive airway pressure (CPAP), in which a device pumps air through a face mask that's strapped over your nose and sometimes your mouth. CPAP is the most common treatment for obstructive sleep apnea, in which sagging flesh in the throat disrupts normal breathing during sleep and causes people who have it to repeatedly awaken with a gasp.

In the study, researchers instructed 181 participants to use CPAP masks. All of them had both apnea and nocturnal gastroesophageal reflux—nighttime heartburn—in which stomach acid backs up into the esophagus, the tube that leads from the mouth to the stomach. The 165 people who continued to use the CPAP machines during the study had a 48 percent improvement in their reflux symptoms, says John O'Connor, M.D., assistant professor of medicine at Duke University Medical Center in Durham, North Carolina, and one of the study authors. The higher the amount of air pressure the machine exerted, the more the symptoms subsided. The 16 people who stopped using the devices experienced no improvement in reflux symptoms. The results were published in January 2003 in the journal *Archives of Internal Medicine.*

How it works. The CPAP device treats apnea by increasing air pressure in the throat, keeping tissues pressed back out of the airway and allowing easier breathing. It also increases pressure in the esophagus, Dr. O'Connor says. This keeps acid in the stomach where it belongs or pushes it back if some slips through the valve that divides the esophagus from the stomach.

The two conditions share a link in many people, he says: obesity. "Almost all patients with sleep apnea are overweight, and so are a significant proportion of those with reflux," he says. Being overweight sets the stage for floppier tissues in the throat and increases pressure in the abdomen, compressing the stomach and pushing acid upward into the esophagus.

If you have reflux but not apnea, CPAP treatment is not the best choice for you, Dr. O'Connor says. Several medications are available that effectively treat reflux more conveniently than wearing a face mask at night. But if you have apnea in addition to nighttime heartburn, it's worth discussing your symptoms with your doctor to find out if you'd be a good candidate for CPAP therapy, he says.

Availability. CPAP devices cost more than $300 and are available with a doctor's prescription from a number of medical supply companies. Insurance plans typically cover them. ■

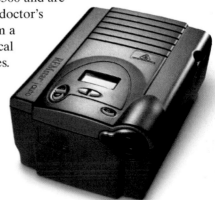

The mask is connected to a machine that provides pressure to keep airways open and the "door" to the stomach closed.

Key Discovery

New Celiac Study Goes Against the Grain

The bread aisle at the supermarket may be a more hazardous place than previously suspected. According to the findings of a large study published in the February 2003 issue of *Archives of Internal Medicine* that measured the prevalence of celiac disease—a condition made worse by eating certain grains—the disease strikes 1 of every 133 Americans. This makes it about 100 times more common than previously thought, says lead researcher Alessio Fasano, M.D., co-director of the Center for Celiac Research at the University of Maryland.

Celiac disease is an autoimmune disorder, a condition in which the immune system attacks the body—in this case, the lining of the small intestine. But it's unique, Dr. Fasano says, because it's the only autoimmune disease with a known environmental trigger. That trigger is gluten, a protein found in wheat, barley, rye, and possibly oats.

If you have unexplained abdominal troubles, look to your diet as a possible cause. More people than previously thought have a sensitivity to gluten, a protein found in many grains, including wheat.

When someone with celiac disease eats gluten, the immune system turns against the small intestine. The ensuing damage can interfere with nutrient absorption from food, leading to malnutrition. Symptoms can include diarrhea, constipation, and

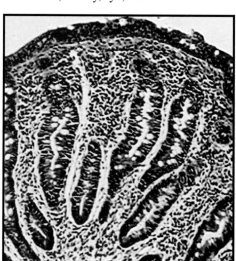

Nutrients are absorbed into the blood through villi, finger-like projections in the small intestine.

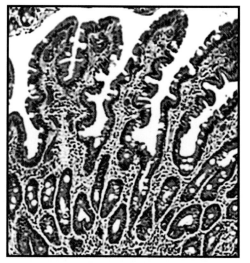

In celiac disease, the body destroys the villi, leading to poor absorption of nutrients.

abdominal pain. Weakness, tiredness, and weight loss can also result. Celiac disease can run in families. Symptoms may appear in babies soon after cereal is introduced. They can develop in adults, too.

The new study involved more than 13,000 children and adults from across America. Some of them were known to be at increased risk for celiac disease, either because they had symptoms, they had a relative with the disease, or they had a condition that's associated with celiac disease, such as short stature, arthritis, osteoporosis, or infertility.

According to the findings, 0.75 percent of people (1 out of every 133) who don't have these risk factors have celiac disease. That percentage skyrockets to 4.5 among people who have a close relative with the disease, such as a parent or sibling. For people with osteoporosis, it's also higher—about 2.5 percent. And it's even higher (4 percent) for people who are short in stature and those with unexplained infertility (6 percent). The malnutrition from the disease can lead to all of these conditions.

Historically, celiac disease has been most associated with Caucasians, but it may be found in similar numbers in other racial groups in America, Dr. Fasano says. However, this study offers limited information on nonwhites, since minorities accounted for only a small number of the participants.

Testing for celiac. Since celiac disease often causes no symptoms and can be difficult to diagnose, Dr. Fasano suggests that people with a family history of the disease or another condition associated with it should ask their doctors for testing. Celiac disease can be diagnosed by a blood test. If the results are positive, the diagnosis is usually confirmed by inserting an endoscope through the mouth and taking a tissue sample from the small intestine. The treatment is straightforward: Avoid gluten.

If unusually short children are diagnosed with celiac disease before puberty, they can make up their lost height once they begin the proper diet, he says. An infertile woman may be able to get pregnant once the disease is corrected. And, he says, if people fix their diets before early adulthood, they can reverse the osteoporosis that celiac disease causes. ■

ALSO in the NEWS

"Good" Bacteria in Gut Linked to Natural Antibiotic

You may already know that "good" bacteria in your digestive tract help fight off "bad" bugs such as Listeria, which can cause food poisoning. But there's more to the story, according to a  new laboratory study. It seems that in mice, the good bacteria spur cells in the intestine to make a protein that acts as a natural antibiotic. Humans don't produce the protein, called angiogenin-4, but we do make a number of other "protein antibiotics" that may be regulated by friendly bacteria, says researcher Lora Hooper, Ph.D., an instructor at Washington University in St. Louis. "I'm sure this is just the beginning of the story," she adds. The findings were reported in the online version of the journal *Nature Immunology* in January 2003. ■

Milk Linked to Crohn's Disease

Even if you aren't lactose intolerant, it's possible that the milk you drink may be wreaking havoc on your intestines. According to a study published in July 2003 in the *Journal of Clinical Microbiology*, Crohn's disease, an inflammatory bowel condition causing diarrhea, weight loss, and tiredness, may be linked to bacteria found in cow's milk. The British scientists behind the research said they detected the bacterium, called *Mycobacterium avium paratuberculosis* (MAP), in 92 percent of Crohn's patients versus only 26 percent of people in a control group. "The rate of detection of MAP in individuals with Crohn's disease is highly significant and implicates this pathogen in disease causation," they wrote. Earlier tests have shown that MAP can survive current pasteurization procedures. The British medical charity Action Research, which backed the study, calls for more stringent pasteurization to kill the MAP bug, as well as tests for MAP in dairy herds and improved hygiene on dairy farms. The study's lead author, John Hermon-Taylor, noted that MAP may also contribute to irritable bowel syndrome. ■

Drug Development

Crohn's Drug Slams the Door on Trouble-making Cells

By 2005, people with Crohn's disease may be able to gain the upper hand over their condition with a new type of drug that shoos away troublemaking cells in the intestine before they can do their dirty work.

Crohn's is a type of inflammatory bowel disease that typically strikes young people, causing inflammation and damage throughout the digestive tract. Although experts still don't know what triggers the inflammation, it's the source of serious symptoms— including bleeding, diarrhea, and pain—and may require surgery. The new drug, natalizumab (Antegren), acts like a guided missile, targeting specific immune cells implicated in the disease. Drugs currently used to treat Crohn's, including steroids, affect the entire immune system.

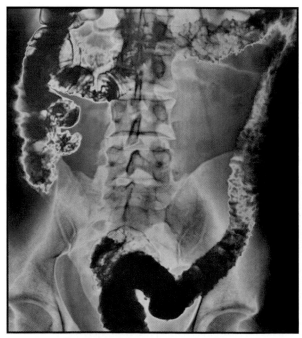

Crohn's disease often strikes the small intestine or the colon. It can affect different parts of the digestive tract at once.

Antegren showed promise in a study published in a January 2003 issue of the *New England Journal of Medicine*. In the study, 248 people with Crohn's were divided into four groups and given either two doses of placebo (dummy pills); one dose of Antegren and one dose of placebo; or two doses of Antegren, at either a lower or higher dosage. Those who received two treatments with Antegren experienced a decrease in symptoms more often than those who received placebos. And all of the groups that received the drug scored better on an index that measured the severity of their disease.

In the same issue of the journal, another study reported success in treating multiple sclerosis (MS) with Antegren. In MS, the protective myelin sheath on nerves is destroyed or damaged, forming lesions (sclerosis) in the brain. The resulting disruption of nerve function causes blindness, difficulty moving, and other symptoms, depending on where the lesions occur.

In the MS study, 213 patients received either a placebo or one of two different dosages of Antegren, all given monthly for six months. Those who received the medication developed only about one-tenth the number of new lesions as those who received the placebo. The groups treated with Antegren also had about half the number of relapses as the placebo group, and they reported greater well-being.

How it works. In Crohn's disease, immune cells called lymphocytes trigger and prolong inflammation after they enter the gastrointestinal tract from the bloodstream. On the surface of the cells are molecules that help the lymphocytes find their way to the area and stay there, says Subrata Ghosh, M.D., professor at Imperial College in London and lead author of the study. Antegren blocks the molecules, preventing the migration of the cells to the inflamed intestine and giving the area a chance to heal. In MS, the drug works by blocking the same type of molecules on the surface of immune system cells, which keeps them from entering the brain.

Antegren will probably be used for patients who have severe problems with Crohn's and haven't responded to conventional drugs, Dr. Ghosh says.

Availability. Antegren is in Phase III clinical trials, the last phase of testing required before a drug can gain FDA approval, as a treatment for both Crohn's and MS. It's expected to be available as a Crohn's treatment, if all goes well, in 2005. Availability as an MS treatment will take longer. ■

Progress in Prevention

A Road Map for Longer Life with Diabetes

Proper food, medications, and plenty of movement / will give your whole body a world of improvement.

Apologies to Benjamin Franklin, who penned similar rhymes urging people to work hard and live sensibly. But he probably would have written this one, too, had he seen the new evidence that the right diet and lifestyle can keep people with type 2 diabetes healthier, if not wealthy and wise.

An eight-year Danish study, reported in a January 2003 issue of the *New England Journal of Medicine*, looked at 160 people with type 2 diabetes, the most common form of the disease. These patients also had early signs of kidney disease and were at increased risk of developing cardiovascular disease, as most

Regular exercise can help keep diabetes complications at bay. And who says it can't be fun?

Obesity May Be the Culprit in Type 1 Diabetes Increase

Type 2 diabetes, typically associated with being overweight, is becoming increasingly common in children. But there's also been a rise in type 1 diabetes, caused by the destruction of insulin-producing beta cells in the pancreas. In fact, the incidence of type 1 diabetes per 1,000 children in the United States has doubled or even tripled since 1960.

Now, a study published in October 2002 in the journal *Diabetes Care* suggests that the obesity epidemic linked to type 2 may also be responsible for the increase in type 1. European researchers studied data on 499 children diagnosed with type 1 diabetes before they turned 15 and compared it with data on 1,337 healthy children in the same population. They found that children with diabetes were significantly taller and heavier from the time they were about 1 month old until age 6 than those without the disease. They also found that breastfeeding the children for any length of time cut the risk of diabetes by one-fourth, duplicating findings from other studies.

Although the researchers don't know exactly why the correlation between weight and type 1 diabetes exists, an analysis in *Child Health Monitor*, which tracks pediatric research, suggests it may be related to how much children are fed in their early years and to the fact that increased weight may put more strain on insulin-producing beta cells. ■

ALSO in the NEWS

Effects of Fructose Not So Sweet

If you're bothered by unexplained rumblings and pain in your belly, the culprit could be the fruit juice in your refrigerator. Fruit juice is high in fructose, a sugar that's not digested as well as other sugars, says Peter Beyer, M.S., R.D., associate professor in the dietetics and nutrition department at the University of Kansas Medical Center.

Beyer and fellow researchers gave 15 healthy adults 25 grams of fructose on one day and 50 grams on another. (A 16-ounce container of juice can contain about 25 grams.) At least half the people had gas, bloating, and gurgling noises after the 25-gram dose, he says, and even more had those problems—plus mild diarrhea—after the larger dose. The researchers presented their findings at the October 2002 scientific meeting of the American College of Gastroenterology.

If you have these sorts of problems regularly, try drinking only small portions of juice at a sitting, and drink it only with meals to help your body absorb the fructose better, Beyer suggests. To confirm a problem with fructose intolerance, ask your doctor for a hydrogen breath test. This simple test is a way to find out if fructose is being properly digested by your small intestine or instead traveling undigested to your colon. When the bacteria that naturally reside in the colon eat the fructose, they produce hydrogen gas, which can be measured in your breath. The test is available at many large hospitals. ■

people with diabetes are. In fact, heart attacks are what ultimately kill some 80 percent of people with diabetes.

In the study, half of the participants were given conventional treatments, such as insulin to control high blood sugar and blood pressure–lowering drugs such as ACE inhibitors. The goal was to get the patients' readings within the limits recommended by the Danish Medical Association, such as total cholesterol below 190 mg/dL and blood pressure less than 135/85 mm/Hg.

The other 80 people in the study pursued goals that were "much more ambitious," says Oluf Pedersen, M.D., chief physician at the Steno Diabetes Center in Copenhagen and senior author of the study. They ate lots of fish and vegetables and less saturated fat. They exercised regularly. They took smoking-cessation classes. They met regularly with a doctor, a nurse, and a dietitian for education and counseling. They took more frequent and higher doses of medications such as statin drugs to lower cholesterol and ACE inhibitors to lower blood pressure. In addition, they took vitamin/mineral supplements and low-dose aspirin for heart health.

At the end of the study, those who followed the intensive therapy were more than 50 percent less likely to have cardiovascular disease than the people in the other group. Also, their risks of eye, kidney, and nerve damage from diabetes had fallen by more than 50 percent.

Drop in on your doctor. To achieve the same improvements in your blood sugar and cholesterol levels and blood pressure, you need continued support, education, and motivation from your doctor, Dr. Pedersen explains. You should visit your physician every few months for a checkup, which could include a physical examination and blood tests. Discuss which risk factors need to be treated most aggressively.

"Type 2 diabetic patients should take their disease as a challenge and do their very best to change their lifestyle," Dr. Pedersen says, and stick to a medication regimen to keep their risk factors under control. ■

Key Discovery

Wedding Cake Another Risk Factor for Diabetes

Being married "in sickness and in health" takes on new meaning for many couples when one of the spouses has type 2 diabetes. That's because, according to a British study of nearly 500 people, those married to someone with type 2 diabetes are more than twice as likely to develop the disease as people whose spouses don't have it.

The spouses in the study also showed an increased risk of having the abnormal blood sugar levels that lead to diabetes, and they had higher levels of triglycerides, a type of blood fat known to raise heart disease risk. The findings were published in the March 2003 issue of the journal *Diabetes Care*.

Birds of a feather? One reason diabetes may strike both members of a married couple is that people tend to choose partners who are similar to them in terms of body type and ethnicity, says study coauthor Tahseen Chowdhury, M.D., a diabetes specialist at the Royal London Hospital. Being overweight increases the chances of developing the disease, as does being a member of certain ethnic groups. In the United States, those include African-Americans, Native Americans, people of Asian and Pacific Island descent, and Latinos.

A more important explanation, however, is that spouses tend to share similar diet and exercise patterns. Eating healthful foods and getting plenty of exercise are critical for avoiding and treating type 2 diabetes. If one spouse has bad habits, the other is likely to have them, too.

Dr. Chowdhury suggests that when either spouse has diabetes, treating it should be a family affair. "Spouses of patients with diabetes should be very vigilant with their own health," he says. In addition, the researchers suggest that such spouses be screened regularly for diabetes during checkups. Children of parents with diabetes are also at higher risk and therefore need to adopt healthy diet and exercise habits to avoid it, he says. ■

High-Tech Help
Virtual Stomach Promises Better Pills

A three-dimensional tablet in the virtual stomach. The arrows indicate how fast the tablet is traveling, and the colors represent the shear force on the pill.

When you swallow an extended- or timed-release tablet, it vanishes into your stomach, where it eventually breaks down and releases its contents. A new computer simulation offers surprising insights into exactly what happens to that pill during its fantastic unseen voyage.

A team of researchers led by James Brasseur, Ph.D., professor of mechanical engineering at Pennsylvania State University, created a "virtual stomach," which may someday help drug companies make their extended-release tablets more effective or reveal which drugs should be taken with which kinds of meals.

How they did it. The "virtual stomach," which runs on a massive cluster of computers, produces animated, two-dimensional outlines of a stomach on a computer screen. A small colored pill can be electronically "dropped" into the stomach, where it drifts about, slowly leaking a cloud of medication as it dissolves. To program the computer model, Anupam Pal, Ph.D., the Penn State postdoctoral student who developed the simulation, fed the computer information taken from magnetic resonance imaging (MRI) movies of the human stomach. He also used movies of dog and cat stomachs made with X-ray machines, as well as measurements of pressure in human stomachs. AstraZeneca, a pharmaceutical company, is supporting the development of the computer model.

What it shows. The simulation has led to interesting discoveries about delayed-release medications and about how the stomach works, Dr. Brasseur

says. For instance, the vigorous muscle motions that mix the contents occur only in the bottom one-third of the stomach. The upper part acts mainly as a holding chamber, although it does squeeze material down toward the bottom. Think of a fruit smoothie in your blender: At the top, the slush is relatively calm; the real churning happens at the bottom, where the blades are whirling.

Researchers were also surprised by how much of a role a tablet's density plays in determining how it moves in the stomach. When the pill is in the calmer upper part of the stomach, it doesn't break down quickly. But when a denser—and therefore less buoyant—tablet falls into the more active lower portion, the stomach fluids that are shifting back and forth rub away at the tablet, which can quickly wear down its surface, says Dr. Pal.

When the researchers simulated a stomach filled with a smooth, squishy food—such as mashed potatoes—and dropped in a virtual tablet only slightly denser than the stomach contents, the tablet quickly fell to the bottom section, where it was more rapidly broken down, he says. In the future, drug manufacturers may be able use this information to control the absorption of drugs by adjusting the density of pills and recommending that they be taken with certain foods. ■

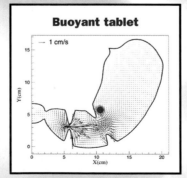

Buoyant tablet

A chart of the stomach with a tablet that floats. Pills that float instead of sinking take longer to break down. Food can affect how fast a tablet sinks.

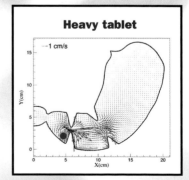

Heavy tablet

A chart of the stomach with a tablet that sinks. Denser tablets fall to the bottom of the stomach sooner and are therefore broken down faster.

Drug Development

Can the Ulcer Bug Stomach a New Vaccine?

In the early 1980s, a pair of Australian physicians discovered that spiral-shaped bacteria named *Helicobacter pylori* are the real culprits behind most peptic ulcers—not stress or diet, as doctors and the public alike had previously thought. Antibiotics that knock out *H. pylori* have become a standard treatment for ulcers. Even better would be a vaccine that could eliminate the bug in people who have it and prevent infection in people who don't—especially since strains of the bacteria are emerging that are resistant to many common antibiotics.

Just such a vaccine is in the works. Antex Biologics, a Maryland-based biopharmaceutical firm, announced that in 2003 its vaccine, called Helivax, would begin testing in two clinical studies designed to evaluate its effectiveness and safety.

Although most people who harbor *H. pylori* show no symptoms, in some people it causes ulcers. In fact, about 80 to 90 percent of peptic ulcers are caused by *H. pylori*. (Peptic ulcers are sores in the lining of the stomach or the beginning of the small intestine.) The bug weakens the mucous coating that protects the stomach lining, allowing acid to damage it. Infection by the bacteria also puts you at a two- to sixfold higher risk of stomach cancer—whether or not you develop an ulcer—and it may play a role in inflammatory bowel disease, says Vic Esposito, Ph.D., chairman, CEO, and chief scientific officer of Antex.

How it works. Previous attempts to develop an *H. pylori* vaccine have been hampered by the fact that the bacterium is difficult to grow in the lab, Dr. Esposito says. Researchers have typically focused on cloning specific proteins from *H. pylori* and using them to teach the body's immune system to recognize and fight the bug. But Antex has found a way to mass-produce the bacteria in 400-liter tanks. They are grown to a certain point, then killed, and the whole cells are used in the vaccine. This is similar to the approach used in vaccines against polio, hepatitis, and flu viruses, Dr. Esposito says.

About 80 to 90 percent of ulcers are caused by *H. pylori*. The bug weakens the coating that protects the stomach lining.

Tissue samples taken from participants in earlier studies showed that the vaccine causes the immune system to produce antibodies in the stomach and small intestine to work against the bacteria, he says.

Availability. The present trials are scheduled to be completed by mid-2004. If all goes well, Dr. Esposito says, the vaccine could be available in 2007. ■

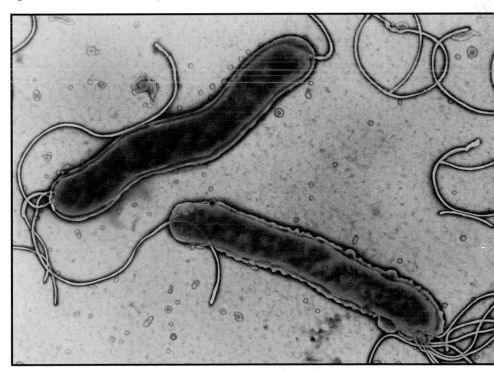

H. pylori, above, is the bacterium that causes most ulcers. About half the people in the world are infected with it. While most people have no symptoms, in some, the bacterium triggers ulcers. A new vaccine could eliminate *H. pylori* for good.

EYES
AND EARS

THANKS TO SEVERAL NEW DEVELOPMENTS, GLASSES AND TRADITIONAL CONTACT LENSES MIGHT BECOME OBSOLETE.

New technology used in laser eye surgery avoids the night vision problems that can plague people who undergo LASIK. Even people who don't qualify for traditional LASIK may be candidates.

Not interested in LASIK? Soon you may be able to have permanent contact lenses implanted instead. And older adults who need cataract surgery—which often leaves people with vision bad enough to require glasses—could get perfect sight with a new kind of lens that can be adjusted *after* it's surgically implanted. For people who've lost their vision due to corneal blindness, there's new hope in the form of the world's first artificial cornea, which means no more waiting for a donor cornea.

Doctors who focus on another sense—hearing—are also making progress in treating some intractable problems. A simple procedure using a $50 vibrating device may provide help for Meniere's disease, while the discovery that the phantom sounds of tinnitus originate in the brain is pointing the way toward new treatments, perhaps using magnets.

High-Tech Help
Clearing Up Fuzzy Night Vision

If you couldn't discern where the carpet ended and the floor began, you might trip. If you couldn't see exactly where one object ended and another began, you'd have trouble driving at night. This aspect of vision is known as contrast sensitivity, and it's one that cataract surgery doesn't do a very good job of correcting. Now, a new artificial lens may solve that problem by providing the equivalent of "high-definition TV" clarity.

Called the TECNIS Z9000, the lens uses so-called wavefront technology to correct for tiny aberrations in the spherical shape of the eye. A study of 30 patients who had the TECNIS lens in one eye and another lens in the other "found a statistically significant improvement with this lens in a variety of testing situations with nighttime driving," says Mark Packer, M.D., clinical assistant professor at the Oregon Eye Institute in Portland. The lens also reduced glare from headlights. "The amazing result was that the people who were looking through this modified lens could see as well with glare as those with the standard lens could see without glare," he says. The study results were published in the November 2002 issue of the *Journal of Refractive Surgery*. The lens is currently approved only for cataract surgery. ■

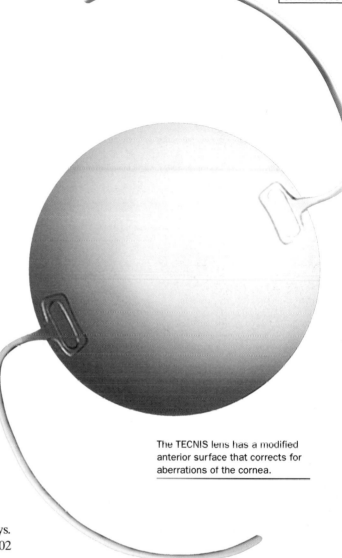

The TECNIS lens has a modified anterior surface that corrects for aberrations of the cornea.

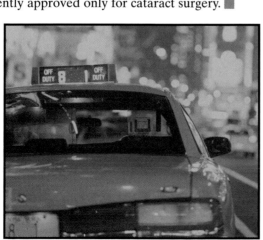

To someone with a loss of contrast sensitivity, this taxi cab would appear gray and hazy.

With the implantable TECNIS lens, the cab would appear sharper and more distinct.

High-Tech Help
Sharpening Vision with a Shape-Shifting Lens

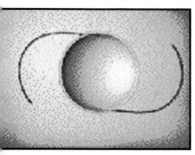

The Light Adjustable Lens can be adjusted using lasers *after* it's been implanted in the eye.

There's a little secret most people don't know about cataract surgery, the most common surgical procedure in the United States. Although the surgery is extremely successful at restoring normal vision, about half of the people who have it still need to wear glasses afterward. A new lens under investigation may change that picture.

During cataract surgery, doctors remove the cloudy lens, usually leaving intact the membrane, or capsule, that encloses the lens. They then insert an artificial lens into the empty capsule through the same tiny slit they used to remove the contents. This not only gets rid of the cataract, it also helps correct vision because a lens of the appropriate optical "power" is used. As the eye heals, however, it may change shape slightly, causing the artificial lens to be either too powerful or not powerful enough (vision problems are related to the shape of the eyeball). A new type of lens, called the Light Adjustable Lens (LAL), avoids this problem because it can be adjusted *after* it's implanted.

How it works. The LAL is made of silicone embedded with light-sensitive molecules called macromers. After the lens is implanted and the eye heals, the strength of the lens can be adjusted by shining a beam of ultraviolet light into either the center or the edges of the lens. The light reacts with the macromers to change the shape of the lens based on where the light is aimed and on the intensity and duration of the light delivered. The LAL can be adjusted several times as needed. Once perfect vision is achieved, the prescription is "locked in" by blasting the entire surface of the lens with light.

"I think it's the breakthrough of the decade in my field," says Robert K. Maloney, M.D., a Los Angeles–based ophthalmologist and spokesperson for the American Academy of Ophthalmology.

Dr. Maloney sees additional applications for the lens, such as providing "super vision"—even better than 20/20. "You would literally have vision like an eagle," he says. It could also be used to eliminate the need for reading glasses, often required as people move into middle age and develop presbyopia (difficulty with close work), because it could be adjusted to provide a kind of bifocal effect.

Availability. Human clinical trials on the LAL began in early 2003 in Mexico. The first lens was implanted in a blind person to test its safety, and the second lens was given to a patient undergoing cataract surgery. That patient emerged from the surgery still a bit nearsighted, and the lens was successfully adjusted afterward. The LAL will be implanted in about 25 eyes during the first phase of testing. Another three years of testing are expected before the device is submitted to FDA for approval. Clinical trials should begin in the United States sometime in 2004. ■

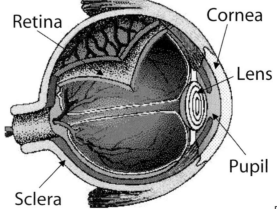

During cataract surgery, doctors remove the eye's lens and replace it with a new one. But since the eye changes shape as it heals, the "power" of the lens may need adjusting.

High-Tech Help
First Artificial Cornea Approved

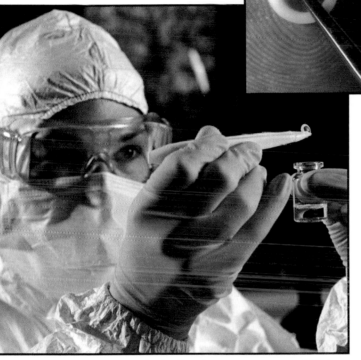

Developed in Australia, the AlphaCor can reverse corneal blindness with no need for a donated cornea.

An estimated 10 million people worldwide suffer from corneal blindness, yet only 100,000 corneal transplants are performed each year because of the difficulty in obtaining healthy corneas from cadavers. Soon, that may no longer be an issue. In December 2002, the FDA approved the world's first soft artificial cornea, called AlphaCor, for sale in the United States.

How it works. The artificial cornea, in development for more than a decade by the International Lions Eye Institute, is a curved, flexible plastic disk. The central part is transparent, just like a lens, while the rim is soft like a sponge, which enables the patient's own eye tissue to grow onto it and hold the lens in place. Recipients of transplanted donor corneas often need to take strong drugs to suppress their immune system so it doesn't reject the new lens as foreign tissue, but the drugs aren't necessary with the artificial cornea.

The implantation procedure is similar to that for a donor cornea. Part of the existing cornea is removed, and the AlphaCor is inserted through a tiny slit at the top of the eye, which is stitched closed after the operation. Then a flap of tissue taken from the conjunctiva (the outer layer of the white of the eye) is used to cover the surface of the front of the eye to make a kind of natural bandage. After three months, the flap of tissue and a thin layer of cornea are removed, exposing the AlphaCor and allowing light to enter the eye. Most patients have some, if not all, of their sight restored.

In clinical trials conducted in Australia and Asia, the artificial cornea worked better than a human corneal graft for some high-risk patients and caused fewer clinical complications. In one trial in which AlphaCor was implanted in 41 patients, more than 80 percent had some vision restored within a year after the surgery.

Availability. The AlphaCor will be available only through surgeons accredited through the ArgusConnect accreditation program. To locate one of these doctors, see the company's Web site, www.argusbiomedical.com. ■

RESEARCH ROUNDUP

Putting Your Eye Where Your Mouth Is (or Vice Versa)

Talk about making something out of (nearly) nothing. A team of Japanese doctors successfully restored the sight of several patients by growing an artificial cornea from membranes taken from the patients' mouths. It took three weeks to turn a 0.8-inch square of membrane into a cornea, growing it on a bed of tissue obtained from a placenta. The surgery was successful in eight patients but failed in a ninth because of the effects of another illness, according to the Associated French Press. The results of the experiment were presented at a meeting of the Japanese Society for Regenerative Medicine in March 2003. ■

High-Tech Help
Sign Language Glove Lends a Hand to the Deaf

Ryan Patterson displays his award-winning invention, which he hopes will offer more independence to deaf people.

Colorado high school senior Ryan Patterson was sitting in a Burger King when he observed a deaf teenager trying to order. The teen signed the order to an interpreter, who relayed it verbally to the clerk. "That would be a bummer—to be unable to go out on your own and order food," Patterson thought. Soon after, he read about a deaf high school student who attended school with a translator tagging along everywhere she went. The proverbial light bulb went on.

Patterson, using little more than a leather golf glove, a circuit board, a laptop computer, and some basic electronic parts (costing under $200), designed a sign language translator for his school's science fair. The device translates finger-spelling sign language into words on a computer screen.

How it works. Ten sensors placed along the fingers of the glove send data to a microprocessor, which transmits the information wirelessly to a small portable receiver. The screen—about the size of those on cell phones—displays the words.

The invention won Patterson the grand slam of science competitions, including the Siemens Westinghouse Science and Technology Competition and the Intel International Science and Engineering Fair. It's also won him about a quarter of a million dollars. In late 2002, *Time* magazine named his glove one of the top inventions of the year, and in April 2003, *Teen People* listed him as one of 20 "teens to watch."

"It's really cool to be honored like that," says Patterson, a blond young man who looks as if he'd be more comfortable on the ski slopes than in a laboratory. After wrapping up his freshman year at the University of Colorado-Boulder in the spring of 2003 (where he's majoring in—what else?—electrical and computer engineering), he planned to spend the summer refining and improving his invention.

Availability. Although Patterson patented his invention (just beating out a similar patent from Japanese electronics giant Hitachi), manufacturers have yet to approach him, and the glove exists only as a prototype. One reason is the cost: Producing it would be very expensive as it's now designed, he says. By the time he finishes with it, though, that should just be one more problem resolved. ∎

ALSO in the NEWS

The Earlier the Better for Cochlear Implants

Cochlear implants—small electronic devices surgically implanted deep in the inner ear (at right is the transmitter, implanted under the skin near the ear)—can provide a sense of sound, although not actual hearing, to someone who is profoundly deaf. They have long been controversial when used in children, with some people in the deaf community concerned that their use would kill off the deaf culture and many insisting that implants shouldn't be considered until children turn 18 and can make their own decisions. But research from the University of Texas at Dallas suggests there may not be time to wait. The study, which examined the brain activity of children with normal hearing and deaf children who received cochlear implants at varying ages, found that deaf children should receive the implants by age 3 1/2. If they receive them any later, the researchers found, the neurological pathway for hearing doesn't fully develop. ∎

High-Tech Help

With Future Contacts, More Drug Meets the Eye

If you've ever tried to put drops in your eyes, you know how frustrating the process can be. Half of the medicine goes sliding down your nose, while the other half might, if you're lucky, make it into your eye for a minute before being washed away via your tear ducts into your nose and from there into your bloodstream, where it can cause serious side effects. For instance, timolol (Timoptic), used to treat glaucoma, can cause heart problems. Overall, only about 5 percent of eye medications go where they need to go.

Derya Gulsen (right) injects a specially designed glass mold with a solution containing drug-loaded nanoparticles to create the prototype lenses held by Dr. Anuj Chauhan (left).

Now, researchers at the University of Florida think they may have found a way to get drugs into the eye—and keep them there—through specially designed contact lenses. Although the idea of delivering drugs via contacts isn't new, previous attempts failed because they basically involved soaking the lenses in the drug solution and then inserting them into the eye. This method resulted in many of the same problems as with eyedrops, says Anuj Chauhan, Ph.D., an assistant professor of engineering who is developing the drug-containing contacts. The new lenses are different.

How it works. Dr. Chauhan's approach encapsulates tiny amounts of the drug within nanoparticles, or oil-based particles, within the plastic of the contact lens. Because the particles are so tiny, they don't interfere with vision, and because the drug is encapsulated, it seeps out over time, providing a steady dose of medicine. The idea is that the lenses—which could also be used to improve vision—would be disposable after being worn for up to two weeks at a time. Dr. Chauhan presented his research at the American Chemical Society's national meeting in March 2003.

Availability. The research is quite preliminary. So far, Dr. Chauhan has produced a lens material and demonstrated that it's possible to put a drug (he used the anesthetic lidocaine) within the material and that the drug is released through it. Any commercial product is at least 10 years away, he predicts. ■

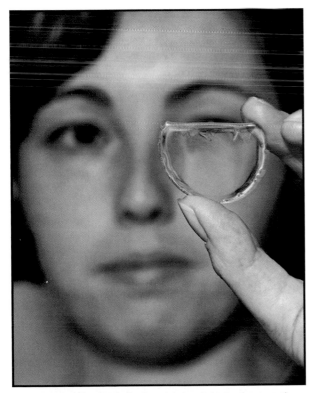

The prototype of a drug-laden lens (obviously larger than a real lens would be). The disposable contact lenses would be a new and improved way to deliver drugs to the eyes.

169

Surgical Solutions
A New Laser, a Better Glaucoma Treatment

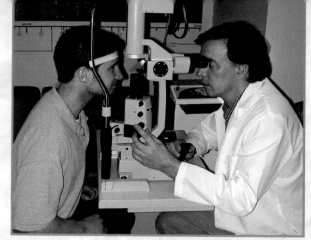

A patient undergoes the new laser treatment for glaucoma.

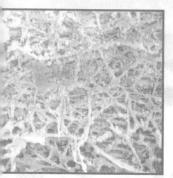

Clogs in this meshwork cause fluid backups in the eye. Pulses of light shake the meshwork, dislodging stuck particles.

An estimated 2 to 3 million Americans have the insidious eye disease glaucoma, the leading cause of blindness in the United States. The most common form, called primary open-angle glaucoma (POAG), affects 1 percent of all Americans and comes on silently, with no swelling or pain—just a slow buildup of pressure and the equally slow destruction of the optic nerve. Treatments typically involve daily medications, most of which have significant side effects, or surgery, which is often effective for only a short time and usually can't be repeated when the pressure builds again. Now, a small company in Boston is hoping that its new laser treatment can provide another option.

Glaucoma results from a buildup of fluid in the eye. Normally, fluid travels through various parts of the eye and drains through a spongy meshwork, called the trabecular meshwork, where the cornea and iris meet. If the fluid passes through this drain too slowly, pressure builds and can eventually cause damage to the optic nerve that can lead to blindness.

The most common laser surgical procedure, argon laser trabeculoplasty (ALT), releases the pressure by making small burns in the mesh, causing the drain holes to stretch. But it's effective in only about 60 percent of patients, and for half of them, the effects wear off within a few years. Because the lasers emit such powerful beams, they can burn the eye tissue and leave permanent scars, so patients can undergo the procedure only once or twice.

How it works. The procedure developed by SOLX, based at the Photonics Center at Boston University, relies on a different kind of laser, called a titanium sapphire laser. Instead of stretching the meshwork, the laser emits quick pulses of energy to shake it, somewhat like shaking out a blanket after a day at the beach. The motion dislodges any particles that may be blocking the flow of fluid and normalizes pressure without damaging the eye.

"If you produce minimal change in the eye, you have the possibility of retreatment," says Francisco Fantes, M.D., professor of ophthalmology at the University of Miami's Bascomb Palmer Eye Institute. Dr. Fantes is familiar with the SOLX technology and calls the clinical trial data impressive.

One study of 100 patients conducted by researchers in Madrid, Spain, found that the SOLX procedure, called gonioscopic laser trabecular ablation (GLTA), reduced pressure in the eye more than ALT did. Another study involving patients who had already had ALT produced similar results. Those who had GLTA were able to cut the amount of medication they required by 72 percent. If they were taking only one drug before the surgery, they didn't need it afterward.

SOLX's greatest competition will probably be lasers approved by the FDA in October 2002 for a procedure called selective laser trabeculoplasty (SLT). It also uses a low-intensity laser and can be repeated several times. But the GLTA laser can penetrate deeper into the eye, says Dr. Fantes, making it more effective. In fact, studies found that GLTA penetrates almost 90 percent of the trabecular meshwork, compared to about 15 percent for SLT, making it better able to clear out any "clogs." Additionally, GLTA patients required significantly fewer medications after surgery than SLT patients.

Availability. SOLX was approved for use in Europe in August 2003. It was expecting FDA approval of its laser in fall 2003. Once approved, says Dr. Fantes, GLTA may be considered a first-stage treatment for POAG instead of drugs. ■

ALSO in the NEWS

New First-Line Treatment Okayed for Glaucoma

What was once a last-ditch treatment for glaucoma may now become standard, thanks to FDA approval in December 2002 of the drug latanoprost (Xalantan) as a first-line treatment.

Previously, Xalantan was approved only for glaucoma patients in whom other medications had failed, yet it is still the most prescribed drug for glaucoma, both because of how well it works and because it has to be administered only once (via eyedrops). It is believed to lower pressure within the eye by increasing the rate at which fluid flows out of the eye. The most commonly reported side effects include blurred vision, burning and stinging, redness, itching, the feeling that something is in the eye, darkening of eye color, and irritation of the clear front surface of the eye. ■

Acne Drug Shows Promise for Eye Disease

Researchers suspect that the acne drug isotretinoin (Accutane) may be able to prevent not just pimples but also a certain type of blindness. Researchers at the University of California, Los Angeles, injected the drug into mice bred to have the same genetic defect that causes Stargardt's macular degeneration, an inherited form of blindness that usually begins in late childhood. It occurs when pigment that's a by-product of vision and is normally washed away builds up on the eye.

For some reason, Stargardt's mice raised without light don't go blind, so researchers decided to try Accutane because of one of its side effects: It prevents the eyes from getting enough light. Two months after the treatments began, the pigment had stopped accumulating in the mice's eyes, with no negative effects on their daytime vision. The findings were published in an April 2003 issue of the *Proceedings of the National Academy of Sciences.*

Researchers warn, however, that people with Stargardt's should not start asking their doctors to put them on Accutane. Without human studies to determine effective dosages (and even if it works), taking the drug could not only be worthless when it comes to eyesight but could even be harmful. Stay tuned for more research results. ■

Kids Who Wear Glasses Really Are Smarter

Although heredity plays a major role in whether your kids are nearsighted, the amount of reading and studying they do may also have an effect. Research published in the December 2002 issue of *Investigative Ophthalmology & Visual Science* found that nearsighted children spend an average of two hours more a week studying and reading for pleasure, and they spend less time playing sports than non-myopic kids. Not surprisingly, nearsighted (myopic) kids also scored higher on a test of basic reading and language skills than did children with normal vision. And lest you think the difference is related to more electronic game playing and television watching, well, the researchers thought of that, too. Both sets of children spent the same amount of time playing video games and watching TV. Before you snatch that book out of your child's hands, though, check your own eyesight. The researchers found that by far the largest risk factor for myopia in children was myopia in one or both parents. ■

Questioning Yearly Eye Exams for Diabetics

People with diabetes are susceptible to diabetic retinopathy, in which blood vessels in the retina are damaged. It's the leading cause of blindness in adults up to age 74, but if it's caught early, vision loss can be prevented or delayed. That's why people with diabetes are advised to have vision screenings at least once a year, although there's never been any research confirming that those yearly visits are really worthwhile.

Now, a study published in a January 2003 issue of the *Lancet* suggests that people with diabetes who have no signs of retinopathy on one exam, have had diabetes for less than 20 years, and are not taking insulin could go up to three years before having another screening. Researchers reached that conclusion after evaluating 7,500 patients with type 2 diabetes. Because people who have had the disease for more than 20 years and those who use insulin are more likely to develop retinopathy, they should be screened at least annually, the researchers reported. ■

Alternative Answers

Good Vibrations: Sweet Music to Meniere's Patients

Imagine knowing that at any time, you could lose your hearing and become so dizzy you collapse on the floor, vomiting. Obviously, working, driving, and even walking would be quite risky, since you'd have no control over when such spells hit.

That prospect is reality for an estimated 615,000 Americans who have Meniere's disease, an abnor-mality of the inner ear that causes severe dizziness, a roaring sound in the ears, fluctuating hearing loss, and the sensation of pressure or pain in the affected ear. Now, a physician at the University of Rochester in New York has found that using a simple $50 "tuning fork" apparatus can be more effective than surgery for treating the condition.

How it works. Meniere's disease results from a buildup of fluid in the inner ear, but no one really knows what causes the buildup. The disease is diffi-cult to treat. About 20 to 30 percent of patients fail to respond to conventional medical treatment (mainly, drugs to reduce fluid volume) and require ear surgery. Even with surgery, 20 to 40 percent of patients don't improve.

Paul Dutcher, M.D., associate professor in the division of otolaryngology at the university, wondered why two forms of surgery for the condition—one that removes a middle ear bone and another that involves drilling through the bone and opening up a fluid-containing sac in the inner ear—produced similar results. He realized that the only common factor was drilling the bone. The drilling causes the skull to vibrate, and those vibrations, he hypothe-sized, may knock loose tiny particles that wind up in the inner ear, clogging the system and resulting in fluid accumulation. "It's basic plumbing," he says.

To test his theory, Dr. Dutcher had patients lie in the same position as they would for surgery, then used an oscillator (an instrument that creates vibra-tions) over the middle ear bone of the affected ear. He used the device on patients for 30 minutes once a week for four weeks, and voilá—70 to 80 percent of the patients improved. He presented the results of a small pilot study on 29 patients in September 2002 at the annual meeting of the American Academy of Otolaryngology–Head and Neck Surgery Foundation.

Availability. Since his presentation, Dr. Dutcher has heard from several physicians around the coun-try who are trying his technique. He cautions that it will be another five years or so before enough data is collected to say that it definitely works. Still, several of his patients who had the procedure are still doing well two years after the treatment, and even those who experienced relapses responded to another course of treatment. If the safety and effectiveness of the procedure are verified, says Dr. Dutcher, patients may someday be able to treat themselves with the $50 oscillator. ∎

In this novel Meniere's treatment, an oscillator (the black device under the headband) seems to knock loose particles in the ear.

High-Tech Help
Jamming the Signal to Switch Off Tinnitus

Dr. Christian Gerloff invented a possible new treatment for tinnitus.

If you've ever been to a really loud rock concert, you may have experienced an annoying ringing in your ears afterward. But people with a condition called tinnitus live with constant or intermittent phantom sounds—from ringing to buzzing to whirring or roaring—all the time. It often occurs for no apparent reason, although previous exposure to very loud noise increases the risk.

Traditionally, tinnitus is treated with psychological training procedures (also referred to as retraining) in which patients are taught to cope with the noise so they can continue to live normally. Although most patients report some improvement after retraining, says tinnitus expert Christian Gerloff, M.D., of the University of Tuebingen in Germany, the noise rarely disappears completely.

A preliminary study conducted by Dr. Gerloff and his colleagues has now found that rather than being imaginary, in most cases, tinnitus emanates from abnormal activity in a part of the brain. "It means that, in some patients, tinnitus can be something like an acoustic phantom perception," he says, similar to phantom pain in amputees. "In other words, the noise is not generated in the ear but directly inside the brain, like an illusion."

To turn off that signal, Dr. Gerloff and his team conducted a small pilot study in 14 patients with intractable, chronic tinnitus. They used a procedure called transcranial magnetic stimulation to stimulate regions of the brain involved in processing auditory input in order to interfere with the electrical activity in those portions of the brain. By doing so, they were able to temporarily "jam" the signal causing the noise, disrupting the tinnitus for several seconds

in most of the patients. Results of the study were published in the February 2003 issue of *Annals of Neurology.* The finding could one day lead to new treatments for the condition, says Dr. Gerloff. But first, he says, "Controlled clinical trials are now necessary to evaluate whether this method can permanently reduce and thus cure tinnitus." Stay tuned for more information. ■

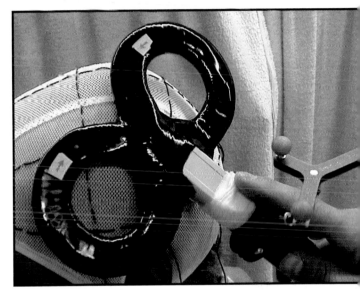

By using a magnet to stimulate a region of the brain called the left temporoparietal cortex, doctors were able to temporarily reduce tinnitus symptoms. There was no reduction when other areas of the brain were stimulated.

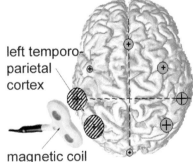

left temporo-parietal cortex

magnetic coil

173

Surgical Solution

Implantable Lens: LASIK Sees Future Competition

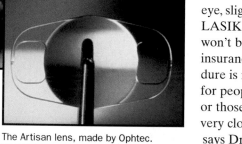

An intraocular lens may be the ticket to perfect vision for millions of people. The lens in this eye, pictured at right, is implanted over the eye's natural lens.

The Artisan lens, made by Ophtec.

Since 1996, 3.2 million people in the United States have had LASIK surgery to correct their vision. But they represent just a fraction of the 160 million Americans who wear glasses. Some of them can't afford the surgery, and others don't qualify—often because they're too nearsighted or their eyes have some factor (pupils too large or corneas too thin, for instance) that makes them poor candidates for the surgery. These are people who grew up wearing spectacles as thick as Coke bottles. Now, a permanent implantable lens offers the promise of clear sight to an estimated 6 million people, possibly by late 2004.

How it works. In the procedure known as phakic intraocular lens implantation, the lens (think of it as an implanted contact lens) is slipped into the eye over the existing lens through a tiny slit that closes on its own once the implant is inserted, explains Robert Gale Martin, M.D., of Carolina Eye Associates in Southern Pines, North Carolina. Dr. Martin has been participating in clinical trials of one

version of the lens made by STAAR Surgical. Several other manufacturers also have such lenses under investigation.

"The best part is that it's entirely reversible," says Dr. Martin. People in the study report that their eyes feel just the same after the lens is inserted as they did beforehand, and no infections have been reported in the 650 implants performed during the STAAR trial in the United States. In fact, people who initially had LASIK surgery on one eye and a lens implanted in the other asked to have a lens put into the LASIK eye as well because they said they could see much better with it.

Some doctors worry about the possibility of long-term side effects, such as glaucoma, cataracts, and macular degeneration, but because the lens can be removed at any time, researchers say potential problems can be averted.

Availability. The FDA is considering several applications from medical device companies seeking to market implantable lenses. The surgery is expected to cost about $3,000 per eye, slightly more than LASIK, and like LASIK, it won't be covered by many insurance plans. The procedure is not recommended for people with small eyes or those whose irises are very close to their corneas, says Dr. Martin. ■

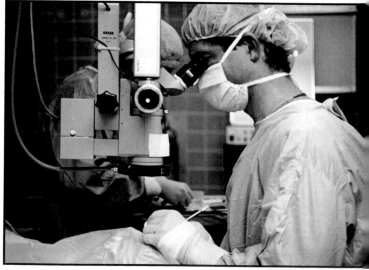

Dr. Robert Gale Martin implants a lens—still under study—that could one day make LASIK a thing of the past.

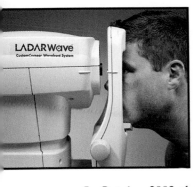

High-Tech Help

The Next Wave in LASIK Surgery

Some people interested in LASIK surgery for bad vision choose not to have it for fear of night glare, a common side effect. Others are poor candidates for the procedure. New technology could be the answer to both problems.

In October 2002, the FDA approved a medical device used in a procedure called wavefront-driven customized ablation. In clinical trials, nearly 80 percent of people who underwent the new laser surgery had vision superior to that achieved with conventional LASIK.

How it works. The device, called LADARWave, uses special technology to measure and adjust for what are called higher-order aberrations in the eye. Lower-order aberrations include nearsightedness and farsightedness, but experts believe higher-order aberrations—tiny defects in the shape of the cornea—are what contribute to common night vision problems, including glare and halos around lights such as headlights.

The LADARWave transmits a ray of light into the eye that reflects off the back of the retina, out through the pupil, and into the device, where the light is captured and arranged into a pattern—a kind of map of a person's individual corneal aberrations, both higher and lower order. This map is then used to guide the laser during the surgery, ensuring more precise reshaping of the cornea—and better eyesight.

The new surgery can be used to correct the vision of people who have already had LASIK, and it can even be performed on some people who don't qualify for regular LASIK.

Availability. Use of LADARWave technology is likely to spread relatively slowly because the equipment is so expensive. ■

Prior to surgery, the LADARWave makes a detailed three dimensional map of the cornea.

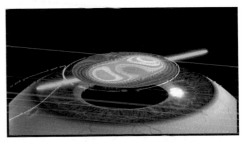

The map makes it possible to correct tiny flaws in the shape of the cornea to provide better vision.

RESEARCH ROUNDUP

Throw Away Those Reading Glasses

The need for reading glasses ranks right up there with the first gray hair as a sure sign of aging. As eyes age, they lose flexibility. The lenses become harder and less elastic, while the muscles surrounding them grow stiff. The condition, called presbyopia, makes it more difficult to focus on close tasks, such as reading, sewing, or computer work. Until now, the only answer was bifocal glasses, bifocal contact lenses, or reading glasses, but a new form of surgery appears to offer another option.

Called conductive keratoplasty (CK), the painless procedure uses a needle-like probe to deliver radiofrequency energy to the cornea. The nondominant eye (everyone has one eye that's stronger than the other) is overcorrected, making it slightly nearsighted. It's like creating bifocals from your eyes: One eye to see far, the other to see near.

In one study of 70 people, 70 percent of patients had 20/20 vision six to nine months after the surgery, compared with nearly none before, and almost 90 percent had 20/25 vision, compared with less than 7 percent before. The three-minute procedure has already been approved for correcting farsightedness, and in mid-2003, the FDA was considering whether to approve it for presbyopia. The ruling is expected in late 2003 or early 2004. ■

HEART
AND CIRCULATORY SYSTEM

THE WORLD'S DEADLIEST AND COSTLIEST CONDITION IS **HEART DISEASE.**

The challenges of treating and preventing it have spurred scientists to make lifesaving advances that once would have seemed fantastical. Heart repair without opening the chest? Doctors can now use robots to operate through pencil-size holes. A pacemaker without the pacemaker? Researchers are recruiting heart cells to do the job themselves. Early detection of heart disease with a simple blood test? It's a reality.

Prevention, of course, is still the best cure, and that means keeping your cholesterol under control, among other things. A drug called Zetia not only provides a whole new mechanism for lowering cholesterol, it can also team with existing drugs to really get those counts down.

There are new breakthroughs for the rest of your circulatory system as well. People who have sickle cell disease may soon be able to prevent painful episodes known as crises by inhaling nitric oxide gas. And there's a new and painless way of eliminating varicose veins with simple injections of a sugar-water solution. Finally, the long search for a safe blood substitute has gotten a boost from an unexpected source.

Key Discovery

Casting About for a Blood Substitute

If you're ever unlucky enough to need a blood transfusion in an emergency medical situation, you may not be thrilled to hear a doctor say, "Give this patient a unit of sea worm blood." But it beats one of the alternatives: "We're out of blood."

HIV/AIDS, mad cow disease, and a host of other health threats have cut the world's blood supply to uncomfortably low levels. The situation has sent scientists scrambling to come up with a safe substitute, and in June 2003, French researchers unveiled a most intriguing candidate: The common lugworm, a sand-burrowing sea creature often used for bait. It turns out that its blood is strikingly similar to human blood. In lab tests with mice, infused sea worm blood did what a blood substitute is supposed to do—that is, deliver oxygen to organs—without triggering any immune system reactions. The results were encouraging enough to merit more study, including tests on humans.

Medical experts worldwide consider it a matter of when, not if, artificial blood will replace the real thing in emergency rooms, on battlefields and accident scenes, and even at nonemergency surgery sites. Three blood substitutes derived from cow's blood are in advanced stages of research and may gain FDA approval in coming years. One of them, HemoPure, is in use in South Africa and has been approved for use in dogs in the United States.

Consider the advantages of blood substitutes: Unlike donated human blood, they require no refrigeration, have a shelf life of two years or more, carry no risk of viral disease, and can be available in unlimited quantities. There's also no chance of mixing up blood types: Artificial blood is one-type-fits-all.

A longstanding quest. A person who has lost blood has an urgent need: to keep oxygen moving from the lungs through the vessels to the organs. The blood component charged with this task is the protein hemoglobin, which is why most potential blood substitutes focus on getting hemoglobin into the bloodstream. One reason the now 50-year-old quest for artificial blood has been so frustrating is that hemoglobin misbehaves badly when it's freed from its usual confines inside blood cells. It tends to fall apart, so it can't carry any oxygen, and its fragmented remains can poison the kidneys. Also, free (that is, non-cell-bound) hemoglobin will bind with nitric oxide in blood vessel walls, preventing that gas from keeping the vessels relaxed. That shoots blood pressure up to dangerous levels.

With the cow-based blood substitutes, modern biotechnology has solved those problems by modifying the cows' hemoglobin molecules so they hold together in the bloodstream for at least 24 hours—long enough to get a patient through an emergency. (Any blood substitute is a temporary fix; everyone needs real human blood eventually.) The modified hemoglobin molecules are also bigger, so they can't enter blood vessel walls and react with the nitric oxide there.

The lugworm advantage. Lugworm hemoglobin, though, is already 50 times larger than human hemoglobin. That fact makes the French investigators hopeful for a medical miracle—a hemoglobin source that doesn't need to be modified but just collected, purified, and used.

If the idea holds up after more advanced testing, sea worm "farms" could eventually be created in coastal areas to harvest enough of the little creatures for an adequate substitute blood supply. In a few years, we may be able to say, "He's got the sea running in his veins" and mean it literally. ■

The common lugworm, also called a sea worm, could be the source of the blood substitute scientists have long sought.

Diagnostic Advance

Diagnosing Heart Disease from a Drop of Blood

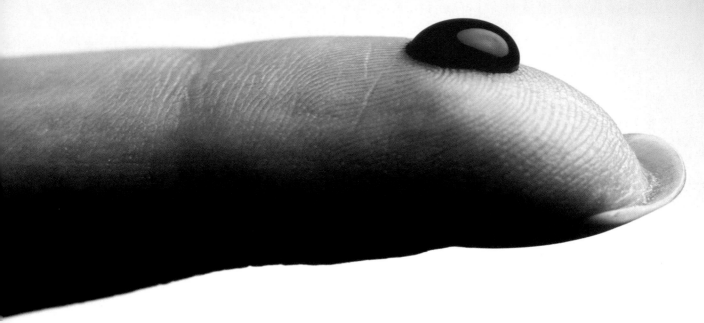

You've been told plenty about what puts you at risk for heart disease—smoking, obesity, high blood pressure, elevated cholesterol levels, and more. But how do you know for sure if you actually *have* heart disease?

So far, the most useful diagnostic tool has been angiography, which involves injecting dye into the coronary arteries through a long, narrow tube inserted up through the groin so that X-rays can reveal any blockages. But this procedure is invasive, not to mention expensive. Wouldn't it be infinitely better if you could be tested for heart disease simply by giving a blood sample?

British researchers from Imperial College London and the University of Cambridge think so, and they revealed just such a diagnostic test in November 2002. The test is so quick, cheap, and dependable that its inventors envision a day in the near future when entire populations can be routinely screened for heart disease. By providing early warning of heart attacks in the making, the test could save thousands of lives a year in the U.K. alone, the researchers estimate.

The new test is referred to by the unwieldy name of proton nuclear magnetic resonance–based metabonomics. From the patient's point of view, it's very simple—giving a bit of blood and waiting for the results. But what's done with the blood sample in the lab is anything but simple. Modern imaging equipment (nuclear magnetic resonance, or NMR) is used to analyze the sample at the molecular level. In study results published in November 2002 in the journal *Nature Medicine,* the technique had a 92 percent success rate at spotting which samples came from people with heart disease and which didn't.

How it works. The key to finding heart disease in a drop of blood lies in a new method of analysis that the researchers call metabonomics. It focuses on molecules called metabolites (glucose and cholesterol are well-known examples). Researchers use high-frequency radio waves to measure the magnetic properties of these molecules in the blood sample. Then they feed the data into a computer program that turns the information into a pattern, or "fingerprint." Heart disease shows up as a recognizable metabonomic pattern.

Availability. Before metabonomic tests have any chance of replacing angiography, larger and more rigorous studies must be completed. They got under way at Papworth Hospital, a cardiology center near Cambridge, England, in 2003. If the test passes muster, the researchers say, it could be ready for the public as early as 2005. And that may be just the beginning. In theory, any disease that yields a metabonomic fingerprint could be diagnosed with the new technique. Researchers are already looking into the feasibility of using metabonomics to diagnose osteoporosis, diabetes, arthritis, and Alzheimer's disease. ■

FingerPrint Technology

FingerPrint technology provides a cheap, rapid, noninvasive alternative to angiography for the diagnosis of heart disease.

Take a blood sample and put it in an NMR machine

15 mins Generate a spectrum, which is a "metabolic fingerprint"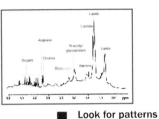

Look for patterns unique to heart disease

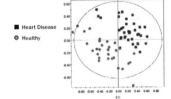
■ Heart Disease
○ Healthy

15 mins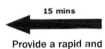

Provide a rapid and reliable diagnosis

Results generated by a collaboration between the laboratories of Dr. David Grainger (Cambridge University), Prof Jeremy Nicholson (Imperial College, London), and Dr. Peter Schofield (Papworth Hospital NHS Trust), supported by TCP Innovations Limited, Metabometrix Limited, and FingerPrint Diagnostics Limited

ALSO in the NEWS   A Lifesaving Device for the Home

There's a smart new electronic device for the home on the market, but unlike the latest digital camera or stock-quoting cell phone, this one has a more serious purpose: keeping you alive. Automatic external defibrillators (AEDs)—the hand-held machines that shock stopped hearts back into action—won FDA approval for home use in November 2002. By June 2003, the manufacturer was announcing Father's Day specials that knocked 15 percent off the list price of the already popular machines. Approval came after similar devices had become standard issue for airports, sports venues, and other public places where fast action can revive victims whose hearts unexpectedly stop beating (a condition known as sudden cardiac arrest)—but home is where most cardiac arrests happen. Emergency help takes an average of six minutes to arrive at a private residence—longer in traffic-clogged urban centers—and the chances of survival shrink by 20 percent with each passing minute. In fact, few cardiac arrest victims survive if their hearts aren't "shocked," or defibrillated, within 10 minutes. That's why a home defibrillator can mean the difference between life and death, since a loved one can use it long before the paramedics show up. To use it, you simply press a pad to the person's chest, and the device gives computerized commands to tell you when, or if, to give the shock. In July 2003, experts announced that AEDs were safe for use in cardiac arrest patients as young as 1 year old. To buy a home unit, you'll need a prescription from your doctor and about $2,300. ■

Key Discovery

Heart Cells Learn to Keep the Beat

The 600,000 heart patients worldwide who receive pacemakers each year are surely grateful that a machine can keep their hearts beating when their bodies can't. But if there were a way to get the job done without implanting an electronic device in their chests, they'd most likely choose that option in (ahem) a heartbeat. Now that a team of researchers has successfully tested a bold new technique that reprograms certain heart cells to take over pace-making chores, it's just a matter of time before such an alternative is available.

Dubbed the biopacemaker when laboratory suc-cess (in guinea pigs) was announced late in 2002, the new technique would not only free heart patients from their hardware burden, it would also provide more versatile pacemaking that can adjust to changes in physical exertion levels in a way that pacemaker implants can't. Furthermore, such a biopacemaker is a potentially important option for patients who are at too high a risk for infection from implanted pacemakers.

How it works. When things are working right in the human heart, two types of cardiac cells supervise the heartbeat by emitting electrical impulses to trigger contractions in all the other heart cells. When these "pacing" cells are diseased, damaged, or otherwise incapacitated, the heart-beat falters, and fatal circulatory collapse looms. This is where traditional mechanical pacemakers have saved the day by emitting the carefully calibrated electrical impulses that create a heartbeat. But the biopacemaker

Dr. Eduardo Marban and his colleagues pioneered the work on the so-called biopacemaker.

researchers, from Johns Hopkins University Hospital in Baltimore, solved the problem in an entirely different way: They used gene therapy to stimulate other, healthy heart cells to pitch in to "conduct" the rhythm section.

The researchers speculated (correctly, as it turned out) that all adult heart cells have the capacity to perform pacing duties. So why don't they? Because a steady supply of potassium to the heart suppresses the innate pacing function in all but the designated pacer cells. This is a good thing in healthy hearts, since too many "conductors" increase the chances of mistakes by the "orchestra." When the pacing cells stop working, however, substitutes are needed.

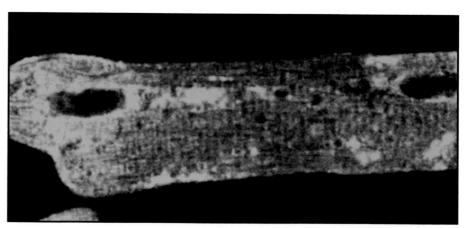

This guinea pig heart cell is producing green fluorescence protein (GFP), a sign that it has taken up the instructions to become a pacemaking cell. The virus that delivered those instructions also delivered the GFP instructions.

Regular heart cells can be prompted into performing backup pacing duty by altering their potassium levels.

That's where gene therapy comes into play. The researchers injected each guinea pig's heart with a virus that served as a vehicle to carry a specially encoded gene into the protein segments of the DNA responsible for pumping potassium into heart cells. The gene reduced the potassium levels in the cells,

and sure enough, that freed them up to fire off the electrical jolts that qualified them as bona fide acting pacemaker cells.

Availability. It's a long road from manipulating guinea pig cells to coming up with a viable biopacemaker that will work safely in humans. The most optimistic guess is that it will be four years before a human treatment is ready. ■

RESEARCH ROUNDUP

A Better Way to Rule Out Heart Attacks

You feel pressure in your chest, and you're sweating and feeling panicky. You're sure you're having a heart attack—but are you? Almost four out of five people rushed to emergency rooms with heart attack symptoms are not actually having heart attacks. Now doctors have a new blood test at their disposal to help rule out false alarms. Approved by the FDA in February 2003, the test is known as albumin cobalt binding (ACB).

When heart tissue is starved for oxygen, as it is during a heart attack, a blood protein called albumin changes properties, binding less easily to cobalt, a metallic element. For the ACB test, emergency room personnel simply add a bit of cobalt to the patient's blood sample. The chemical reaction that takes place provides a good indication of whether a heart attack has taken place.

ACB can be used only negatively—that is, to rule out heart attacks rather than to confirm that one has occurred. Also, it isn't foolproof, which is one reason it was approved for use only in conjunction with two existing tests—an electrocardiogram, which measures the heart's electrical activity, and a test for toponin, another blood protein.

The three tests make a good team. One study showed that when the ACB test was added to the other two, doctors were able to rule out heart attacks 70 percent of the time, up from 50 percent. That means more very relieved people can be sent home earlier, and precious emergency room resources can be better directed to where they're needed most. ■

Exercising Harder—Not Longer—Helps the Heart

While experts were debating whether to recommend a half-hour or a full hour of daily exercise, new research showed that it may not matter. When it comes to staving off heart disease, a 12-year study of 44,452 male health professionals revealed that what counts most is not how long you exercise, but how hard.

For example, among men who preferred walking for exercise, those who walked briskly were less likely to develop heart disease than slower-paced walkers, regardless of whether they walked for more or less time. The researchers also found that incorporating weight training—with its emphasis on short, intense movements—into an exercise routine significantly reduced heart disease risk.

The study authors recognize that some of the men may have been exercising harder precisely because they were already healthier than most, which could explain their reduced risk of heart disease. Still,  along with their findings, published in the *Journal of the American Medical Association* in October 2002, they suggest that for men at least, increasing exercise intensity and adding weight training—even if that means shorter workouts—may be a heart-healthy strategy worth considering. ■

Surgical Solution

A da Vinci Masterpiece: Robotic Heart Surgery

As lifesaving as a heart operation can be, the prospect of having your chest cracked open so surgeons can get in there and go to work is daunting, to say the least. But the day is coming soon when heart surgery will routinely be a closed-chest procedure, with a few tiny holes substituting for a football-size chest excavation site and precision-guided computerized robotic arms taking over for human hands.

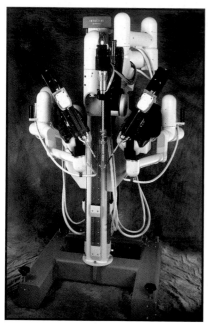

A robot's arms, with instruments attached, perform heart surgery as a doctor controls them.

That day got closer in November 2002, when the first research results based on actually performing the robotic procedure were announced. The verdict: All 15 "open-heart, closed-chest" surgeries performed at Columbia-Presbyterian Medical Center in New York City came off without major complications. Just one required follow-up surgery five days later. The rest were completely successful.

The advantages of robotic heart surgery go beyond easing the dread factor a bit. According to the study, the closed-chest patients were out of the hospital two to four days earlier than what's typical for conventional open-heart surgery patients, and they were strong enough to return to work 50 percent sooner. There's less pain during recovery and less scarring as a lifelong souvenir of the surgery. The procedure itself did take a bit longer, but that's expected to change as surgeons become more familiar with the technique.

How it works. Robotic heart surgery is the latest application of the da Vinci Surgical System, a high-tech piece of medical equipment if ever there was one. It allows the surgical team to insert a camera through a pencil-size chest incision and two remote-controlled robotic arms through two other equally small holes. Surgical materials are inserted as needed through a fourth hole. The instrument-wielding robotic arms perform the actual operation, controlled with joysticks by a surgeon as he views the image at a nearby console. So, yes, mere mortals are still in charge, but the da Vinci system allows a degree of precision and steadiness unmatched by human hands.

Availability. The completed Columbia-Presbyterian study is a major step toward making robotics the norm for heart surgery. The procedure performed in this case was the closure of an unwanted opening between the heart's two upper chambers,

Robotic assisted cardiac surgery significantly reduces the trauma—and the recovery time—for the patient.

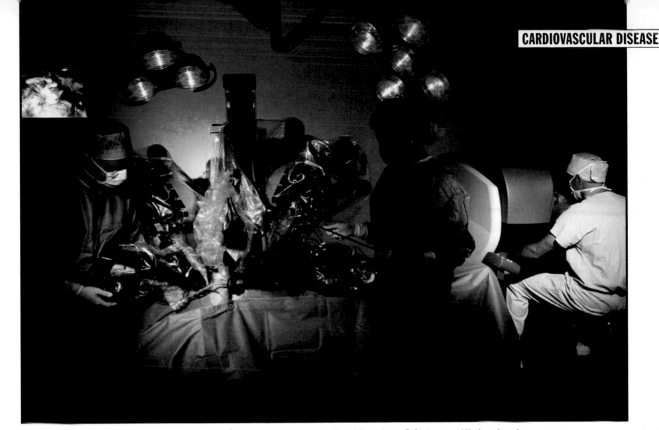

The doctor seated at the control console is performing surgery on a patient lying about 8 feet away. His hand and wrist movements are translated precisely by instruments—held by tiny mechanical wrists—inside the patient.

a congenital condition called atrial septal defect. Earlier use of robotics to repair the mitral valve, which controls blood flow between the left atrium and left ventricle of the heart, was so successful that the da Vinci system now has FDA approval for that procedure. The big prize will come with the release of successful study results for closed-chest coronary artery bypass surgery, the lifesaving, heart attack–avoiding procedure that reroutes blood flow around clogged arteries near the heart, bypassing the dangerous blockages.

Robotic bypass surgery has already been performed successfully many times, and formal evaluations of its safety and effectiveness (clinical trials) were nearing completion in 2003. They should show—with all due respect to former presidential candidate Ross Perot's political philosophy—that you *can* fix the problem without opening the hood. ∎

Green Isn't Your Cup of Tea? Try Black

Green tea has reaped a lot of attention lately for its heart benefits, but a new study of tea drinkers brings good news for lovers of the darker version of the world's most popular beverage. After examining the health records and sipping habits of more than 3,000 men and women in Saudi Arabia, researchers found a clear correlation between black tea consumption and a lower risk of heart disease.

In the study, published in the January 2003 issue of the journal *Preventive Medicine,* people who drank at least six cups of black tea a day reaped the most heart-health benefits. That's a tall order even in tea-loving England, let alone a coffee country like the United States. Still, the study authors point out that even lesser amounts deliver some flavonoids, the plant chemicals believed to be responsible for tea's salutary effect. Flavonoids, abundant in both black and green tea, help protect the cardiovascular system by acting as antioxidants, which neutralize cell-damaging molecules called free radicals.

As with most other studies that find in favor of tea, this one is somewhat flawed, since there's always the possibility that drinking tea is merely the preferred habit of people who are already healthy. If you're not crazy about green tea, though, at least you're in healthy company if you drink black instead. ∎

Surgical Solution

Drug-Coated Stent Popularity Balloons

A new way to unclog blocked coronary arteries took a giant step closer to becoming common practice in April 2003, when the FDA issued its eagerly awaited approval of drug-coated stents. Cardiologists immediately started using words such as "remarkable" and "revolutionary" to describe the stents—tiny wire mesh tubes that not only prop open coronary arteries but also emit a drug that helps prevent the stent itself from becoming clogged.

There's good reason for the enthusiastic adjectives. The FDA go-ahead for the new stents in the United States, following on the heels of their approval in Europe, means that a much higher percentage of people with serious heart disease will be able to avoid open-heart surgery as well as heart attacks.

Bypassing bypass surgery. In the past, if arteries near your heart were blocked or narrowed, making you a prime candidate for a heart attack, your only choice was to undergo bypass surgery, in which doctors remove a blood vessel from elsewhere in the body and use it to reroute blood flow around the blockage. A more recent and far less invasive option is balloon angioplasty. Instead of opening up the chest, doctors guide a narrow balloon-tipped tube up from the groin and into the blocked artery, then inflate the balloon to expand the artery so blood can flow freely.

Angioplasty works as well as bypass surgery—but only temporarily, since the arteries soon collapse or narrow again. To avoid that backward step, doctors began leaving behind a tiny, cylin-

Angioplasty Advances

Stents, the tiny mesh-like tubes placed in arteries to keep them open after angioplasty, become blocked again in 20 to 30 percent of patients. A drug coating on the stent significantly reduces this risk.

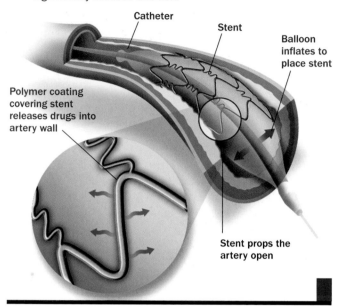

Catheter

Stent

Balloon inflates to place stent

Polymer coating covering stent releases drugs into artery wall

Stent props the artery open

drical, hollow tube called a stent to prop the artery open, much like scaffolding in a mine tunnel. That helped, but not enough, because the stents themselves tended to become blocked with scar tissue, a process called restenosis. Because restenosis often makes repeat procedures necessary, less invasive angioplasty remained a distant second to very invasive bypass surgery as the treatment of choice for coronary artery disease. The drug-coated stents are expected to change all that.

The stents are treated with a drug such as sirolimus (also called rapamycin), which inhibits the proliferation of cells that create the scarring. A 2002 study published in the *New England Journal of Medicine* credits the drug

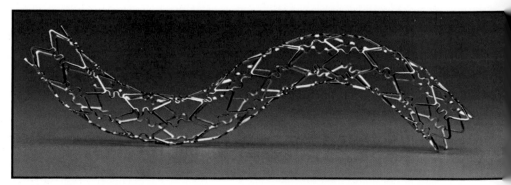

The Cypher stent is coated with a drug to prevent the stent from becoming clogged inside the artery.

coating with drastically reducing restenosis in heart patients with stents. More important, among the study subjects, the rate of "major cardiac events" (such as heart attacks) after receiving a stent dropped from 28.8 percent to just 5.8 percent if the stent was drug coated.

More angioplasties on the way. Cardiologists say that the FDA approval means that virtually all stents used in angioplasty will soon be coated with sirolimus or another drug, paclitaxel. They also predict that because of the reduced restenosis rate with drug-coated stents, physicians will be more likely to recommend angioplasty rather than bypass surgery to heart patients with serious coronary artery blockage.

Cost seemed to be a drawback for a while, since drug-coated stents are three times as expensive as uncoated ones. But evidence published in the *American Heart Journal* in March 2003, then updated at a meeting of the American College of Cardiology, showed that the newer stents are actually more economical in the long run than regular stents and that angioplasty with any kind of stent is more cost-effective than bypass surgery. ■

RESEARCH ROUNDUP

A Slice of Rye for Your Health

Fiber is a famous ally of older adults, but now we know which fiber source is the seniors' best friend. The winner is whole grain cereal fiber, especially in the form of dark bread—and for good reason. University of Washington researchers, in a study published in an April 2003 issue of the *Journal of the American Medical Association,* found that eating two slices of fiber-rich, whole grain bread such as wheat, rye, or pumpernickel a day reduces the risk of the deadliest enemy of the over-65 set—heart disease. The more such fiber (also found in bran and whole grain cereals) you eat, the more your risk is reduced.

The study is an eye-opener for two reasons. For one thing, it shows that fiber from grains is a better heart helper than fruit or vegetable fiber (although, of course, there are plenty of good reasons to eat fruit and vegetables, including their fiber content). The other reason is that whole grain cereal fiber benefits your heart even if you don't start eating it until late in life. ■

Progress in Prevention

Low Doses of Blood Thinner Ward Off Killer Clots

Along with hospital-acquired infections, medical errors, and bad food, there's another danger you need to worry about when you or a loved one is hospitalized: deep vein thrombosis (DVT), blood clots that form in the leg after a long period of inactivity. DVT becomes particularly dangerous

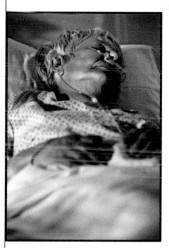

In bed-bound patients, blood clots in the legs pose a threat.

when a blood clot breaks loose, travels through the circulatory system to the heart, and finally lodges in the lung, causing an often fatal condition called pulmonary embolism. DVT contributes to an estimated 60,000 to 200,000 deaths in the United States each year, many of them among people who are hospitalized or confined to nursing homes or rehabilitation centers.

Now, a major study published in an April 2003 issue of the *New England Journal of Medicine* has found that a long-term, low-dose course of the common (and inexpensive) blood thinner warfarin (Coumadin) can help prevent recurrence of these blood clots without negative side effects.

Currently, people who have had a blood clot or embolism are treated for six months with higher doses of Coumadin. The drug is then stopped because of fear of bleeding complications—which is most likely why those people have a 6 to 9 percent risk of experiencing another blood clot within the following year.

The participants in the study received Coumadin for up to four years, with no negative results and a

64 percent reduction in DVT compared with those who didn't receive the drug.

The news was deemed so important that not only did the journal release the results on its Web site several weeks prior to publication, but experts who gathered to discuss the prevention and treatment of DVT in March greeted the announcement with applause. The value of the treatment was so obvious that the study's sponsor, the National Institutes of Health (NIH), stopped the study early so all of the participants could benefit from it.

The ABCs of DVT. Deep vein thrombosis made headlines several years ago with reports of "economy class syndrome"—blood clots in the leg suffered by people crammed into coach airline seats during long flights. More recently, in April 2003, NBC news reporter David Bloom, 39, died of a pulmonary embolism while covering the war in Iraq. Experts speculate that a clot may have formed because of the cramped quarters Bloom traveled in, coupled with dehydration.

Other risk factors for DVT include orthopedic surgery, cancer, chronic heart or respiratory failure, varicose veins, smoking, and use of birth control pills and hormone replacement therapy. But the risk is substantially higher for people in hospitals and nursing homes, says Samuel Z. Goldhaber, M.D., who directs the Venous Thromboembolism Research Group at Brigham and Women's Hospital in Boston, which conducted the NIH study. "The rate increases with age and with additional medical illness," he says. It also rises with obesity, "and, unfortunately, in this country, we have a pandemic of obesity."

Despite these facts, studies find that doctors often don't take the necessary precautions to prevent such dangerous clots from forming, says Dr. Goldhaber, including treating patients with blood thinners *before* they develop clots, having them wear special compression stockings to increase blood flow in the legs, and making sure they move regularly.

You can't blame just the doctors, though. "Not only the doctors but also the patients and their families have some responsibility," Dr. Goldhaber says. So, if you feel a cramp in your leg that gets worse and doesn't go away, or you have any unexplained shortness of breath or chest pain—common symptoms of DVT—tell your doctor about it. And if you have a relative who's confined to bed, ask the health care provider, "What are you doing to prevent DVT in my loved one?" suggests Dr. Goldhaber.

Also, take matters into your own hands on long car or plane trips, doctors advise. Get out of that cramped seat occasionally and walk around. ■

Key Discovery
Say "Nuts" to High Blood Pressure

Here's the kind of health news everybody likes to hear: Tasty, dry-roasted soy nuts can reduce your blood pressure and therefore lower your risk of heart disease. These snacks don't merely nudge your blood pressure down a tad. According to research presented to the American Heart Association in November 2002, eating a half-cup a day can drop your blood pressure readings as much as some prescription blood pressure medications.

Soy nuts aren't nuts, of course. They're simply roasted soybeans that taste and crunch like nuts. Plenty of research over the years has solidified soy's reputation as a heart-healthy food. Recently, the attention turned from soy's cholesterol-lowering benefits to its effect on blood pressure. In the second half of 2002, a Spanish study found that substituting soy milk for cow's milk significantly lowered blood pressure. Canadian research found evidence that eating soy in any form—milk, beans, tofu, you name it—helps reduce blood pressure, at least in men.

What the study shows. The soy nut study focused on women—specifically post-menopausal women, who are at much higher risk of heart disease than younger women. The researchers, from Boston's Beth Israel Deaconess Medical Center, put 60 such women on the same diet for eight weeks, except that half the women ate 58 grams of roasted soy nuts each day instead of the equivalent amount of protein (about 25 milligrams) from other sources. Then the soy eaters switched with the nonsoy eaters, and they all followed the diets for another eight weeks.

The results: While in the soy nut group, women experienced a much more significant drop in blood pressure on average than those in the other group. Those whose blood pressure was too high at the start of the study lowered it by 10 percent while eating soy nuts daily. Those who started out in the normal blood pressure range saw a 5 percent drop.

No one is certain why soy helps lower blood pressure. It's rich in plant chemicals known as isoflavones, and a lot of research has attributed soy's heart-saving benefits to these chemicals. But the Canadian study found that even soy products that are low in isoflavones (such as soy-based hot dogs and ice cream) seemed to lower blood pressure in men, indicating that other beneficial mechanisms may be at work. The Spanish researchers point out that soy milk is rich in the amino acid argi-nine, which converts in the body to nitric oxide, a chem-ical that relaxes blood vessels.

How to enjoy soy nuts. While well-stocked super-markets may offer dry-roasted soy nuts, you're more likely to find them at a health food store. You can eat them straight out of the bag, use them as croutons on salads, or put them in soups or casseroles. ■

Want High Blood Pressure? Then Hurry Up!

Are you the type who honks at red lights so they'll change faster? If so, better check your blood pressure. After following more than 3,000 men and women for 15 years, researchers found that impatient people are two to three times more likely than their more laid-back counterparts to develop high blood pressure, a risk factor for heart disease. This is the first time impatience has been linked to high blood pressure independently of other characteristics of the "Type A" personality, such as hostility, aggressiveness, and competitiveness. Also noteworthy was the relatively young age (18 to 30) of the volunteers when the study began in 1985, meaning that a hurry-up attitude in your youth could lead to high blood pressure before middle age. ■

Blood Pressure Drugs: Which Works Best?

Point
Counterpoint

The big announcement had all the hall-marks of a major breakthrough in the stepped-up war against high blood pressure (hypertension). A huge study that spanned eight years and looked at more than 33,000 hypertension patients in 623 medical centers in the United States, Canada, and the Caribbean had come to a startling conclusion: The oldest, simplest, and least expensive blood pressure–lowering drugs on the market turned out to be the best choice more often than the newer drugs that had come into favor. When the findings were released at the end of 2002, the study authors recommended that the older drugs, called diuretics, be considered first for treating high blood pressure.

The study (known by its acronym, ALLHAT) drew immediate fire from plenty of cardiologists and hypertension specialists who objected to the idea that any blood pressure drug merits being singled out as a first choice. Many doubted that ALLHAT had made the case for diuretics' superiority at all. The ALLHAT team held firm, however, and its diuretics-first advice was included in the new 2003 guidelines for dealing with high blood pressure (dubbed JNC-VII).

We asked one of the study's key authors and a prominent critic of its conclusions to explain their sides of this broiling medical controversy. But first, here's a lineup of the three main drug types compared in the ALLHAT study.

Diuretics ease the pressure on blood vessel walls by drawing water from the bloodstream.

Calcium channel blockers expand arteries to give blood more room to flow.

ACE inhibitors loosen artery walls by blocking a chemical that would otherwise stiffen them.

Point ▶

Barry Davis, M.D., Ph.D., was an ALLHAT study author who had full responsibility for the integrity of the data and the accuracy of the data analyses in the published version. He is a physician/statistician at the School of Public Health of the University of Texas Health Science Center at Houston.

Q: Why should diuretics be the first choice for controlling hypertension?

A: In our study, diuretics were shown to be superior to calcium channel blockers and ACE inhibitors in preventing one or more forms of cardiovascular disease. Also, JNC-VII, the new guidelines for controlling high blood pressure, have recommended diuretics as a first choice after considering the totality of all the evidence from ALLHAT and other studies.

◀ Counterpoint

Michael A. Weber, M.D., is past president of the American Society of Hypertension. Professor of medicine and associate dean for research at the College of Medicine of the State University of New York Downstate Medical Center in Brooklyn, Dr. Weber has published much commentary critical of the ALLHAT study.

Q: Why shouldn't diuretics be the first choice to treat high blood pressure, as ALLHAT concluded?

A: The problem is that with many patients, diuretics may not be the best option. We can't overgeneralize from ALLHAT. The average age of the ALLHAT subjects was close to 70, and there were a large number of African-American patients, for whom diuretics work well. There's good evidence, however, that for white people under age 65, diuretics do not have a meaningful blood pressure–lowering effect. So I know that if I have a white patient who is not elderly, diuretics aren't going to get the blood pressure down. Also, people with diabetes and those who have heart or kidney conditions do better with drugs like ACE inhibitors or angiotensin-receptor blockers.

Q: What does such a recommendation accomplish that's better than leaving doctors to use their best judgment based on the individual patient?

A: JNC-VII looked at the totality of the evidence. For mostly every patient (except those who cannot tolerate a diuretic), the evidence is fairly compelling that diuretics are better. Many guidelines for treatment are based on looking at all the available evidence, which individual doctors can't always do.

Q: Didn't all the blood pressure drugs tested turn out to be equally effective at preventing heart disease in general?

A: The drugs tested in ALLHAT were equivalent in preventing coronary heart disease and total mortality. But diuretics were better at preventing heart failure and other forms of cardiovascular disease. Heart failure is a very serious condition in terms of mortality and cost.

Q: Don't most people with hypertension need more than one drug anyway?

A: Yes, so diuretics should be part of the regimen.

Q: How could professionals disagree so vehemently over this issue?

A: There is not much disagreement among most professionals. The inclusion of the ALLHAT findings in the JNC-VII guidelines is a good indication of ALLHAT's broad acceptance. The problem is that those who question ALLHAT's results are very vocal. Their reasoning is not clear. The evidence from the largest hypertension trial ever conducted speaks for itself.

Q: What are people who are concerned about blood pressure supposed to make of all this?

A: If they are not on a diuretic, they should ask their doctors why they aren't. The cheapest antihypertensive drugs are the best.

Q: Didn't the study show that people on diuretics fared better against heart disease in the long run?

A: In the two most important areas—fatal or nonfatal heart attacks and death—there was absolutely no difference between the ACE inhibitor and the diuretic, despite the fact that the study didn't use the ACE inhibitor in an optimal way.

Q: But then the tie was broken, so to speak, by the diuretics' performance in preventing heart failure.

A: That's passionately disputed by experts in the field. Making a diagnosis of heart failure is difficult, and even more so in this study, because a diuretic can hide the symptoms of heart failure. So we don't really know what the true incidence of heart failure was. Heart failure is serious. People tend to die from it very soon.

So if there was really a dramatic decrease in heart failure rates for those on the diuretic, it should have been reflected in the death rate. It wasn't.

Q: Does it matter that diuretics are less expensive?

A: It's doubtful whether they're in fact cheaper. Unlike the other blood pressure drugs, diuretics have metabolic effects. For example, they cause the body to lose potassium, and they can increase uric acid, which can lead to gout. And they increase blood sugar, which increases the likelihood of diabetes. To make sure everything is safe, we must do regular blood tests. If we find problems, they must be treated. So when you total it all up, we're not at all sure that diuretics are the cheaper treatment, even though they're less expensive to buy.

Q: How could professionals differ so much on a topic like this?

A: Actually, there are few instances where you have a unanimous point of view on how to treat a condition. The controversy in this case comes from the suggestion that there is one drug that will trump all. There's no such thing. Most people with hypertension will need a combination of drugs, so debates about which is the best single drug are inappropriate.

Q: What are health consumers to make of all this?

A: The most important thing is that we've made better progress in treating hypertension than anywhere else in the world. We have a good selection of medicines that can control high blood pressure. Physicians often prefer newer drugs because they are effective and so well tolerated, but diuretics still have a role to play.

Progress in Prevention

Panel Sounds Off on a "Silent Killer"

Think your blood pressure is in the "normal" range? You'd better ask your doctor, because that range just got smaller. According to new guidelines released in the spring of 2003, if you have a reading between 120/80 and 139/89, you have "pre-hypertension"—in other words, you're on your way to developing high blood pressure (hypertension), and you need to take preventive measures right away.

The guidelines are part of a report issued by a panel of experts (the Joint National Committee on the Prevention, Detection, Evaluation, and Treatment of High Blood Pressure) from more than three dozen health organizations. Their message: It's time to get serious about high blood pressure. From now on, doctors and their patients are urged to take more and quicker action against this "silent killer," the

"Normal" blood pressure just got a little lower.

number one risk factor for heart attack, stroke, heart failure, and kidney damage.

Earlier intervention. If you have pre-hypertension, it's too early for medication but not too early for lifestyle modifications that will keep you behind the line that marks the beginning of high blood pressure. The guidelines recommend losing weight, exercising, consuming less salt, and limiting alcohol intake. Most important is adopting what's known as the DASH (Dietary Approaches to Stop Hypertension) diet, which emphasizes fruits, vegetables, and low-fat dairy products. A guide to the DASH diet is available online at www.nhlbi.nih.gov/health/public/heart/hbp/dash/new_dash.pdf.

Some hypertension experts don't buy into the new category, worrying that it will cause unnecessary anxiety among people who are essentially healthy. European blood pressure treatment guidelines, also released in 2003, don't recognize a pre-hypertension range and consider any reading between 130/85 and 139/89 to be "high normal," which requires no action.

Still, it's understandable why the U.S. panel felt the need to take stronger measures. More than 50 million Americans have high blood pressure, and only about a third of them are able to get the problem under control with drugs or lifestyle changes. That 35 percent control rate is better than Europe's, but it still leaves about 30 million people at high risk for heart disease. Even more people will be at risk for high blood pressure as the population ages. At the current rate, more than 90 percent of people over 55 with normal blood pressure eventually cross the line and develop high blood pressure.

The new guidelines also focus on aggressively reducing blood pressure among people who already have it. Here are some of the highlights.

● **Diuretics are your first-choice drugs.** But a number of special high-risk complications and other "compelling conditions" call for the use of other blood pressure–lowering medications, such as alpha blockers, cal-

The DASH diet, replete with fruits and vegetables, has proven effective at lowering high blood pressure.

cium channel blockers, ACE inhibitors, or angiotensin-receptor blockers.

- **Concentrate on the top number.** If you're over 50, the top number in a typical blood pressure reading—for example, the 140 in a 140/90 reading—is a more important risk factor for heart disease than the bottom number. It's the measurement of systolic blood pressure, when the heart has contracted and sent a surge of blood into circulation. Get that number down, and the other number (your diastolic blood pressure) will follow.

- **You'll probably need at least two drugs.** More is often better when it comes to blood pressure medication. People with hyperten-sion will usually need at least two different drugs to get their blood pressure under control—that is, at least back down to the pre-hypertensive range, or less than 140/90. People who have high blood pressure as well as diabetes or chronic kidney disease need to get their blood pressure all the way down to 130/80 in order for it to be considered controlled.

Finally, in the report's words, "The most effective therapy prescribed by the most careful clinician will control hypertension only if the patient is motivated to take the prescribed medication and to establish and maintain a health-promoting lifestyle." In other words, lowering your blood pressure is up to you. ■

Drug Development
New Cholesterol Drug Boosts Statins' Performance

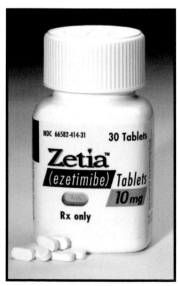

This new drug provides more control over cholesterol.

Atorvastatin (Lipitor), simvas-tatin (Zocor), and other so-called statin drugs have achieved near-won-der drug status because of their cholesterol-lowering prowess. Even so, as many as 60 per-cent of the 13 mil-lion Americans with statin pre-scriptions fail to reach their target cholesterol levels and thus remain at serious risk for heart disease and possibly a heart attack. The FDA took a big step toward filling this treatment gap with its approval in November 2002 of a new medication called ezetimibe (Zetia).

Zetia is not a statin knock-off by any means. Rather, it's the first in an entirely new class of cholesterol-lowering drugs that not only reduce cholesterol on their own but also work in tandem with statins to get much better results than either drug could on its own. In studies, Zetia taken alone lowered "bad" (low-density lipoprotein, or LDL) cholesterol by an average of 18 percent. When Zetia was given for eight weeks to people who were already taking statins, LDL dropped by 25 percent more than it had with statins alone.

Besides pushing down LDL levels, Zetia also low-ers triglycerides (another dangerous blood fat) and raises levels of artery-cleansing HDL (high-density lipoprotein, the "good" cholesterol). According to preliminary research released in 2003, Zetia even appears to reduce counts of C-reactive protein, a marker for inflammation—now considered a signifi-cant risk factor for heart disease. (See page 14.) Again, all of these benefits are magnified when the drug is teamed with statins.

How it works. The reason Zetia complements statins so well is that it attacks the problem from a different angle. Statins set up shop in the liver, where they slow down the body's cholesterol-making factory by inhibiting an enzyme that stimulates cholesterol production. Zetia, on the other hand, works in the intestine to prevent the absorption of cholesterol, so it's eliminated from the body before it can clog arteries.

Availability. Zetia is already being prescribed across the United States. Talk to your doctor about it if your cholesterol levels are high even though you've been taking statin drugs. ■

RESEARCH ROUNDUP

Game of ACAT and Mouse Points the Way to Unclogged Arteries

A new discovery paves the way for a drug that could virtually eliminate atherosclerosis (hardening of the arteries). Studies in mice have pinpointed an enzyme responsible for converting the cholesterol made by the body into forms that circulate through the blood, including artery-clogging LDL (low-density lipoprotein). Mice genetically altered to lack the enzyme, called ACAT2, were found to be virtually free of atherosclerosis. A drug that blocks ACAT2 could perhaps produce the same results in humans.

Pharmaceutical companies had already developed ACAT-inhibiting drugs, but later research revealed that there are two forms of the enzyme. ACAT1 exists throughout the body, while ACAT2 is concentrated in the liver and small intestine—the areas where cholesterol is made and absorbed. That may explain why knocking out ACAT2 now seems a more promising cholesterol-lowering strategy than targeting both forms of the enzyme.

The study authors, who published their results in the February 2003 issue of *Proceedings of the National Academy of Sciences,* believe a future drug that targets ACAT2 without disturbing ACAT1 will be a huge step forward in heart protection. ■

Key Discovery
Sickle Cell Pain Relief: Just a Breath Away

In the near future, children and other people with sickle cell disease may be able to literally breathe away its frequent pain attacks with an inhaler. New research carried out at Children's Hospital in Boston showed that inhaling nitric oxide, a chemical known to improve circulation, noticeably soothed youngsters' pain.

The findings point to an entirely new way to treat the devastating genetic blood disorder, as well as an alternative to morphine and other strong pain medications that are often needed. That would be a long overdue blessing for the 70,000 Americans, mostly of African descent, who inherit the genetic flaw that distorts red blood cells—the normally rounded cells that carry oxygen throughout the body—into a sick-

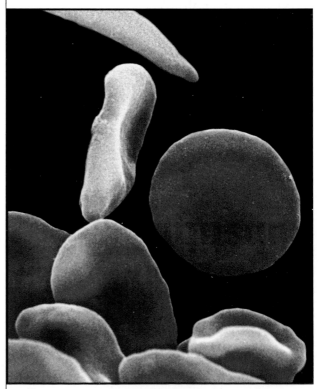

Normal red blood cells and sickle-shaped cells. Sickle shapes result from abnormal hemoglobin, the pigment in red blood cells.

Reader's Digest

The Reader's Digest Association, Inc.

A Word Of Thanks...

In the unceasing effort to service our customers' orders efficiently and promptly, it is all too easy to neglect the simple courtesy of saying "Thank You."

Therefore, to show our appreciation for the interest you've shown in our products, we'd like to extend an exceptional opportunity to you today.

Because we know you as a person concerned about health issues, we invite you to review the enclosed collection of specially-selected books -- we think you will find they can make life better for you and your family. As our thanks for any purchase you may make, shipping and handling is FREE!

This opportunity is being offered only to loyal friends like you. It's our way of saying "thanks" to you for saying "Yes" today!

Keira Krausz
for Reader's Digest

Please see inside for all the details ►

GET WELL AND STAY WELL!

STRENGTHEN YOUR IMMUNE SYSTEM

Get your immune system functioning at full capacity! Your immune system is your best ally in the battle to stay healthy, but stress, diet, environment, and lifestyle choices can overtax your body's defenses and make you susceptible to illness and fatigue. Here's the help you need in the fight against disease. Send for your copy of *Strengthen Your Immune System* and release your body's natural healing power!

- More than 250 helpful full-color photographs and illustrations
- Vitamin, mineral and supplement charts • 320 pages
- Regularly priced at $29.96 but it's yours for only 2 installments of $7.49 each, just $14.98 total – that's half the price! **FREE shipping and handling!** (#021303)

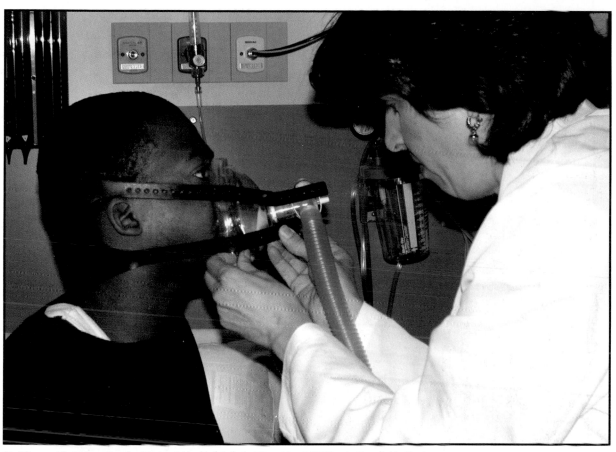

An 18-year-old sickle cell patient is treated with inhaled nitric oxide at Children's Hospital in Boston.

le shape, like a quarter-moon. The jagged cells create traffic jams in the bloodstream, blocking small blood vessels, holding up oxygen delivery to tissues, and leading to organ damage over time. In the short run—as early as infancy—it can provoke "crises," acute episodes of blood flow restriction that cause pain severe enough to send many to the hospital.

Nitric oxide promises to resolve or perhaps even prevent these crises by getting to the cause of the pain (poor blood flow) rather than merely treating the pain itself.

How it works. Sickle cell patients are deficient in the very substance they need most: nitric oxide, a chemical that widens blood vessels and improves blood flow. That's because sickle cells are fragile and are often destroyed prematurely. When that happens, the oxygen-carrying hemoglobin proteins inside them are released to float free in the bloodstream, where they destroy any nitric oxide they encounter. Inhaling nitric oxide gas seems to raise blood levels of nitric oxide enough to widen blood vessels and clear the traffic jam.

That certainly appeared to be the case at Children's Hospital, when 20 sickle cell patients ages 10 to 21 were given face masks to breathe through for four hours during a crisis episode. Half breathed nitric oxide and half breathed regular room air. According to the results of the study, published in March 2003 in the *Journal of the American Medical Association,* those who inhaled nitric oxide reported a greater decrease in pain than the others, especially after the fourth hour of treatment.

Availability. As encouraging as these results are, approval of nitric oxide as a treatment for sickle cell crises will require larger studies involving more patients. Such studies are currently under way. Meanwhile, nitric oxide inhalation already has a positive track record. It's currently used to treat respiratory failure and pulmonary hypertension, a rare condition marked by narrowing of the blood vessels in the lungs. ■

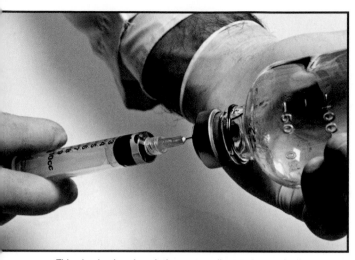

This simple glycerin solution can eradicate unwanted veins.

Key Discovery

Glycerin Shots a Sweet Solution to Spider Veins

Getting rid of unsightly leg veins with a simple injection just got quicker, cheaper, and surer, thanks to a new glycerin solution that makes such veins disappear without a trace, often in just one session. Best of all, unlike saline injections, which cause such discomfort that they discourage many people from seeking any treatment at all, glycerin shots are relatively pain-free.

The glycerin solution—essentially sugar water—has been used for many years in Europe in a slightly different configuration to remove small varicose veins, but it remains fairly obscure in the United States. That could soon

change. In June 2003, Mitchel Goldman, M.D., a San Diego–area dermatologic surgeon who pioneered the current formula, published results based on his own clinical experiences. After injecting small varicose veins in one leg of each of 13 patients with glycerin and the other leg with STS (sodium tetradecyl sulfate, another superior alternative to saline), Dr. Goldman found that glycerin cleared away veins more quickly and with less temporary bruising, swelling, and discoloration.

How it works. Any agent used in sclerotherapy (vein removal by injection) destroys the unwanted vein by killing the cells that form the vessel wall. It's that simple: no wall, no vein. Saline gets the job done by acting as a chemical irritant, which is one reason it's so painful ("barbaric" is the word Dr. Goldman uses). STS is a detergent that works by stripping the cells of their proteins. Glycerin, on the other hand, dehydrates the cells to death. Since it's thicker than the other substances, glycerin is less likely to be drained away through the vessel and more likely to work slowly and effectively right where it's put.

According to Dr. Goldman, glycerin works best for small varicose veins—spider veins—about the width of a pencil point. For problem veins up to the width of the pencil itself, STS is still the treatment of choice. By using the right agent for the right vein—and treating the entire vein "complex" that's generating the unwanted surface veins—the job can be completed in one or two sessions instead of the multiple return visits traditionally required.

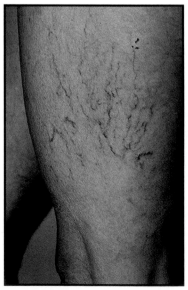
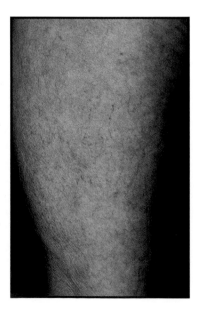

Spider veins, or small varicose veins, before and after glycerin injections. The treatment could start to gain in popularity in the U.S.

Availability. Glycerin is available to dermatologists. For now, the challenge may be to find a doctor who is familiar with using it as a sclerotherapy agent. Varicose vein removal is usually considered cosmetic surgery, so it's not covered by insurance. The cost is somewhere in the neighborhood of $400 per leg per session. ■

ALSO in the NEWS

Smokers Light the Way to Healthier Arteries

Research involving smokers, who are at increased risk for heart disease, has revealed three new ways to take care of stiffening blood vessels before the problem can lead to something more serious. In two separate studies from Ireland and the United States, published in early 2003, a drug called allopurinol, a supplement called taurine, and good old vitamin C were each shown to reverse an early stage of atherosclerosis, or hardening of the arteries. In this stage, called endothelial dysfunction, the artery walls lose so much flexibility that they can't expand to accommodate any increase in blood flow. The condition is common in—but not limited to—smokers.

In the Irish study, smokers with this condition who were given 2 grams of vitamin C or 1.5 grams of taurine (an amino acid abundant in fish) for five days demonstrated measurable improvement in blood vessel function. In the U.S. study, smokers were given one 600-milligram dose of allopurinol, a prescription drug commonly used to treat gout, then given a drug that stimulates artery expansion. The allopurinol clearly improved the arteries' ability to respond.

The fact that smokers were recruited as ideal models of endothelial dysfunction points to a fourth strategy for healthy arteries: Don't smoke. ■

Key Discovery

Gene Therapy Could Save a Leg

Early success with an experimental gene therapy may mean that people with severe circulatory problems in their legs will be able to avoid surgery—and possibly amputation—in the future.

Today, if you suffer from artery-blocking atherosclerosis in your lower body, you have pretty much the same options as people with blocked coronary arteries: angioplasty (opening the arteries by inflating tiny balloons inside them) or bypass surgery (rerouting blood around the blockage by grafting a blood vessel from elsewhere in the body). Unfortunately, not all people respond to treatment, and as many as 40 percent of those with severely blocked vessels must eventually undergo amputation. In the future, however, some of those people may be able to keep their limbs intact, thanks to a groundbreaking new approach.

In early 2003, doctors from the Jobst Vascular Center in Toledo, Ohio, announced that they had treated atherosclerosis of the leg by stimulating the growth of new blood vessels with gene therapy. They did it by injecting 51 patients' muscles with a genetically engineered growth factor called non-viral fibroblast growth factor Type 1, or NV1FGF. The growth factor in turn instructs certain cells to create small new "feeder" blood vessels that allow blood to flow around the blockage.

The treatment did not cause any serious side effects, and patients showed signs of improvement. "Many of the patients who were studied in the trial had ulcers on their feet that had been there for a long time," says Anthony Comerota, M.D., director of the Jobst Vascular Center. "Many patients were in constant pain. After treatment with NV1FGF, their pain diminished, their ulcers healed, and the blood pressure in their ankles increased." The next step: a larger, Phase II study that will compare the progress of gene therapy recipients with that of patients who get placebo (dummy) injections. ■

MUSCLES
BONES AND JOINTS

"FIX ME!" IS WHAT A GROWING NUMBER OF ACTIVE ADULTS WITH TENDON PROBLEMS ARE TELLING **THEIR DOCTORS.**

Thanks to advances in the past year, orthopedic surgeons now have three new minimally invasive ways to answer the call. One technique uses nothing more than an empty hypodermic needle to rid the tendon of pain-causing scar tissue. Another pulses low-energy shock waves through the skin to promote healing. And if surgery is needed, it can now be done with gentle heat therapy through a tiny incision.

Pain is being tamed on other fronts as well. A drug called Humira eases arthritis symptoms in as little as a week. For people with fibromyalgia, a compound called milnacipran has proven astonishingly effective in studies and may be available by mid-2005. Another distressing condition, lupus, may succumb to a dramatic new treatment—namely, completely rebuilding the immune system after first destroying it down to the last cell. Drastic as it sounds, the treatment has already worked for several volunteers.

Last but not least, Forteo, the world's first bone-growing drug, promises to slash the risk of fractures for women with osteoporosis.

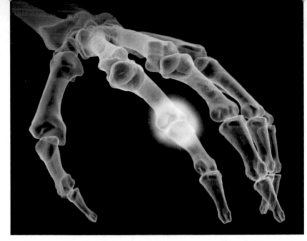

In rheumatoid arthritis, inflamed joints cause pain, swelling, and stiffness. If it's left untreated, severe joint damage may result.

Drug Development
New Rheumatoid Arthritis Drug Spares Immune System

There's a new rheumatoid arthritis medication at your doctor's disposal, and unlike other drugs in its category, there's no need to take immune-suppressing medicine along with it. Adalimumab (Humira), approved by the FDA in December 2002, is what's known as a monoclonal antibody. These drugs are lab-produced copies of antibodies, the body's invader-fighting molecules. Other monoclonal antibodies are already in use for rheumatoid arthritis, but because they're partially derived from mouse proteins, they provoke the human immune system to wage a battle against the foreign substances, forcing patients to take immune-suppressing medication along with the drugs. With Humira, which is derived from only human proteins, that's not necessary.

In no fewer than four major studies, Humira worked like gangbusters to alleviate rheumatoid arthritis symptoms and slow the disease's progression. A significant number of patients reported pain relief after taking it for just a week.

How it works. Rheumatoid arthritis is treated differently than the more common osteoarthritis because its cause is completely different. The joint damage isn't the result of wear and tear (as with osteoarthritis) but of an immune system that runs amok, attacking the body's own tissues. Humira

TOP Trends

FOR AGING BOOMERS, LIFE'S A SPRAIN

"They're coming in droves," says Nicholas A. DiNubile, M.D., a Philadelphia orthopedic surgeon. "They" are men and women in their forties and fifties with the laudable goal of keeping themselves fit in middle age. What's bringing them to the doc in such high numbers? Dr. DiNubile calls it boomeritis—a collection of joint, tendon, and muscle woes emblematic of the first generation that's ever made an all-out effort to stay active on an aging frame.

Ankle sprains are among the most frequent injuries. The chances of reinjuring a formerly sprained ligament soars each time you get out on the court or the running path—even if the original injury happened decades before. That's because most ankle sprains *never* heal completely on their own. So if you're still in the game, play some defense, Dr. DiNubile advises. Have your ankles checked for lingering weaknesses before you stress them again. An orthopedic surgeon can recommend exercises. And consider using ankle supports (from an orthopedic supply store or your doctor) that fit inside your shoes. ■

THEY WANNA BE LIKE MIKE

Doctors have known for some time that women and girls are far more prone to a torn ACL (anterior cruciate ligament)—a serious knee injury—than men and boys are. Orthopedic researchers are convinced that typical "female" movements during sports are responsible for the difference. The main problem, they say, is that girls tend to jump in a more stiff-legged way than boys do. When they land, their knees absorb more of the shock. Girls also tend to do their cutting and shifting—quick lateral moves common on the court or field—while standing more upright, which puts even more strain on their knees.

Now, thousands of young women and girls in California are learning to jump and move like boys. Studies of the early participants in the PEP (Prevent Injury, Enhance Performance) retraining program developed at the Santa Monica Orthopaedic and Sports Medicine Research Foundation have shown that it works—so well, in fact, that PEP has become standard team training in organized amateur women's soccer. But any girl as young as 10 can benefit from the training. Interested parents can contact Santa Monica Orthopaedic at hollysilverspt@aol.com ■

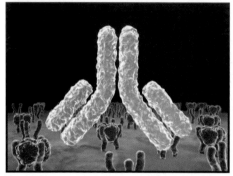

A buildup of TNF proteins (purple) in the joints causes painful swelling in rheumatoid arthritis.

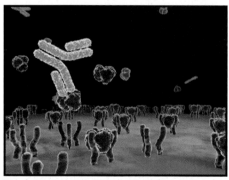

Humira is a man-made antibody (yellow), virtually indistinguishable from antibodies found in the body.

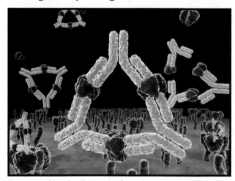

The antibody targets the troublesome proteins, blocking them by binding to them.

Because Humira is made from human proteins, it doesn't provoke an immune response.

blocks these misguided immune attacks by inhibiting a renegade protein called TNF, short for tumor necrosis factor. TNF is largely responsible for the inflammation that causes so much pain, swelling, stiffness, and even deformity in the joints of people with rheumatoid arthritis.

TNF inhibitors, including Humira and the older "semi-human" monoclonal antibodies, are powerful drugs that not only reduce pain and inflammation but also slow and even halt structural damage to the joints. They're turning out to be star players among the cast of monoclonal antibodies, and they may someday be used against other chronic inflammatory diseases. They are also being studied as possible treatments for congestive heart failure.

Availability. Humira is available now. It's taken by self-administered injection every other week. Because rheumatoid arthritis often causes crippling joint destruction in patients' hands, specially designed syringes—prefilled with the proper dosage—are sold in drugstores. ■

Steroid Shots Safe for Knees

Synthetic hormone-based drugs called steroids can provide months of pain relief when injected directly into arthritic knee joints. But even though steroids, such as prednisone and hydrocortisone, have been in use for decades, there's always been a concern that repeated treatments could harm the joint and make the arthritis worse in the long run. Now, after conducting the first long-term study of the safety of steroid injections to relieve knee arthritis pain, Canadian researchers report that even repeated injections don't appear to be harmful.

In a well-designed study of 68 women and men with severe osteoarthritis of the knee, researchers from the University of Montreal found that people injected every three months with 40 milligrams of the steroid triamcinolone acetonide showed no more joint degradation after two years than those who received shots of saltwater. Translation: Steroids seem to be safe in the long term for arthritis pain. The study, published in the February 2003 issue of the journal *Arthritis & Rheumatism*, also confirmed that steroid shots reduce pain and stiffness and increase the range of motion of arthritic knees. ■

Key Discovery
Broken Hips: Linger in the Hospital, Live Longer

A 75-year-old woman loses her balance and falls, fracturing her hip. Her family sees to it that she gets good medical care, and after a brief hospital stay, she comes home to start her rehabilitation. But the shortness of breath and loss of appetite that bothered her in the hospital grow worse. She's readmitted but never recovers, and she dies six months later.

Sadly, this story is a fairly common one. Of the 350,000 people (mostly elderly) hospitalized with hip fractures each year, as many as 13.5 percent die within six months.

Now, research has revealed a risk-lowering strategy that's as simple as can be: Make sure that patients recovering from hip fractures aren't discharged too early from the hospital. If they are, the research shows, their chances of dying shoot up by a staggering 360 percent.

How it works. A hip fracture—really a break in the femur (thigh bone) up near the hip socket—isn't just painful. It's life-disrupting, keeping patients from walking or even standing up. Treatment often strives for "early mobilization"—that is, getting you on your feet again as soon as possible. The problem is that more often than not, fracture patients also have other health problems—either preexisting conditions made worse by the fracture and its treatment or new troubles that started after the fracture. The researchers insist that overall health—not just progress in the healing of the fracture—should guide doctors when they choose the go-home day.

To help that happen, researchers at the Mount Sinai School of Medicine looked at the hospital records and follow-up reports of 559 hip fracture patients in New York City–area hospitals over a two-year period. Then they used the information to come up with a list of potentially dangerous health problems that indicate a patient is not ready for discharge. Dubbed "acute clinical issues," they include high fever, high or low blood pressure, poor appetite, shortness of breath, and an altered mental state. Patients who were sent home before any one of these issues was remedied were much more likely to die soon after. The study was published in a January 2003 issue of the *Archives of Internal Medicine*.

The researchers urged doctors to keep patients hospitalized until all such problems are stabilized. And what's the message to those with hip fractures? As eager as you may be to resume your normal life, a longer hospital stay could mean a *longer* life. ◼

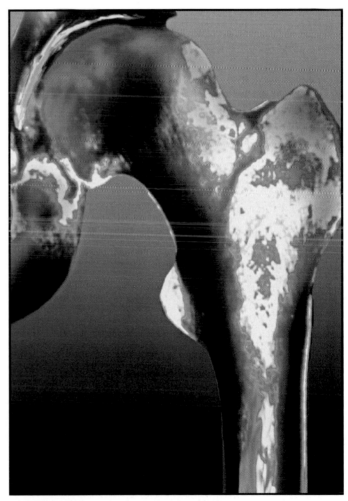

Of all fall-related fractures, hip fractures are responsible for the most deaths and significantly reduce quality of life. To lower your risk, exercise to improve your balance and lower body strength, get rid of any tripping hazards in your home, and use a nonslip mat in the shower.

Drug Development
Fibromyalgia Drug Shows Promise

A long nightmare may be nearing an end for as many as 11 million people with fibromyalgia in the United States. For years, they've endured the relentless pain, fatigue, and low mood of this chronic condition, with no approved drug treatments to help. As recently as the 1990s, modern medicine refused to even recognize the syndrome. And the pain relievers that were offered for fibromyalgia symptoms had a distinct downside: They didn't work.

At long last, pharmaceutical researchers are convinced they have found a drug that does: milnacipran. According to study results announced in 2003 by drug developer Cypress Bioscience, the drug is poised to give fibromyalgia patients back their lives. About half of 125 study participants were given milnacipran once or twice a day for 12 weeks. The other half were given a placebo (an ineffective substance used for comparison).

At the end of the study period, the patients were rated for their levels of pain, mood, and fatigue. The subjects who received milnacipran showed a "statistically significant" improvement over those given placebos. Seventy percent reported an overall improvement in their symptoms, and 37 percent reported that the intensity of their pain was cut at least in half. As a final survey question, all of the subjects were asked, "How do you feel?" Seventy-five percent of those on the drug said they felt much better than at the beginning of the study, while a majority of the placebo group reported feeling the same or worse.

How it works. Fibromyalgia pain isn't like most pain, and milnacipran doesn't work like most pain relievers. When you

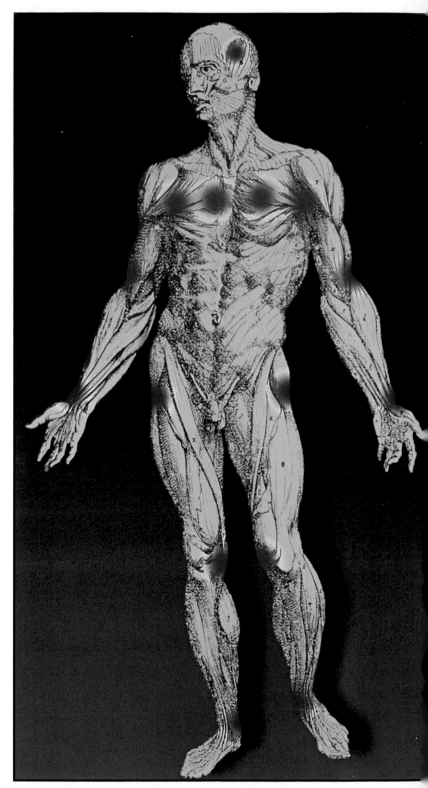

Difficult to diagnose and treat, fibromyalgia causes pain at "tender points" in the body. Fibromyalgia may be diagnosed when a patient has significant pain in at least 11 of 18 tender points when a doctor presses them lightly.

Daniel Clauw's research may lead to the first drug for fibromyalgia.

Hard Science Took the "Mush" Out of Fibromyalgia

If Daniel Clauw, M.D., had listened to his colleagues early in his career, he probably wouldn't be doing cutting-edge fibromyalgia research now. He certainly wouldn't have headed up the key study of the drug called milnacipran, which may become the first fibromyalgia treatment available in the United States.

"As a young junior faculty member, I began to see fibromyalgia as a real problem that, like all real problems, could be understood by applying scientific principles," says Dr. Clauw, director of the University of Michigan's chronic pain and fatigue research group. "People tried to dissuade me, though. They said it was a poor career choice—too unpredictable, too mushy." It wasn't until just a few years ago that fibromyalgia was recognized by the medical community as a disease. Previously, it was considered at best a collection of unrelated complaints and at worst a figment of overactive imaginations. Perceptions had to change before a drug like milnacipran could be taken seriously as a treatment.

As Dr. Clauw predicted, science itself started to turn things around. "Research used techniques where you could see objective evidence of the pain that people were reporting," he says. "As these studies accumulated, there was more acceptance that there was a real problem."

Armed with a growing consensus that fibromyalgia was real, as well as evidence from Dr. Clauw and others that the neurotransmitters norepinephrine and serotonin were a promising treatment focus, pharmaceutical companies such as Cypress Bioscience and Pfizer went in search of a treatment.

But they didn't look in the lab; they looked to Europe. "Basically, they scoured the world for existing drugs that fit the criteria they were looking for," Dr. Clauw says. "We ended up testing milnacipran after Cypress licensed the compound from a company in France, where fibromyalgia isn't recognized as a disease. The French don't even have a word for it."

Longtime fibromyalgia sufferers might be forgiven a twinge of bitterness. While much of the medical community was pooh-poohing their condition, the drug that could help them was already approved and in use as an antidepressant in 20 countries. But any bitterness will surely turn to relief if milnacipran makes it to market in 2005 as predicted. And they'll also be grateful that Dr. Clauw stuck to his guns and specialized in fibromyalgia research.

"I viewed it as an opportunity to accomplish something," he says. "And with milnacipran, that appears to be the case." ■

think of pain, you usually assume it's due to some kind of damage or inflammation in specific parts of the body. Fibromyalgia, though, is a malfunction in the way the entire nervous system processes pain. As one expert puts it, "It's as if the volume control in the central nervous system is turned way up and stuck there." Milnacipran adjusts the levels of key brain and nerve chemicals called neurotransmitters to turn the volume down.

Milnacipran is the first of a new class of drugs called norepinephrine serotonin reuptake inhibitors, or NSRIs. If that sounds a lot like the well-known class of antidepressant drugs called SSRIs (selective serotonin reuptake inhibitors), it's no coincidence. Depression and fibromyalgia have a lot in common—their symptoms overlap, and they're both characterized by imbalances in brain chemicals.

Essentially, scientists have adapted the antidepressant strategy of adjusting levels of the brain chemicals serotonin and norepinephrine. The result: a pain-relieving, mood-elevating, fatigue-fighting fibromyalgia drug.

Availability. An identical compound already exists as an approved antidepressant drug in much of Europe. However, milnacipran is not approved for any use in the United States, so it can't be prescribed yet for fibromyalgia. Phase III studies of the drug, to confirm its effectiveness and monitor side effects, began in 2003. If they go well, researchers expect milnacipran to be approved by mid-2005. A similar drug, pregabalin, being developed by Pfizer, has also shown good results and could be available at about the same time. ■

Drug Development

Attacking Lupus by Rebooting the Immune System

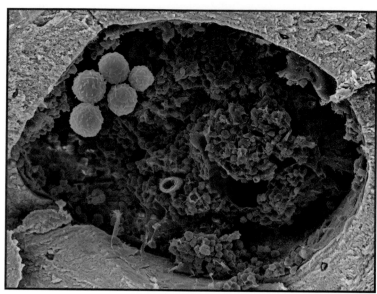

Because they survive high-dose chemotherapy, bone marrow stem cells may be the key to a new lupus treatment that involves wiping out the immune system.

The idea has to be intriguing for the estimated 500,000 to 1.5 million Americans with lupus, the often painful, tissue-destroying disease that can seriously damage joints and key organs. Since lupus is an autoimmune disease—that is, it's caused by a constantly malfunctioning immune system—why not simply wipe out the entire immune system and start a better one from scratch?

Outrageous? Maybe not. A team of researchers from Johns Hopkins Bayview Medical Center in Baltimore tried it on 14 lupus patients and reported that nearly four years later, 3 of the patients had been essentially cured, 2 more were mostly symptom-free, and 6 others were controlling their disease much better than before.

The chosen weapon of mass immune system destruction was cyclophosphamide (Cytoxan), a chemotherapy drug used to kill cancer cells. Cytoxan is also currently used (not always successfully) as a lupus treatment, but only in low doses administered over six months. For this study, however, one huge dose of the drug was used to obliterate the immune system—and hopefully, the disease along with it.

For this study, one huge dose of the drug was used to obliterate the immune system—and hopefully, the disease along with it.

How it works. A person's immune system can recover from this drastic approach because high-dose chemotherapy spares stem cells, the multipurpose "starter" cells in the bone marrow that are resistant to chemotherapy. After the chemical blast, these surviving cells immediately go to work to rebuild a new, disease-free immune system. In fact, a key feature of the study was the researchers' decision not to help the reconstruction process by removing bone marrow before the treatment and reintroducing it afterward.

Previous attempts at high-dose chemotherapy for lupus used this "hedge"—and that may be precisely why they failed, since they may have reintroduced diseased cells along with the set-aside stem cells. The Johns Hopkins researchers, on the other hand, trusted in the stem cells' ability to survive on their own, and their leap of faith seems to have paid off.

It's doubtful that most lupus patients will be willing to have their immune systems demolished—even temporarily—based on a study involving only 14 people. But the crash-and-reboot strategy holds promise for a future lupus cure. It could also potentially help with other autoimmune diseases, such as rheumatoid arthritis.

Availability. The next step will be a larger study comparing megadose chemotherapy with standard treatments in 100 lupus patients at medical centers in Philadelphia, Baltimore, and Madison, Wisconsin. The researchers began signing up volunteers in 2003 and expected to continue enrollment into 2004. For information about participating, call the Johns Hopkins Lupus Center at (410) 614-1573 or send an e-mail to stdman@jhmi.edu. ∎

Drug Development
Bone-Growing Drug Gets the Green Light

Calcium. Estrogen. Calcitonin. Fosamax. Actonel. Evista. There's no shortage of treatments for the 10 million Americans, most of them postmenopausal women, hampered by the bone-thinning disease osteoporosis. But as varied as that list is, all of the current options work the negative side of the equation, slowing bone loss rather than encouraging new bone growth. And that approach puts a limit on long-term benefits.

Things changed in November 2002, when a bone growing drug called teriparatide (Forteo) won FDA approval. Forteo actually reverses the disease's damage by speeding up the formation of new bone tissue. One major drawback is that the drug isn't available in pill form, only as an injection—a daily shot in the thigh or abdomen. Also, Forteo carries a warning from the FDA because it appeared to cause bone tumors in lab mice when they were given large doses of the drug over an extended period of time. No such problems emerged during the human trials, however. The benefits of Forteo are clear. Not only has it been shown to grow bone tissue and boost bone density better than other established drugs, it also has been shown to reduce fractures.

In 2001, a multinational study published in the *New England Journal of Medicine* showed that postmenopausal women with osteoporosis who were injected with 20 micrograms of Forteo a day for 18 months reduced their risk of new vertebral fractures by

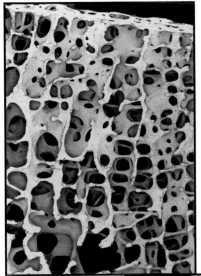

In osteoporosis, dense bone (left) becomes brittle and porous (below). It can lead to fractures, often of the hip, spine, or wrist. The new drug Forteo is the first to increase the rate of bone formation. Weight-bearing exercise (such as walking) is another way to boost bone density.

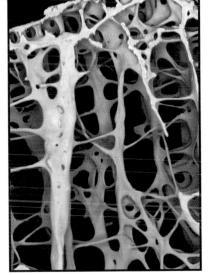

Milk at 10, Strong Bones at 50

Kids who ignore the age-old parental command to "drink your milk!" may live to regret it. New findings show that women over 50 who drank less than a glass of milk a day as girls have significantly lower bone density and twice the risk of fractures compared with those who drank a glass or more a day. And there's no undoing past damage: In the study, the added risk existed no matter how much milk the women drank as adults or how much calcium they took.

Childhood and adolescence are key bone development stages that require sufficient calcium intake. Calcium supplements taken during those years help, but you have to keep taking them to sustain the benefits. Milk, on the other hand, appears to impart bone-strengthening benefits that last well past menopause, even if you don't drink it as an adult. The study, published in the January 2003 issue of the *American Journal of Clinical Nutrition,* stops short of concluding that the more milk you drink in childhood, the more benefits you receive. But it clearly shows that drinking your milk while your bones are growing pays big dividends later—when you're trying to save them. ■

65 percent. That was a better performance than the 40 to 50 percent (at best) reduced risk achieved with other drugs. Forteo also cut the risk of fractures elsewhere in the skeleton by more than 50 percent.

How it works. Your bone mass is ever-changing, with bone cells constantly being destroyed and replaced. As long as the balance of old and new cells is maintained, bones remain dense and strong. With age, however, the breakdown process often outpaces new bone formation. That leads to weaker, "airier" bones that can fracture easily. Indeed, the word *osteoporosis* means "porous bone."

Forteo stimulates bone-growing cells known as osteoblasts.

All osteoporosis treatments slow the pace of bone breakdown. That does improve bone density, because the new bone cells that are still being created naturally get a chance to catch up in their job of filling in the "airy" parts. Still, overall bone mass continues to shrink, which is why the strengthening effect of those drugs tends to plateau after a year or two.

Forteo works differently. It's a genetically engineered form of a human hormone called parathyroid. By mimicking the action of this hormone, the drug increases calcium levels in the blood while decreasing phosphorus levels. That combination stimulates bone-growing cells known as osteoblasts, giving people with osteoporosis a much-improved chance of avoiding fractures and posture problems.

Availability. Forteo was approved primarily for post-menopausal women whose fracture risk is considered high, but doctors can prescribe the drug for anyone with osteoporosis. ■

RESEARCH ROUNDUP

The More You Lift, the Stronger Your Bones

If you are past menopause and you're looking for ways to protect your bones from osteoporosis, you've no doubt heard the mantra "moderate weight-bearing exercise." But if you interpret "moderate" as a signal to take it easy, your bones may be missing out. New research shows that when it comes to lifting weights to fortify bones, more is definitely better.

In the study, published in the January 2003 issue of the journal *Medicine & Science in Sports & Exercise*, 140 women ages 44 to 66 performed eight different weight-training exercises three times a week. The researchers encouraged the women to use a weight load that was 70 to 80 percent of their "one-repetition maximum"— that is, the heaviest weight with which they could do an exercise once. When a study subject's one-repetition maximum increased because she'd gotten stronger, the amount of weight she lifted for that exercise was increased accordingly. Those who made the most progress reaped the most bone-density benefits, especially In the hip area—the most troublesome fracture site for women with osteoporosis.

One note of caution: Trying to find your one-repetition maximum on your own could lead to injury, fitness experts say, especially if you're an older person. Unless you're training with an expert, the surest way to make progress is to start with lighter weights and increase the weight to the point where you can just barely complete 12 repetitions. ■

Key Discovery
Light Up and Feel the Pain

Just when you thought there couldn't possibly be more harmful effects to attribute to tobacco, a team of British researchers has discovered a surprising one: Smoking hurts. At least that's one interpretation of a new study revealing that smokers are at higher risk for muscle and joint pain than nonsmokers. Even ex-smokers among the study subjects complained more of pain than those who had never smoked, raising the possibility that there's something about tobacco smoke that causes long-term damage to muscle tissue or neurological responses.

The researchers uncovered the tobacco-pain link by surveying more than 12,900 Britons about their smoking habits as well as their experiences with lower-back, neck, arm, and leg pain. After analyzing the data, they found that smokers and ex-smokers of both sexes reported more overall pain than lifetime nonsmokers and were much more likely to have experienced episodes of pain severe enough to interfere with their normal activities. Most striking: Subjects who were still smoking were 50 percent more likely to have experienced muscle or joint pain in the previous year than people who had never smoked. The study was published in the January 2003 issue of *Annals of Rheumatic Diseases*. Previous studies have also connected smoking to increased pain.

How it works. The fact that there's an association of some kind between smoking and pain doesn't necessarily mean that smoking causes the pain, but there are at least two ways that it could, the researchers point out. The nicotine in tobacco could ratchet up pain perception with its stimulant effect. And smoking could actually damage musculoskele-tal tissue, possibly by reducing the blood supply to the tissue or interfering with the delivery of vital nutrients to muscles and joints.

The researchers went beyond previous studies on pain and tobacco by "correcting" the data to allow for the fact that people in physically demanding blue-collar jobs are more likely to experience pain and to smoke. But it's also possible that the type of person who takes up smoking may be the same type of person who's prone to musculoskeletal pain, or that those who have more frequent pain may be more likely to take up smoking as a result. The researchers urged further study to find out if the link is coincidental. In the meantime, you have plenty of reasons not to light up. ■

Earlier studies have shown that smokers have a much higher incidence of chronic low-back pain. Now, a large study indicates that smokers have more muscle and joint pain and more pain overall.

Alternative Answers

Serving Up a New Solution to Tennis Elbow

It happens to even the fittest of recreational sports buffs: One day they're blasting shots like Serena Williams at her best, and the next day they're watching from the sidelines because a minor tendon tear has put them in too much pain to play. If the joint injury is serious, they might consider orthopedic surgery. But common cases of tennis elbow, jumper's knee, and other tendon injuries are best taken care of by rest and patience. Patience can wear thin, though, especially if the pain refuses to go away. After several months or more of being sidelined, anyone with a chronic tendon problem is probably wishing for a treatment that's less drastic than surgery but more aggressive than doing nothing.

The answer has been found at the tip of a needle. Making use of recent advancements in ultrasound imaging, a new technique helps doctors solve tendon problems by aiming an empty hypodermic needle at them. Radiologist Levon N. Nazarian, M.D., and

sports medicine specialist John McShane, M.D., treated more than 300 people with "ultrasound-guided needle therapy"—with good results. In January 2003, the doctors reported to the Radiological Society of North America's annual meeting in Chicago that pain was reduced and function restored in 65 percent of those patients. What's more, because a needle probe is so much less invasive than surgery, recovery time was typically much shorter.

How it works. Tendons attach muscle to bone. They're sinewy and elastic but prone to tears when overused or misused, especially if they belong to an older person. A typical tendon injury is tennis elbow (lateral epicondylitis), an inflammation of the tendons on the knobby sides of the elbow. Unlike bone, injured tendons create scar tissue as they heal. That hard, dense tissue continues to cause pain as it's dragged across the bone when the muscle contracts.

Traditional treatment involves injecting a corticosteroid drug into the joint to reduce inflammation, and it's only a temporary fix. But with the new technique, the needle point is used as a scraping tool to break up the scar tissue and clear the way for healthy new tendon tissue to form. That's essentially what's involved in arthroscopic surgery (which requires an incision), but in this case, it can be done with a mere needle puncture because ultrasound provides real-time imaging to help guide the doctor's needle to the scar tissue.

Availability. Dr. Nazarian recommends ultrasound-guided needle therapy for chronic tendon problems that don't warrant surgery but cause persistent symptoms. Currently, the procedure is being performed only at Thomas Jefferson University Hospital in Philadelphia, where the researchers developed it, and by a handful of doctors elsewhere who have been shown the technique. But Dr. Nazarian anticipates more widespread availability as knowledge of the procedure spreads.

"It's not brain surgery," he says. "Any facility with somebody who knows how to handle an ultrasound machine and somebody competent to wield a needle inside a tendon can do it."

Since the technique is based on already accepted practices—namely, ultrasound and the removal of scar issue—it needs no formal approval. But doctors usually don't rush to adopt a new procedure until it passes muster in a rigorously controlled clinical study. Dr. Nazarian and Dr. McShane have submitted an application for funding for just such a study, which could take place in 2004. ■

High-Tech Help

Gentler Shock Waves Offer Painless Tendon Treatment

For several years, professional athletes were flocking to Canada to take advantage of a nonsurgical therapy that uses low-energy shock waves to quickly heal tendon injuries. But as of 2003, they can stay home and get the same results—and so can thousands of ordinary Joes and Jills who are looking for a fast and painless way to end tendon problems such as tennis elbow, jumper's knee, and chronic tendinitis.

The therapy, which has been available in Canada and Europe for years, is usually called by its brand name, Sonocur. Its big advantage is that nothing pierces the skin—not a surgical tool, not a probe, not even a needle. Patients feel only a slight tapping sensation as shock waves are pulsed at the damaged area. Sonocur uses much lower energy than older versions of shock wave therapy (originally used to break up kidney stones). That makes for a more patient-friendly treatment, usually consisting of three short sessions in a doctor's office, with no need for the general anesthesia that the painful high-energy treatment often required. The lower-energy shock waves also do a better job of healing tendons.

How it works. Low-energy shock waves promote new blood vessel growth in the damaged area, which helps bring natural healing agents to the site. They also stop the pain caused by the injury or inflammation (although researchers aren't sure how). As welcome as that pain relief may be, neither it nor the new vessel growth "cures" damaged tendons. Rather, each of the two improvements makes it easier (and quicker) for your body to do its own healing work,

with your help. "The treatment lets you feel good enough to do the exercises and physical therapy needed to really improve the tendon permanently," says Gary Covall, M.D., an orthopedic surgeon and principal investigator of the large study that led to FDA approval of Sonocur in 2002.

Availability. Sonocur was approved specifically for tennis elbow, but doctors are also using it on injured tendons in other parts of the body, including the knee, shoulder, and hip. It remains to be seen how soon after a tendon injury the use of Sonocur will be recommended and whether insurance companies will pay for it. In the confirming study, the "worst of the worst" cases were used—people who had tried everything short of surgery and still showed no improvement after two years. But Dr. Covall sees no reason why low-energy shock wave therapy shouldn't be used to speed recovery much earlier than that—perhaps as soon as a few months after an injury, as it is in Canada and Europe. ■

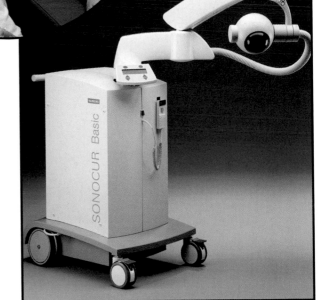

Sonocur, which heals tendon injuries with low-energy shock waves, is a painless, noninvasive alternative to surgery.

Surgical Solution

A Warm Welcome for Heat Surgery

Inflamed or damaged tendons have become increasingly common, thanks to the active but aging baby boom generation. And sometimes, there's just no getting around the need for surgery to take care of especially stubborn injuries. Now, a new kind of surgery available in the United States repairs tendons with a tiny "wand" that's inserted through a small (1-inch) incision and heals with mild heat. The procedure takes about 20 minutes, requires only mild sedation, and gets people back to their regular activities in a matter of days.

That's a far cry from conventional tendon surgery. The "open" procedure involves reaching the tendon through large incisions and scraping away diseased tissue with small spoon-like instruments. After surgery, rehabilitation is lengthy, and compli-

cations aren't uncommon. Hockey players and NFL linebackers may figure such a radical procedure is worth the trouble, but it's not the kind of thing that typical victims of tennis elbow or jumper's knee want to endure.

Most joint injuries are caused by overuse. Endlessly repeated motions (such as tennis strokes) can damage tendons—the dense, fibrous attachments responsible for moving bones when the muscles generate energy. Usually, the best treatment is simply to wait for the tendon to heal itself, perhaps with the help of new noninvasive healing aids such as ultrasound-guided needle therapy or low-energy shock wave treatment. (See pages 206 and 207.) But if the problem goes beyond painful inflammation (tendinitis) to more serious degradation of the tendon fibers, called tendinosis, it can hurt just to lift a coffee cup or walk up stairs, let alone play sports. Surgery may be needed, and that's where the new heat-based surgical method comes in.

How it works. Dubbed Topaz by its manufacturer, ArthroCare Corporation, the new technology is a modification of existing "ablation" methods that surgeons use when they need to burn through tissue. Because its high-energy radiofrequency heat is so intense, ablation has never been an option for treating tendinitis or tendinosis. But Topaz's controlled ablation (or Coblation, as ArthroCare calls it) uses a much gentler heat source that allows an orthopedic surgeon to safely "dissolve" damaged tendon tissue rather than burn it away. One therapeutic goal of the surgery is the removal of this scarred or damaged tissue, called debridement. But the heat treatment also hastens healing by promoting new blood vessel growth in the area.

Availability. Spurred by FDA approval in 2002, several encouraging studies, and a positive progress report to the American Academy of Orthopaedic Surgeons in February 2003, the Topaz technique became widely available in 2003. It can be used for tendon problems in the knee, shoulder, elbow, ankle, and wrist, but it's recommended only for people who haven't responded well to at least six months of other treatments. Surgery is still a last resort, but Topaz has made it a less drastic one. ■

Surgery with Topaz uses a wand to dissolve damaged tendon tissue with gentle heat. It requires only a 1-inch incision, and patients recover in a matter of days.

patient profile

The surgery known as Topaz allowed Silvia Dauphin to play tennis again—without pain.

Life Is No Longer a Pain in the Elbow

Silvia Dauphin got tennis elbow the old-fashioned way—by playing tennis. But there was nothing old-fashioned about the way she finally freed herself of the resulting tendon pain that had been worsening since she was in her twenties.

At age 44, Dauphin answered an ad in a San Diego–area newspaper and became a volunteer subject in the final testing phase of a new electrosurgery technique that heals tendons with heat. Several months after her surgery, she was pain-free, and the new treatment, known as Topaz, had won FDA approval.

Dauphin found that ad at just the right time. She had gradually damaged the tendon in her right elbow as a young player, before much was known about safe grips and suitable racket weights. That led her to give up tennis for most of her thirties, but she took it up again so she could introduce her daughter to the sport and return to assistant coaching for a high school team. "I love to play so much that I didn't really care about the pain," Dauphin says. "I'd just suffer afterward and ice it down for hours."

She tried the usual tendinitis treatments—including high doses of anti-inflammatory drugs ("They just killed my stomach," she says), pressure armbands, and a couple of cortisone shots ("They worked, but the pain came back in a few months"). Eventually, she learned that her tendon problem had advanced beyond inflammation (tendinitis) to more serious structural damage (tendinosis). Meanwhile, the pain got worse. "It got to the point where I had to switch arms just to lift plates out of the cupboard," she says. "I figured I was going to live with this my whole life."

Surgery was the only answer. What was it like to have a wand-like instrument aiming heat at the damaged tendon tissue through a small incision? Dauphin can't tell you. "They asked me to count backward from 10, and I didn't make it to 6 before the anesthetic took effect," she says. What she can tell you is that the procedure didn't take much more than 10 or 15 minutes. "When I woke up, I looked at my right elbow and saw about an inch of sutures, but I didn't feel any pain," she says. "They gave me some Vioxx [an anti-inflammatory drug], but I only took the first one. I didn't need it."

She was told to take it easy for six months, but she felt so good after four months that she started doing some light rallying on the tennis court. Later, the overhead shots and zinging serves returned to her game as well. "I was amazed," she says. "I could do business as usual. I never feel my tendon at all now."

So Silvia Dauphin traded in her pain for a 1-inch mark on her elbow. "That scar?" she says. "It's nothing." ■

REPRODUCTION
AND SEXUALITY

FORGET SARS. THE NEXT BIG MEDICAL STORY OUT OF CHINA MAY BE A NEW METHOD OF BIRTH CONTROL FOR MEN. World-wide research into male contraception is heating up. Meanwhile, new techniques—including a vasectomy that involves a clip instead of a snip—have revolutionized sterilization for both sexes, and the Today Sponge is available again.

There's also news for couples who want a baby, from a natural extract that may boost male fertility and high-tech ways of weeding out "weak" sperm to progesterone therapy to prevent premature births.

For women whose reproductive years are past, the bad news about hormone replacement therapy (HRT) continued. The FDA slapped its toughest warning on all estrogen products, and new study results show that HRT has no effect on general health, energy, or memory. One bright spot: Researchers are working harder to find new treatments for hot flashes, and a drug used to prevent seizures may help.

Finally, turn to page 220 for a sneak peek at the next Viagra.

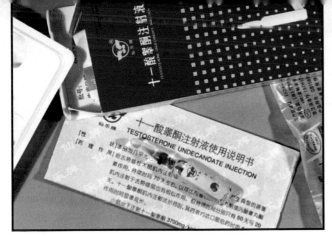

Men in China have been receiving injections of testosterone as part of a study on male contraception.

Drug Development

Beyond Latex: A New Era of Male Contraception

Women have had several reliable forms of birth control for more than 50 years now. But men...well, they're still relying on a method that dates back to the ancient Egyptians—a device quite subject to tearing and slippage, much to women's chagrin.

That may be changing, as technology and science finally catch up to biology. In early 2003, 1,000 men in China were participating in a late-stage study of monthly testosterone injections as a birth control method. The World Health Organization (WHO) and the Chinese government are sponsoring the trial.

How it works. When young, healthy men are given supplemental testosterone, it shuts down production of testosterone in the testes, preventing them from manufacturing sperm, says Christine Wang, M.D., professor at Harbor-UCLA Medical Center and Research and Education Institute in Torrance, California, and a member of the WHO committee overseeing male contraceptive research. The beauty of this system, says Dr. Wang, is that with the exception of infertility, the men experience minimal effects from the testosterone injections. Plus, the infertility is only temporary.

Availability. Each participant will continue the testosterone injections for two years, with the entire study expected to wrap up sometime in 2007. That may mean a birth control method for Chinese men, but in the United

TOP Trends

THE SPONGE IS BACK!

A birth control option that gained cult status after starring in an episode of *Seinfeld* is available again after disappearing from the market nearly 10 years ago. It's the Today Sponge, the squishy little white cylinder that's inserted like a tampon. Production of the sponge ceased in March 1994 after the FDA found problems in the only factory where it was made. Its manufacturer decided the relatively small market for Today didn't justify the expensive modifications the plant required.

In 1998, Allendale Pharmaceuticals bought the rights to the sponge and began the arduous process of finding a manufacturing plant that would meet FDA requirements. In March 2003, it began selling the sponge from a Canadian Website, www.birthcontrol.com, and said it hoped the product would be available on U.S. shelves later in the year, pending FDA approval of the manufacturing process. The sponges are expected to sell for about $2.90 each. ◼

"MORNING-AFTER PILL" GOES OVER THE COUNTER

Since its approval in 1999 as an emergency contraceptive, the so-called morning-after pill has become available without a prescription from pharmacists in four states and will soon be sold over the counter in the rest of the country. The pill, actually a high-dose regimen of oral contraceptives, reduces the risk of pregnancy by 89 percent if taken within 72 hours of unprotected sex. Since its approval, it's been used by an estimated 6 percent of American women—a threefold increase over the number using it in 2000, according to the Kaiser Family Foundation—and is being heralded as one reason for drops in abortion rates in some states.

In April 2003, the maker of Plan B, one of two FDA-approved brands, applied to the FDA for permission to sell the pills without a prescription, but individual states have already moved to make them more easily available. Oregon began offering them over the Internet in December 2002, letting women get a prescription without seeing a doctor. In New Mexico, California, Washington, and Alaska, pharmacists can dispense the pills to women without a prescription. ◼

States, the FDA is likely to require additional studies. To spur progress toward that end, the National Institutes of Health (NIH) invited research centers throughout the country to apply for membership in a network of centers that would participate in research and clinical trials on male contraception, says Dr. Wang. In October 2002, the NIH awarded a $9.5 million grant to the University of Washington in Seattle to establish a new interdisciplinary Male Contraception Research Center as part of that network.

Why is it taking so long to develop a reliable male birth control method? The reasons are many.

● Any male contraceptive would compete on the market with already profitable female contraceptives, limiting company incentives to develop such a product.

● While a woman produces just one egg each month and is fertile for only a few days a month, a man produces up to 100 million sperm per day and is fertile 24/7.

● Getting testosterone into the body isn't easy. To date, there is no viable testosterone "Pill." Instead, the hormone is available through less convenient patches, creams, injections, and implants.

● Since men don't get pregnant and thus don't have quite as much incentive to prevent a pregnancy as women do, there's a question as to how much women could trust them to take a daily pill, a monthly injection, or any other birth control method that isn't immediately obvious, notes Nancy Alexander, Ph.D., director of medical services for contraception at Organon, Inc., a New Jersey–based pharmaceutical company that's working to develop a male contraceptive. ■

Researchers Stumble On Another Contraceptive Contender

A drug used to treat a rare metabolic disorder known as Gaucher's disease shows great potential as a male contraceptive—at least in mice. The drug, NB-DNJ, works by disrupting the way the body produces fatty substances called glycosphingolipids. In people with Gaucher's, these substances accumulate in the spleen, liver, lungs, bone marrow, and, in rare cases, the brain. They also play a critical role in sperm formation, as researchers from the Glycobiology Institute at Oxford University in England discovered while testing the drug in mice.

These sperm have virtually no acrosomes, tiny parts essential for fertilizing an egg.

Sperm treated with the Gaucher's drug. The green is the acrosome.

Specifically, NB-DNJ affects tiny parts on the sperm called acrosomes, which help sperm penetrate the egg's protective coating. It also interferes with the sperm's ability to make its way toward the egg—like tying an anchor to an Olympic swimmer. The drug had no effect on the male sex hormone testosterone, which is necessary for sex drive, or on the fertility of the female mice. When researchers stopped giving the drug to the male mice, the mice regained their fertility with no ill effects. Since the drug (at doses 10 times what may be required for contraception) has been shown to be safe in Gaucher's patients, the way is paved for clinical testing, which could begin in late 2003, researchers noted. The findings were published in December 2002 in *Proceedings of the National Academy of Sciences*. ■

New Male "Pill" under Development

One of the first male contraceptive drugs to be tested in large-scale studies could reach the U.S. market within five to seven years, either in the form of a pill, an implant, or regular injections. It's a combination of testosterone and progestin, the synthetic form of the female hormone progesterone. Progestin not only halts egg production in women but also stops sperm production in men. Unfortunately, it cuts testosterone production, too—which is why researchers have combined it with testosterone. Clinical trials have already begun and will occur at multiple hospitals and research centers around the world. They're the result of a partnership between two multinational pharmaceutical companies that have both been working for years to bring a male contraceptive to market: NV Organon, a subsidiary of the Dutch chemical company Akzo Nobel, and the German firm Schering AG. ■

Key Discovery
Easier Vasectomy: A Clip Instead of a Snip

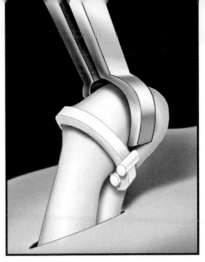

In the Vasclip procedure, a tiny clip is placed around the vas deferens, closing off the tube so that sperm can't pass through.

For all those men out there who swore they'd never voluntarily put their private parts under the knife comes a new form of vasectomy that promises to be quicker, less painful, and snip-free. In fact, its creator thinks the procedure is so different from a traditional vasectomy that it began marketing the device that makes it possible—Vasclip, a tiny plastic clip about the size of a grain of rice—as an "alternative to vasectomy" in the spring of 2003.

How It works. In a traditional vasectomy, the vas deferens, the tubes through which sperm flow on their way out of the testes, are cut or burned (cauterized). With Vasclip, however, clips are snapped around the vas deferens, not unlike putting a clamp on a hose. No cautery is involved.

While a traditional vasectomy takes 15 to 20 minutes, the Vasclip procedure takes less than 10, says David Kirby, M.D., chief of family practice at St. Luke's Hospital in Duluth, Minnesota. "When men are sitting there awake, they're apprehensive, and they get tense," says Dr. Kirby, who participated in clinical trials on Vasclip. "This is much quicker; there's less tissue trauma; there's no cautery, so they don't see or smell the smoke; and since there's less dissection of the tissue, there's a much lower chance of bleeding."

Clinical studies on 124 men found that the new procedure significantly reduced the incidence of complications, with less than 1 percent of men who had Vasclip reporting any significant swelling, compared with up to 15 percent of those who had the traditional vasectomy procedure. And none of the men who had the Vasclip procedure developed infections, compared with up to 6.9 percent of those who had regular vasectomies.

An added benefit: Because there's less damage to the vas deferens with Vasclip, the procedure may be easier to reverse. Nationally, about 500,000 men have vasectomies each year, and 4 to 6 percent try to have them reversed.

Availability. The company, also called Vasclip, began training doctors throughout the United States in the procedure in the spring of 2003. Because the procedure is new, the $350 cost may not initially be covered by insurance. ■

Doctors use this device, which resembles a small stapler, to apply the Vasclip.

ALSO in the NEWS Fish Oil Equals Intelligence

Want to raise a smarter kid? Forget Baby Einstein videos. Try fish oil instead. A study published in the January 2003 issue of the journal *Pediatrics* found that women who took 2 teaspoons of cod-liver oil daily, beginning in their 18th week of pregnancy and continuing until three months after delivery, had children who scored significantly higher on a standardized intelligence test at age 4 than children of mothers who had been assigned to take a placebo (in this case, corn oil). Fish oils such as cod-liver oil contain an important essential fatty acid called docosahexaenoic acid (DHA) that's needed for optimal brain development. The fat is so important, in fact, that infant formula manufacturers have begun adding it to their products. ■

Key Discovery
Sterilization for Women— No Surgery Required

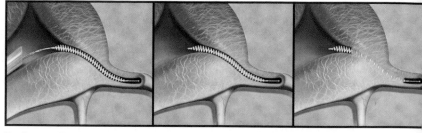

To place an Essure implant, a catheter is inserted, with the implant attached to its tip. Then the catheter is removed. Over the next three months, tissue grows over the implant, blocking the fallopian tube.

Gynecologist David Levine, M.D., is bracing for the vitriol of the urologists. Dr. Levine, who directs the Women's Diagnostic Center at St. Luke's Hospital in St. Louis, Missouri, has been traveling the country training physicians to perform the first permanent sterilization technique for women that doesn't involve surgery, pain, or disability.

patient profile

LaTia Mayer found an easy answer in Essure.

The Easiest Sterilization

For LaTia Mayer, 33, a 7-year-old daughter and a 7-year-old stepdaughter were enough. She and her husband knew they didn't want any more children. But her husband wasn't keen on the idea of a vasectomy, and she wasn't thrilled about a tubal ligation. Then Mayer heard a radio advertisement for a clinical study on Essure. Three months later, she decided to participate. A half-hour after entering the clinic, she was done.

"It was great," says Mayer, a sales administrative receptionist. "Quick, easy, and painless." By 11 that morning, she and her husband were sitting down to an early lunch. "I'm just so glad this came along when it did," she says. "This was the best option. It was wonderful." ■

"We are definitely going to cut into the vasectomy market," he says. "Once men understand that their wives or significant others can have this procedure done as easily as they can, there's no way they'll be able to be persuaded to have vasectomies."

How it works. In November 2002, the FDA approved Essure, tiny metallic implants used to block the fallopian tubes. Doctors employ a special catheter inserted through the vagina, cervix, and uterus to place the implants. Scar tissue forms over them, blocking the fallopian tubes and preventing fertilization of eggs. Unlike tubal ligation and hysterectomy—the only other permanent sterilization techniques available for women—the procedure doesn't require an incision or general anesthesia. It's performed under IV sedation in a doctor's office or ambulatory surgery center, and women can return to their regular activities the following day, says Dr. Levine.

"The patient is on and off the table in 35 minutes," he says, "and 75 percent of the patients we evaluated during the clinical trial didn't even need any pain relief after the procedure."

Women who have had a previous tubal ligation that failed, and those with significant tubal disease from infection or uterine cavity scarring, probably aren't good candidates for the Essure implants, Dr. Levine says. Women need to use backup birth control for three months after the procedure while the scar tissue forms. Unlike a tubal ligation, this procedure cannot be reversed, and women who've had it aren't even candidates for in vitro fertilization.

Availability. Hundreds of gynecologists were being trained in the procedure in early 2003, and it was expected to be widely available throughout the United States by the end of the year. ■

High-Tech Help
Separating the Boys from the Girls

More than 500 birth defects are linked to the baby's gender, including hemophilia and X-linked mental retardation (the most common cause of inherited mental retardation). These defects occur in 1 of every 1,000 live births. Until fairly recently, parents with a family history of such conditions had to either forgo having children altogether, opt for adoption, undergo expensive in vitro fertilization procedures, or roll the dice and hope to avoid the one-in-four chance they would have a child born with the sex-linked condition. Now, a technique called MicroSort, originally developed by U.S. Department of Agriculture scientists to sort bull sperm, sorts male from female sperm, enabling couples to choose the sex of their babies before conception via artificial insemination.

In October 2002, research on the first 300 live MicroSort births was presented at the Society for Reproductive Medicine's national meeting in Seattle. Keith Blauer, M.D., medical director of MicroSort, which is based at the Genetics & IVF Institute in Fairfax, Virginia, reported that the technique was 91 percent successful for couples seeking girls and 73 percent successful for those seeking boys. Just as important: There was no evidence that the procedure damaged the sperm's DNA, because babies conceived using Microsort had the same rate of birth defects as those conceived without it.

How it works. Microsort is based on the fact that "girl" sperm (those with an X chromosome) are much larger than "boy" sperm (those carrying a Y chromosome) and contain about 2.8 percent more DNA, explains Dr. Blauer. In the procedure, a special dye is applied to sperm to highlight their DNA, then the sperm are sent through a machine called a flow cytometer, which uses a laser beam to make the DNA glow. The more DNA the sperm has, the brighter the glow and the more likely that it carries the X chromosome. The sperm are then sorted based on brightness, with the appropriate sperm collected for artificial insemination.

To ensure that the resulting sample contains as much of the right sperm as possible, a small portion is evaluated using a DNA analysis method called FISH (fluorescence in situ hybridization). This technique uses DNA probes that attach to either the X or Y chromosome in sperm and emit a red/pink color (of course) for X-bearing sperm and green (no, we don't know why they didn't choose blue) for Y-bearing sperm.

Parents who undergo MicroSort to avoid a sex-

patient profile

Kathy Krug, with her two boys and a girl on the way. The sex was chosen with MicroSort.

It's a Girl!

It's February 2003, and Kathy Krug of Fairfax Station, Virginia, has just learned that she's pregnant with a girl. She's thrilled, not just because she already has two boys but also because one of her sons has hemophilia, a bleeding disorder that's carried through the mother's genes and passed on only to boys. For this pregnancy, Krug and her husband, Cliff, chose artificial insemination using sperm sorted with MicroSort.

They are incredibly blessed, she says, not only by the existence of the technology but also by the fact that it's available just a few minutes away. She learned about MicroSort through a friend who works at the Genetics & IVF Institute in nearby Fairfax. Without the technique, she and her husband probably wouldn't have tried for more kids, she says, even though they've always wanted a large family.

Krug's identical twin sister, Eileen Prophett of Fairfax, who also has a son with hemophilia, has tried three times to get pregnant using MicroSort and artificial insemination, but with no success. She's hoping the fourth time will be the charm. ■

linked disorder receive the procedure for free, while those who just want a child of a particular gender pay about $2,300. All are taking part in an ongoing FDA-approved trial of the procedure, the early results of which were presented at the October meeting. Eventually, that trial will include 750 participants. So far, about 15 percent of couples used MicroSort to avoid genetic defects, and the rest used it for family balancing, says Dr. Blauer.

Although the concept of choosing a child's gender is controversial, in 2001 the American Society of Reproductive Medicine's ethics committee endorsed using sorting techniques such as MicroSort for family balancing. The committee recommends that the parents be fully informed of the risks of failure, agree to fully accept children of the opposite sex if the gender selection fails, be counseled about having unrealistic expectations about the behavior of children of a preferred gender, and be offered an opportunity to participate in research to track and assess the safety, efficacy, and demographics of preconception selection.

Availability. In October 2002, MicroSort teamed with the Huntington Reproductive Center of Southern California in Laguna Hills to provide a West Coast MicroSort office. But numerous reproductive clinics around the country have cooperation agreements with the Genetics & IVF Institute and send frozen sperm to the institute for sorting, says Dr. Blauer. ■

Diagnostic Advance
New Test Spotlights Damaged Sperm

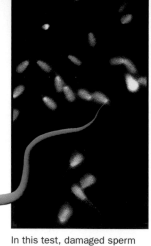

In this test, damaged sperm show up as red; healthier sperm appear green.

When a couple is infertile, many people automatically "blame" the woman. But 30 to 40 percent of all cases of infertility stem from a problem with the man's sperm. Even some men with what seem to be plenty of healthy, active sperm have trouble getting their partners pregnant. And if they do succeed, miscarriage is often the result. Until recently, doctors had trouble teasing out the problem with these men's sperm. But a new test can help.

The test, called sperm chromatin structure assay (SCSA), goes beyond simple sperm counts to look at the health of individual sperm and determine if there are any DNA abnormalities that would make conception and healthy pregnancy difficult or impossible.

How it works. SCSA checks for a condition called sperm DNA fragmentation, explains Philip Werthman, M.D., a Los Angeles–based urologist and male infertility specialist. Remember the double-helix design of DNA, resembling a twisted ladder? With DNA fragmentation, there are breaks in the rungs connecting the two sides of the ladder. This damage can prevent the sperm from fertilizing the egg and even if fertilization occurs, the sperm carries so much damaged DNA that the woman miscarries.

In the test, sperm cells are stained with a fluorescent dye and passed through a laser beam, which causes the dye to emit colored light. Green sperm have very low levels of fragmented DNA, while red sperm have moderate to high levels. Although the egg can sometimes make some minor repairs to damaged sperm, sperm with moderate to high levels are too damaged for the egg to fix.

The test has reinforced the thought that yes, men do have a ticking reproductive clock. Using SCSA, researchers at the University of Washington in Seattle discovered that the sperm of men older than 35 showed more DNA damage than that of younger men. For men with sperm damage that isn't age-related, the good news is that once you identify what's causing the damage—a virus, exposure to chemicals or toxins, heat, a varicose vein squeezing the testicle— the problem can often be corrected, and the sperm will return to normal, says Dr. Werthman.

Availability. SCSA costs about $350, which probably won't be covered by insurance until the FDA approves the test—possibly sometime in late 2003 or 2004. Until then, it's being used on an investigational basis. If you're interested, ask your doctor about it. ■

RESEARCH ROUNDUP

How Sperm Go Egg Hunting

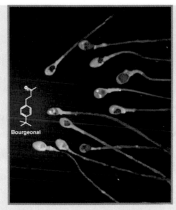

What draws sperm to their destination? It seems they can "smell" a compound that may be emitted by eggs.

Almost ever since we learned there were such things as a sperm and an egg, scientists have wondered how sperm find their way to the egg. It turns out that they have a kind of "nose" and may be capable of "sniffing out" the unique scent of a ready-to-be-fertilized egg

In a March 2003 issue of *Science* magazine, German and American scientists announced they had found a protein on sperm, called hOR 17-4, that's similar to the olfactory proteins in the nose—that is, a protein designed to smell. The idea that sperm can "smell" is not new, but the scientists discovered what the sperm respond to by searching for compounds that bind to hOR 17-4, also known as an odorant receptor. One of those compounds, called bourgeonal, made sperm swim faster and sent them swimming toward areas with high concentrations of the compound, suggesting that eggs may release bourgeonal as a sort of siren call. If that's the case, bourgeonal may one day be used somehow to enhance fertility.

The scientists also identified a compound called undecanal that seems to block the effects of bourgeonal, suggesting a new avenue of research into contraceptives. The next step: verifying that the egg does indeed release bourgeonal or a similar compound. Those studies are now under way. ■

Fertility from the Forest

An extract from the bark of a pine tree that grows along the coast of southwestern France may improve the health of sperm in men with fertility problems. The extract, called Pycnogenol, is one of the most potent antioxidants known. Researchers in West Orange, New Jersey, gave 19 men with fertility problems 200 milligrams of Pycnogenol daily for three months. The patients' semen samples were examined at the beginning and end of the study. The researchers found that the antioxidant significantly improved the quality and function of sperm. The likely reason: Pycnogenol protects sperm from the oxidative damage that threatens all cells (something like the rust that occurs when you leave a shovel outside). The results of the study were published in the October 2002 issue of the *Journal of Reproductive Medicine*. Pycnogenol is sold as an over-the-counter supplement in drugstores. ■

The supplement comes from the bark of the tree.

Pycnogenol, a mix of bioflavonoids (antioxidant compounds also found in fruits and vegetables), is extracted from these maritime pines, which grow on the sandy coast of France.

IVF May Be Linked to Rare Cancer

When specialists in the Netherlands noticed a spike in the occurrence of a rare childhood cancer among children conceived using in vitro fertilization (IVF), they decided to investigate. The cancer, retinoblastoma, is a malignant tumor of the retina, the structure inside the eye that reflects light. The researchers used data from the Dutch retinoblastoma registry, the Dutch cancer registry, and data on IVF births throughout the Netherlands. They compared the rate of retinoblastoma in the IVF babies with the number of expected cases. The result? The risk of retinoblastoma after IVF was 7.2 times higher than in children conceived naturally. While the finding was worrisome, the researchers say, it was hardly conclusive, and more study is necessary. ■

Drug Development
Pregnancy Despite Breast Cancer

You wouldn't think a medicine used to prevent and treat cancer would have much use as a fertility drug. But in the case of tamoxifen (Nolvadex), it may.

The anti-estrogen drug tamoxifen, currently used to treat breast cancer, was originally developed as a morning-after contraceptive, designed to prevent a fertilized egg from implanting in a woman's uterus if she'd had unprotected sex. That tactic was a failure. The drug actually helped women get pregnant, making researchers think it might work as a fertility drug. Now tamoxifen's two benefits— improving fertility and

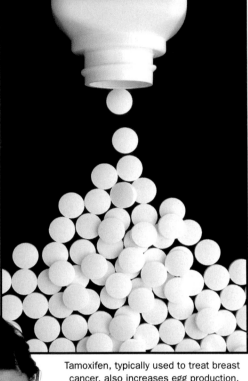

Tamoxifen, typically used to treat breast cancer, also increases egg production.

protecting against breast cancer—have come together to help women with breast cancer get pregnant. Women who have or have had breast cancer can't take traditional fertility drugs designed to increase their egg production. That's because

those drugs work by increasing the production of estrogen, which can trigger the growth of breast cancer. So in the past, women who underwent in vitro fertilization (IVF), either to freeze the resulting embryos before beginning cancer treatment or to help the women become pregnant after treatment, rarely encountered success. Enter tamoxifen. Called a selective estrogen-receptor modifier, or SERM, tamoxifen belongs to a class of drugs that mimic the actions of estrogen in the body but don't seem to have the same potentially harmful effects on breast tissue as natural estrogen.

How it works. "Tamoxifen fools the brain to make it think that the ovaries are not working hard enough," says Kutluk H. Oktay, M.D., of Weill Medical College of Cornell University in New York City, lead author of the new study. "As a result, the brain sends signals to the ovaries to make them work harder, which results in production of extra eggs. We wanted to hit two birds with one stone: While shielding the breast against estrogen, which stimulates cancer cells, we can increase egg production."

In Dr. Oktay's study, IVF in 12 women who used tamoxifen resulted in an average of 2.5 times more embryos than in the group that didn't use any fertility drug. In that second group, half of the IVF procedures didn't result in a single embryo. In the tamoxifen group, at least one embryo resulted for each woman. Tamoxifen was also given to several patients who had been "cured" of breast cancer but were infertile and wanted IVF. Pregnancies resulted in two such patients—one of them 43 years old. The results were published in the January 2003 issue of the journal *Human Reproduction*. ■

Key Discovery
More Bad News for HRT

Last year, we learned that the hormone replacement therapy (HRT) drug Prempro increased the risk of breast cancer, stroke, and heart disease in women. But millions of women stayed on HRT anyway, believing that the benefits—including improved sleep, fewer hot flashes, and simply feeling better—more than made up for the health risks. Alas, that may not be the case.

More results from the Women's Health Initiative (WHI), the government study that first uncovered the health risks of HRT, show that HRT in the form of estrogen plus progesterone has no significant effect on quality of life. "There was no benefit… in terms of general health, energy, mental health, depression, memory, or sexual functioning after one year," says Jennifer Hays, Ph.D., lead author of the study and director of the Center for Women's Health at Baylor College of Medicine in Houston.

Surprising results. Researchers gave the 16,608 postmenopausal women in the WHI study questionnaires designed to evaluate quality of life issues such as energy and fatigue, body pain, and emotional health. They also evaluated memory and other cognitive functioning, sleep quality, sexual functioning, and menopausal discomforts such as hot flashes and night sweats. Half of the women received HRT and the other half received a placebo (dummy pill). One year later, the women were retested.

"And we found nothing," says Dr. Hays. The findings were so unexpected that the researchers went back and ran the data in several different ways. They still found no evidence that HRT improved quality of life. The same was true when they evaluated women who had been on HRT for three years. When they looked at only the youngest women in the study—those closest to menopause, who were most likely to have menopausal problems—they found just one area that showed a lifestyle improvement from HRT: quality of sleep. But the difference was small—about 5 percent.

There was no difference in quality of life even when it came to the one thing that HRT is approved to treat: hot flashes. Although 77 percent of the 2,000 women in the study who complained of hot

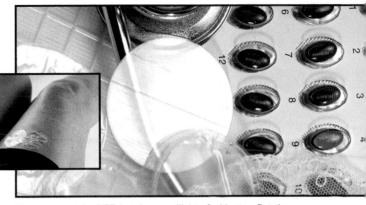

Many women take HRT (patches or pills) to feel better. But the hormones do nothing to improve memory, sleep, or quality of life.

flashes said their flashes improved while on HRT, that improvement didn't translate into an overall improvement in quality of life, says Dr. Hays. And besides, 52 percent of the women on placebos also reported improvement in hot flashes. The study results were published in a May 2003 issue of the *New England Journal of Medicine.* ■

RESEARCH ROUNDUP

Seizure Drug for Hot Flashes?

With hormone replacement therapy—the only FDA-approved treatment for hot flashes—in the proverbial doghouse, researchers are hunting for alternatives. One promising candidate is the anti-seizure drug gabapentin (Neurontin). A study published in the February 2003 issue of *Obstetrics and Gynecology* found that the drug significantly reduced the frequency and severity of hot flashes in menopausal women.

In the study, 59 menopausal women who had at least seven hot flashes a day were given either Neurontin or a placebo. The drug cut hot flashes by more than half after 12 weeks of treatment, while the placebo cut them by about a third. (Hot flashes are notoriously sensitive to the placebo effect.)

Similar positive results occurred in a Mayo Clinic study of 24 women published in the November 2002 issue of *Mayo Clinic Proceedings.* Further studies are likely. (Note that in the first study, four women in the Neurontin group withdrew from the study after experiencing dizziness, rash, heart palpitations, and swelling.) ■

Drug Development
Move Over, VIAGRA

Viagra was the first, but it's not the last of the impotence drugs. Two new competitors are in the same drug class and target the same enzyme.

Believe it or not, it's been five years since Viagra (sildenafil) became the butt of countless late-night television jokes, the mainstay of Bob Dole's advertising career, and one of the biggest-ever moneymakers for drug manufacturer Pfizer. Despite rumors of imminent rivalry, the impotence market has pretty much belonged to the tiny blue pill since its approval by the FDA in 1998. Until now.

Two new impotence drugs are set to give Viagra some serious competition. Bayer and GlaxoSmithKline won European approval in March 2003 to sell their new impotence drug, Levitra (vardenafil), which was approved for sale in the United States in August. In February, drug maker Eli Lilly launched Cialis (tadalafil) in Europe, Australia, and New Zealand. Analysts expected the drug to be approved in the United States by the end of the year.

All three impotence drugs are taken orally, and all work by inhibiting an enzyme called PDE-5. That action relaxes smooth muscle cells in the penis, enabling more blood to flow in and out of the organ and helping to create an erection. But the manufacturers of the two newcomers tout significant differences between their products and the little blue pills.

Cialis, for instance, is said to work for up to 24 hours after it's taken, compared with Viagra and Levitra, which work for about 5 hours. While Viagra must be taken 60 minutes prior to intercourse, Cialis can be taken anywhere between 30 minutes and 12 hours ahead of time. Cialis appears to lose out when it comes to side effects, however, with participants in studies reporting headache, upset stomach, and back pain, compared with the headache and facial flushing experienced by some men taking Levitra. Viagra is also known to cause headache and flushing, as well as altered or bluish vision.

The two new drugs have a long way to go to beat Viagra, however. The *Wall Street Journal* calls it "one of the drug industry's most successful products in recent years," with sales of $1.7 billion in 2002. Doctors have written 120 million Viagra prescriptions since its introduction. ■

Drug Development
Estrogen Gets Black Box WARNING

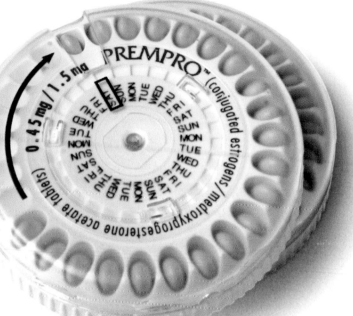

FDA announced that it would require a new, boxed warning accompanying all estrogen products for use by postmenopausal women.

In the summer of 2002, researchers for the federally funded Women's Health Initiative (WHI) announced that the hormone replacement therapy drug Prempro slightly increased a woman's risk of invasive breast cancer and heart disease. The resulting firestorm continued burning into 2003. In January, the FDA announced that it would require a new, boxed warning accompanying all estrogen products for use by postmenopausal women.

The so-called black box is the strongest step the FDA can take to warn consumers of potential risks from a medication. The warning highlights the increased risk of heart disease, heart attack, stroke, and breast cancer and emphasizes that estrogen products are not approved for heart disease prevention. It advises health care providers to prescribe estrogen products at the lowest dose and for the shortest possible duration. It also advises women taking such products to have yearly breast exams, perform monthly breast self-exams, and receive periodic mammography examinations.

Until now, the warning was mentioned only on the product insert for Prempro, the estrogen/progestin product used by women in the WHI study. But after considering the issue and evaluating the evidence, the FDA said it should be assumed that all estrogen-containing products—whether patch, cream, or pill—pose similar risks unless proven otherwise. Five products currently on the market in the United States contain estrogen and progestin, while 15 contain estrogen alone.

The warning may not dissuade millions of women who still want to use HRT. Many women who have problems with menopause "choose to use hormone therapy notwithstanding the risks," says Andrew Kaunitz, M.D., director of menopause services at the University of Florida Health Science Center in Jacksonville and a co-principal investigator in the WHI trial. However, it's a good idea to stop taking the hormones periodically to see if your symptoms return, he says. That's less likely as you get older. ■

RESEARCH ROUNDUP

Where There's Smoke, There Are Hot Flashes

Women looking for an alternative to hormone replacement therapy for relief from hot flashes should try stubbing out their cigarettes. A study published in the February 2003 issue of *Obstetrics and Gynecology* found that smoking may lead to more severe or more frequent hot flashes during menopause. In the study, current smokers were nearly twice as likely to experience moderate or severe hot flashes as women who never smoked, and they were more than twice as likely to suffer from daily hot flashes. The more they smoked, the more hot flashes they had. The researchers also found a link between obesity and hot flashes. Women with a body mass index (BMI) greater than 30, considered obese, were more likely to have frequent and severe hot flashes than women with a BMI under 25, considered a healthy weight. The BMI is a measurement that takes into account height as well as weight. ■

ALSO in the NEWS

Freezing Shrinks Fibroids

About 77 percent of women in the United States will have fibroids (noncancerous uterine tumors) at some point in their lives. While the tumors can be symptomless, some women have severe pain,

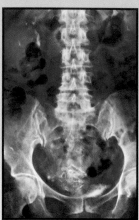

bloating, pressure, and bleeding, which result in more than 200,000 hysterectomies a year. In fact, fibroids are the leading reason for hysterectomy in the United States.

In April 2003, however, Utah researchers reported that using a device that freezes fibroids while they're still in the uterus can shrink the tumors, possibly making hysterectomy unnecessary. The device, called CryoGen Cryosurgical System, is already approved by the FDA for treatment of abnormally heavy menstrual bleeding, another common reason for hysterectomy. The procedure for fibroids, called laparoscopic cryomylysis, takes about 30 minutes and is performed in an outpatient surgery facility or a physician's office. The doctor inserts a slender tube through a small incision in a woman's abdomen, then threads the probe through the tube into the tumor and releases a freezing gas.

In the study, which was presented at a meeting of the American College of Obstetrics and Gynecology, 20 women with large uterine fibroids underwent the procedure. All but one said their symptoms had disappeared or significantly improved within two weeks, and doctors found their tumors had shrunk an average of 57 percent after six months. ■

Progress in Prevention
The Pap Test Gets a Partner

A routine visit to the gynecologist will soon become more revealing. Women will be able to learn not only whether they have cervical cancer but also whether they've been infected with the virus that causes it.

In March 2003, the FDA approved an expanded use for a sophisticated type of Pap test known as the HPV DNA test. It was first approved three years ago for use in women who had abnormal Pap results to determine whether they required additional watching or treatment. Now it's available for all women over 30.

How it works. Doctors still take one sample of cervical and upper vaginal cells, but when they send it to the laboratory, they order the new test along with a traditional Pap. The HPV DNA analysis doesn't check for cancer, but it does test for the human papillomavirus, or HPV, which is known to cause up to 90 percent of cervical cancers. The Centers for Disease Control and Prevention estimates that 50 to 75 percent of sexually active adults will harbor the virus at some point. While most women who become infected get rid of the virus with no problem, some develop a persistent but symptomless infection that can eventually lead to precancerous changes in cervical cells. There is no treatment for HPV, but testing for the virus lets doctors know whether to keep an especially close watch for signs of cancer. If it does develop, the earlier it's found, the better the chance of a full recovery.

If a woman tests positive for HPV, she's given another Pap every 6 to 12 months. Women whose HPV tests are negative and who have normal Paps—meaning no precancerous abnormalities were detected—won't need either test again for three years, according to new guidelines released by the American Cancer Society (ACS) in November 2002 (see "Annual Exam Not Annual Anymore"). Those

ANNUAL EXAM
NOT ANNUAL ANYMORE

The American Cancer Society (ACS) issued new guidelines in November 2002 for cervical cancer screenings that let some women go up to three years between Pap tests and cease testing altogether under certain circumstances after age 70. In January 2003, the U.S. Preventive Services Task Force (USPSTF) released similar guidelines.

THE ACS GUIDELINES STATE:

■ Cervical cancer screening should begin about three years after a woman begins having vaginal intercourse, but no later than 21 years of age. Experts recommend waiting about three years following the start of sexual activity because HPV infections and cervical cell changes that are not significant are common during this time, but they're rarely reflective of possible cancers. Cervical cancer is extremely rare in women under the age of 25.

■ Cervical cancer screening should be done each year with regular Pap tests or every two years using liquid-based Pap tests (ThinPrep) until age 30. At that point, women who have had three normal test results in a row may be screened every two to three years. A doctor may suggest having the test more often if a woman has certain risk factors, such as HIV infection or a weakened immune system. The USPSTF recommendations simply call for a Pap test at least once every three years.

■ Women 70 and older who have had three or more normal Pap test results and no abnormal results in the previous 10 years may stop cervical cancer screening. The USPSTF recommendations say women may stop screenings at age 65 if they meet these criteria.

■ Screening after a total hysterectomy (with removal of the cervix) is not necessary unless the surgery was done as a treatment for cervical cancer or precancer. Women who have had hysterectomies without removal of the cervix should continue cervical cancer screening at least until age 70.

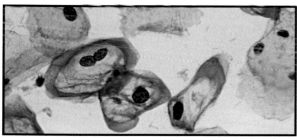

Most cases of cervical cancer are caused by the human papillomavirus, the same virus that causes genital warts.

women have less than a 0.2 percent risk of developing cervical cancer, while the risk for women with an abnormal Pap test and a positive HPV test is 6 percent or higher.

The likelihood that HPV will lead to precancerous cell changes is greatest in women over 30, which is why the FDA approved the test for that age group. According to the ACS, cervical cancer will strike 12,200 American women this year and kill 4,100.

Availability. The HPV DNA test is already available throughout the United States. The big question is whether insurance companies will pay for its routine use. The test costs $50 to $60 (including the Pap), compared with $14 to $30 for a Pap test alone, which is typically covered by insurance. ■

RESEARCH ROUNDUP

Conventional Pap Best

After years of debate over the benefits of a more expensive Pap test called ThinPrep, which many insurance companies refuse to pay for, a large study published in an April 2003 issue of the *British Medical Journal* has found that the conventional Pap test is more reliable at detecting cell abnormalities that could indicate the presence of cervical cancer.

Both Pap tests involve taking a sample of cells from the cervix and upper vagina. In the conventional Pap, the smear is analyzed on a slide in a laboratory. For the ThinPrep test, the cell sample is suspended in liquid and a spot of thin cells is extracted for analysis, thus removing blood, vaginal secretions, and other extraneous matter from the sample and potentially making it easier to read. The study authors concluded that ThinPrep, "which seems less reliable and less valid and is more expensive, should not replace conventional smear tests for cervical cancer screening." ThinPrep costs about $20 more than conventional Pap tests. ■

Progress in Prevention
An Old Solution to the Preemie Problem

More than 476,000 babies annually—1 in 8—are born too early in the United States, a 27 percent increase over the number of premature births 20 years ago. In fact, premature births are the biggest problem in obstetrics, says Paul Meis, M.D., professor of obstetrics and gynecology at Wake Forest Baptist University in North Carolina. And the increase has occurred despite improvements in prenatal care and diagnosis.

While doctors have some ideas about the reasons behind the increase—the use of assisted reproductive techniques such as in vitro fertilization (IVF) that result in more multiple births, better dating of conception, and possibly some environmental effects—they really don't know how to prevent it. But the results of a large study suggest that weekly injections of a synthetic form of the hormone progesterone may hold the key.

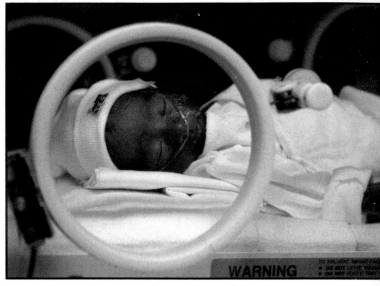
A baby born more than three weeks before its due date is considered premature and is at increased risk for health problems and learning delays. Progesterone injections may help stave off early delivery.

How it works. Progesterone plays an important role in prolonging pregnancy, including quieting the uterine muscle so it doesn't begin contracting, exerting anti-inflammatory effects that suppress the immune system (and prevent it from "attacking" the fetus as a foreign object), and preventing the formation of what are called gap junctions—spaces between individual cells in the uterus that begin the cascade of events that results in labor.

Back in the 1960s and 1970s, some small trials were conducted on the use of progesterone to prevent preterm delivery, but no major studies were ever completed. "We wanted to revisit this old treatment that seemed to have fallen out of favor," says Dr. Meis. His clinic at Wake Forest is one of 19 clinics that make up the Maternal-Fetal Medicine Units Network, which operates under the National Institutes of Health.

The centers enrolled 459 pregnant women who had already had at least one preterm delivery (one-third had had more than one). Beginning in their 17th week of pregnancy, about two-thirds of the women received injections of a form of progesterone called 17-alpha-hydroxyprogesterone caproate, or 17P, and the rest received a placebo (dummy drug). The progesterone drug was approved for other applications and was once sold under the brand name Delalutin as an infertility treatment. It's no longer manufactured but can still be produced by

Bed Rest Put to Rest

For decades, doctors prescribed bed rest for pregnant women at risk for preterm delivery. In fact, more than 1 million women each year spend at least a week of their pregnancies in bed. There's just one problem: It doesn't work.

A review article published in the December 2002 issue of the journal *Obstetrics and Gynecology* reported no evidence that bed rest helps prevent premature births. In fact, of the four trials conducted on the use of bed rest in women who were pregnant with twins, two found no benefit and two showed bed rest actually increased the chance of preterm birth. The study's author, Robert L. Goldenberg, M.D., professor of obstetrics at the University of Alabama in Birmingham, also found no benefit to drinking lots of fluids, using home uterine monitors, or sedation—other methods commonly prescribed to prevent early labor. ∎

compounding pharmacies, which make approved drugs from their individual components.

The difference between the two groups was so significant—the rate of premature births among those who got 17P was reduced by more than one-third—that study officials halted the trial early so the women in the placebo group could receive the drug. Another study currently under way will test the efficacy of the drug used in combination with omega-3 fatty acids, or fish oil, deficiencies of which have been linked to premature births. Combining the two, says Dr. Meis, might reduce the rate of preterm labor even further.

The results of Dr. Meis's progesterone study were published in June 2003 in the *New England Journal of Medicine.*

Availability. Although 17P has not been approved to prevent preterm labor, doctors are still free to prescribe it, notes Dr. Meis, who says he is using it in patients who have already had one premature delivery and are at risk for another. "I think clinicians need to make their own decision as to whether or not to use it. I certainly would not say that it is the standard of care at the present time; I can only advocate its use for women with a previous preterm birth." ■

ALSO in the NEWS

Coffee Gets a Break

As long as you keep your coffee habit under six 10-ounce cups of java a day while pregnant, you're probably not increasing your risk of having a too-small or too-early baby. For years, researchers have debated the issue, with some studies linking even moderate coffee consumption to low-birthweight babies or miscarriage and others showing little effect. In a study published in the March 2003 issue of the *American Journal of Epidemiology,* Yale University researchers evaluated 2,291 pregnant women who delivered single babies between 1996 and 2000. They tested urine samples for levels of caffeine, cotinine, and creatinine (all found in coffee) and continued testing the women throughout the study to monitor their consumption of coffee.

When the researchers compared the results with the babies' health, they found that coffee consumption did not increase the risk of low birthweight or preterm delivery and had no effect on fetal growth. There does seem to be a limit, however, to how much of the black brew is safe. An article published a month earlier in the *British Medical Journal* found that pregnant women who drank eight or more cups of coffee a day had more than twice the risk of stillbirth compared with women who didn't drink any. ■

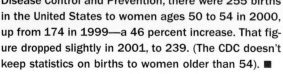

Babymaking after 50 Gets the Green Light

At 50, many women are looking menopause square in the face. But a few are looking at a far different phenomenon: new motherhood, thanks to assisted reproductive techniques such as donor eggs and in vitro fertilization. And according to a study published in the *Journal of the American Medical Association,* for healthy women, there's no clear medical reason not to.

The study looked at 77 women ages 50 to 63, all of whom were postmenopausal and used donated eggs. It found that the women's rates of pregnancy, multiple gestation (twins, triplets, etc.), and spontaneous abortion were similar to those of younger women who received donated eggs. The older women did have a higher risk of preeclampsia (a serious condition involving high blood pressure and fluid retention) and gestational diabetes, and most of their babies were delivered by cesarean section.

The numbers of women over 50 who give birth is small but growing. According to the Centers for Disease Control and Prevention, there were 255 births in the United States to women ages 50 to 54 in 2000, up from 174 in 1999—a 46 percent increase. That figure dropped slightly in 2001, to 239. (The CDC doesn't keep statistics on births to women older than 54). ■

RESPIRATORY
SYSTEM

JIMMY CARTER PROBABLY NEVER MET A PEANUT HE DIDN'T LIKE.

But thousands of other people—those allergic to the legume—would rather chance an encounter with just about anything else. Soon they may have less to worry about, thanks to a revolutionary allergy shot that could turn accidental ingestion of peanuts into a minor threat instead of a deadly crisis.

Speaking of health threats, if you're a long-time smoker age 50 or over, there's now a quiz you can take to find out your risk of developing lung cancer in the next 10 years if you keep smoking, and if you quit now. For people who have emphysema—usually smokers and former smokers—the results of a long-term study on the controversial lung volume reduction surgery are finally out. Find out which emphysema patients are most likely to benefit from the procedure.

Also in this chapter, an allergy vaccine under development that requires fewer injections and lasts longer than current shots, new proof of the link between thunderstorms and asthma attacks, and a good reason to avoid indoor hot tubs.

Drug Development

New Drug Cracks Tough Nut: Peanut Allergy

In some schools around the country, the ubiquitous peanut-butter-and-jelly sandwich is about as welcome as a drug dealer on the playground. That's because an increasing number of children in the United States are allergic to peanuts—about 3.3 percent in 1996, compared with 1.1 percent in 1989.

Unlike an allergy to, say, milk, pet dander, or pollen, a peanut allergy is serious business. In the United States alone, the severe allergic reaction that some people experience after eating peanuts is responsible for some 50 to 100 deaths each year. The only way to prevent this reaction, known as anaphylaxis, is to avoid peanuts—which is surprisingly difficult these days, since everything from gravy to chili to egg rolls can contain some kind of peanut product.

That's why news of an experimental drug for peanut allergies drew such excitement from researchers, doctors, and patients in early 2003. The drug, dubbed TNX-901 for now, prevented reactions in allergic patients when they ingested capsules of ground peanuts. If future studies bear out the positive results, the drug could revolutionize the treatment not only of peanut allergies but of all allergies, says Hugh A. Sampson, M.D., director of the Jaffe Food Allergy Institute at Mount Sinai School of Medicine in New York. Dr. Sampson was the lead researcher for a study on the drug that was published in a March 2003 issue of the *New England Journal of Medicine*.

How it works. Administered by injection, the drug is what's known as a monoclonal antibody—a laboratory-engineered, custom-designed antibody. (Antibodies are proteins that identify and neutralize invaders, such as viruses, that the body perceives as threats.) It's nearly identical to the human antibody immunoglobulin E (IgE), which plays a starring role in allergies. Normally present at very low levels in the body, IgE is found in larger quantities in people who have allergies. If you're allergy-prone, the first time you're exposed to an allergen, your body begins to make large amounts of corresponding IgE antibodies. The antibodies then attach to the surfaces of cells known as mast cells, which in turn spit out chemicals, such as histamine, that are responsible for the wheezing, sneezing, runny eyes, and itching associated with allergies.

By binding to receptors, or "locks," on the mast cells meant for IgE, TNX-901 prevents the real IgE from locking on. "Basically, you've got a lot of mast cells sitting around with very little IgE," says Dr. Sampson. "They're like guns with no triggers."

RESEARCH ROUNDUP

Baby Lotions Linked to Peanut Allergy

There are numerous theories as to why peanut allergies are on the rise, ranging from more women eating peanuts while they're pregnant to the increasing popularity of soy formulas for infants (some experts suspect that soy is a peanut allergy trigger). Now, a study from Great Britain has found that using lotions and creams that contain peanut oil can sensitize children to peanut protein, eventually resulting in peanut allergies. Baby lotions made in the United States don't usually contain peanut oil, but those used in or imported from other countries may—so read the list of ingredients. The study was published in a March 2003 issue of the *New England Journal of Medicine*. ∎

Another Excuse Not to Vacuum

High-end vacuum cleaners with high-efficiency particulate arrest (HEPA) filters are supposed to provide cleaner environs for people with allergies. But do they? Researchers from a hospital in Manchester, England, tested five HEPA vacuum cleaners, along with some older, non-HEPA models, in homes with cats. Then they measured the amount of dander in the air. Rather than clearing the air, both types of vacuums significantly increased the amount of inhaled dander. The HEPA vacuums worked better, however, in a testing chamber. It seems that vacuuming in the home increases airborne dander by pulling it from clothes, skin, and other surfaces. ∎

In the study, Dr. Sampson and his colleagues gave 84 patients with a history of peanut allergies a small, medium, or large dose of the drug once every four weeks for four months. Two to four weeks after the final dose, the patients took a capsule containing ground peanuts. Although some participants experienced a reaction, it was quite mild. It took the equivalent of 9 peanuts to trigger a reaction instead of the 1/2 peanut it took without the drug, and five people ate the equivalent of 24 peanuts with no reaction. That, concludes Dr. Sampson, should translate into protection against most unintentional consumption of peanuts. Even better: The drug should work against other allergies, all of which result from the same IgE/mast cell process. The only downside, he says, is that people will need to continue injections every two to four weeks, possibly for the rest of their lives.

Availability. The drug is several years away from going to market. Phase III clinical trials stalled in mid-2003 because the three companies involved with the drug were arguing over the rights to develop it. In the meantime, a similar drug, called omalizumab (Xolair), was approved by the FDA in June 2003 for treating moderate to severe asthma in adolescents and adults. According to the *New York Times*, some doctors said they would offer it to patients with severe allergies. Xolair and TNX-901 are expensive, though, costing upward of $10,000 a year. ■

If your child has asthma even though there's no history of asthma or allergies in your family, a surprising underlying problem may be to blame.

Key Discovery
Reflux May Lurk behind Asthma in Children

If your child has asthma that's difficult to control, another underlying condition may be to blame. Treat that condition, and your child's need for asthma medication may be drastically reduced, according to the results of a recent study.

The condition is acid reflux, also known as gastroesophageal reflux disease (GERD), in which highly acidic stomach fluid backs up (refluxes) into the esophagus, the long tube that connects the mouth to the stomach. Before you assume that your child doesn't have it, consider this: Previous research indicates that at least half of all children who have asthma also have GERD. Asthma attacks can be triggered when a small amount of the fluid that makes its way to the esophagus is inhaled into the lungs, or when the irritated esophagus makes the person cough as a reflex.

In a small study reported in the April 2003 issue of the journal *Chest*, 27 children with both asthma and evidence of GERD either took medications to treat the reflux (drugs called proton-pump inhibitors) for one year or underwent a common surgical procedure to fix it. As a result, the children's overall need for asthma medications was reduced by more than 50 percent, and their use of inhaled corticosteroids dropped by 89 percent, says Vikram Khoshoo, M.D., Ph.D., lead study author and a pediatric gastroenterologist at West Jefferson Medical Center in New Orleans.

If your child has asthma as well as heartburn or a sensation of stomach acid rising into her throat, ask her doctor whether reflux could be playing a role, Dr. Khoshoo suggests—especially if your family has no history of asthma or allergies, or if the asthma is becoming increasingly hard to treat. ■

ALSO in the NEWS

A Real "Kiss of Death"

Have a food allergy? Before you pucker up for that good-night kiss, you'd better be sure what your darling had for dinner. An article published in the  February 2003 issue of *Mayo Clinic Proceedings* describes the case of a 20-year-old woman who went into anaphylactic shock immediately after kissing her boyfriend. She wasn't allergic to the young man but to the shrimp he'd eaten an hour before. "To my knowledge, this is the first report of a life-threatening reaction to shellfish transmitted by passionate kissing," wrote David P. Steensma, M.D., the Mayo Clinic doctor who treated her. So now, at least for the highly allergic, lovebirds dreaming of where a kiss might lead have another outcome (albeit unlikely) to envision—death. An ironic side note: Both the young woman and her boyfriend worked at a seafood restaurant when the incident occurred. After treating her with epinephrine, doctors prescribed another remedy: Quit the job. ■

New Allergy Shot Is Made to Last

Injections are a painful fact of life for people who undergo immunotherapy to control their allergies. Patients make weekly visits to the allergist for months, and sometimes years, before they become desensitized to the allergen, and they need monthly maintenance shots for years thereafter.

That could change one day soon. A study presented at the American Academy of Allergy, Asthma, and Immunology meeting in March 2003 found that a single six-week series of weekly shots with a new immunotherapy agent called AIC not only significantly reduced symptoms in people allergic to ragweed, it also worked for two years, with no maintenance shots required. The results were part of clinical testing of AIC prior to submission to the FDA for approval. More studies are on the way. ■

Heeding the Call for Asthma Monitoring

One day, cell phones may replace plastic peak flow meters as the best way to monitor lung status in people with asthma. About half of those with asthma have to regularly check their lung capacities by blowing hard into a peak flow meter and tracking the results so their doctors know if their medications should be changed. But it's hard to get people—especially children—to do it. A company based in Oxford, England, has designed software that enables cell phones to capture data from a small electronic flow meter, about the size of an asthma inhaler, that attaches to the phone. The phone reminds owners to use the flow meter twice daily, then sends the results to a computer, which analyzes them. If the computer detects signs of a problem, it e-mails the patient's doctor, who can then contact the patient. The company, E-San, was conducting trials in Britain in mid-2003. The ideal users of the new technology? Teenagers, of course. ■

Thunderstorms Spark Asthma Attacks

Emergency room doctors throughout the world know that when there's a thunderstorm in the forecast, they can expect a rush of patients with asthma attacks. Now they have proof—and a possible cause. Researchers at the University of Ottawa Health Research Institute in Canada examined four years of records from the Children's Hospital of Eastern Ontario, comparing asthma attacks with weather patterns, airborne allergens, and pollution. They found that asthma-related hospital visits jumped 15 percent during thunderstorms, from an average of 8.6 visits on clear days to 10 on stormy days. They suspect the increase is related to fungal spores,  which nearly double in number during thunderstorms. In fact, when levels of these spores are high—storm or not—asthma-related hospital visits increase. The findings were published in the March 2003 issue of the journal *Chest.* ■

Alternative Answers
New Doubts Cast on Echinacea

For many people, the herbal remedy echinacea—taken in capsules, teas, or tinctures—has become as much a part of the cold-and-flu arsenal as chicken soup and hot tea. What no one seems to know for sure, however, is whether it actually *works*. That's because, like many herbs, echinacea hasn't been extensively studied. But if you commonly put stock—and money—in the herb when you're hit with the sniffles, hear this: One of the first "gold standard" clinical trials (double-blind, placebo-controlled) on echinacea found that it worked no better than a placebo (dummy pill) in improving cold symptoms. The results were published in the December 2002 issue of *Annals of Internal Medicine*.

Researchers at the University of Wisconsin at Madison recruited 148 students with colds. Half received capsules containing powdered echinacea; the other half received placebos. Both groups started taking the capsules soon after their cold symptoms began (in most cases, within 36 hours). The students took four capsules six times the first day, then three times daily thereafter until their colds went away. Each day, they completed a questionnaire about their symptoms. The researchers then compared the duration and severity of 15 separate cold symptoms (dry cough, sore throat, runny nose, and so on) on each day of the study. The result? Echinacea capsules had no effect: Colds lasted an average of about six days in each group.

That doesn't mean the herb is worthless, however, says lead researcher Bruce P. Barrett, M.D., assistant professor of family medicine at the university. "I'm not convinced that our trial is the final word," he says, because so many other trials have suggested that echinacea *does* have benefits. Many studies that showed an effect used a tincture (liquid concentrate) of the herb, which may make a difference, and his study was conducted with college-age students, who tend to have relatively healthy immune systems. A greater effect might turn up in the elderly or people with compromised immune systems. Also, the study was small—too small to detect the smallest possible positive effect, he says.

Stay tuned. Several other research groups are conducting other studies on the herb, and even Dr. Barrett is planning another one. In the meantime, if you think echinacea helps you, go ahead and take it. While Dr. Barrett's study didn't find any evidence of benefit, it also found no evidence of harm. ■

RESEARCH ROUNDUP

Nose Spray Takes the Sting Out of Flu Vaccine

Never mind rolling up your sleeve the next time you go to get your annual flu vaccination; you may get it from a nasal spray instead of a needle. FluMist, the first nasal spray flu vaccine available in the United States, was approved by the FDA in June 2003. The delivery system makes it particularly attractive for kids. "They leave the office happy," says Robert Belshe, M.D., director of the Center for Vaccine Development at St. Louis University and lead researcher on studies that tested the vaccine.

FluMist isn't currently approved for children under 5, however, because a safety study found that kids in that age range may be more likely to have wheezing after the treatment. It's also not yet approved for adults 50 and older, because safety and effectiveness haven't been proven for that group. More research is planned. Because this is the first flu vaccine to use live viruses rather than inactivated ones, it's not intended for people with weakened immune systems.

The spray vaccine will protect people from the same strains of flu virus each year as the injected type, Dr. Belshe says. ■

Surgical Solution

Less Lung, Better Life— For Some

To spot someone with the lung-destroying disease emphysema, just look for the characteristic barrel-shaped chest. This physical oddity occurs as oxygen-starved lungs grow larger and take up more space in the chest cavity, causing the diaphragm to flatten and making it even harder for the lungs to move air in and out. In recent years, a potentially lifesaving surgery called lung volume reduction surgery, in which 20 to 30 percent of the lung is removed, has become popular. While not a cure, it seemed to improve breathing by creating more room in the chest.

Evidence on the effectiveness of the surgery was mixed, and with a price tag of $35,000 or more, the procedure is expensive. Medicare, the government insurance program for the elderly, refused to cover it, putting it out of reach for most people with the disease. Now, a landmark study, published in a May 2003 issue of the *New England Journal of Medicine* and paid for by Medicare and other government agencies, suggests that for about 10 percent of people with emphysema, the surgery not only improves quality of life but extends life as well.

How they found out. The study, begun in 1996, enrolled 1,218 people with severe emphysema at 17 sites across the United States. Half received surgery, and half received conventional drug treatment. All were followed for about three years. Researchers studied patient survival, exercise capacity (as measured by a bicycle stress test), lung function, quality of life, shortness of breath, and illness and hospitalization rates. After one year, 15 percent of those who had the surgery significantly increased their exercise capacity, compared with 3 percent in the drug treatment group. They also had higher scores on questionnaires designed to measure their quality of life. After two years, however, the scores for quality of life and exercise capacity returned to their pre-surgery starting point.

A certain subset of patients, however—those whose disease was limited to the upper lobes of the lungs and who were able to do little exercise prior

to surgery—not only lived longer than those in other groups but also had increased lung function. Those whose emphysema was not in the upper lobes, on the other hand, and who were able to do more exercise prior to surgery, showed worse lung function and survival rates.

"We didn't think we'd see any survival advantage," says Barry Make, M.D., senior professor at the National Jewish Medical and Research Center in Denver and one of the researchers for the study. In fact, the only reason researchers chose survival as an outcome was to make sure that those who had the surgery weren't more likely to die than those who took medication.

In August 2003, the Centers for Medicare and Medicaid Services announced that it intended to cover the procedure for certain patients. Since most private insurers follow Medicare's lead, it's likely that the surgery will be covered even for those who aren't eligible for Medicare. Previously, patients had to either pay for the procedure themselves or participate in a study.

Don't expect a mad rush to the operating room, though. Lung reduction surgery is just one therapy among many that can help emphysema, says Dr. Make. Given the number of people with the condition—an estimated 3 million in the United States, most of them over 65—drug companies have also targeted the disease, and a plethora of new treatments is expected in the near future, he says. ■

Lung Reduction Surgery

In minimally invasive lung reduction surgery, a tiny video camera and surgical instruments are inserted through three to five incisions. The camera allows the surgeon to guide the instruments. Lung volume is usually reduced by 30 to 40 percent.

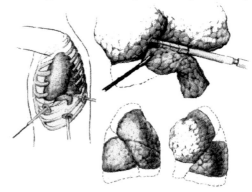

Source: University of Pittsburgh Medical Center

Could this lung-irritating bacterium be lurking in your hot tub? Unfortunately, yes.

Key Discovery
Bubble, Bubble, Hot Tub Trouble

Those bubbles in your hot tub, the ones helping you soak away your stress? Watch out: They could also be making you sick. Doctors at the Mayo Clinic in Rochester, Minnesota, reported two cases of what they're calling hot tub lung disease in the November 2002 issue of *Mayo Clinic Proceedings*.

The disease, a form of lung inflammation, is caused by a bacterium that lives in hot tub water. Called *Mycobacterium avium* complex (MAC), it thrives in the warm, moist environment of a spa, since chlorine loses much of its disinfectant properties at temperatures higher than 84°F, says study author Otis B. Rickman, D.O., a pulmonary critical care fellow at the Mayo Clinic. MAC hitches a ride on the bubbles in hot tubs, which are the perfect size to be inhaled into the lungs, he says.

Hot tub lung disease appears to be related to a hypersensitivity to MAC—almost like an allergy—because the more patients use their indoor hot tubs, the more likely they are to develop the condition, says Dr. Rickman. Symptoms include fever and shortness of breath, with X-rays showing shadows on the lung that can be confused with pneumonia.

Clear the air. Although the bacteria are also present in outdoor hot tubs, says Dr. Rickman, he hasn't heard of a single case occurring there, probably because of the cleansing effects of sunlight on water and the superior ventilation outdoors.

If you're loath to give up your spa room, try disinfecting the hot tub with bromine, he suggests. The chemical seems to do a better job of eliminating MAC than chlorine does. Also, make sure you're maintaining your hot tub according to the manufacturer's directions, including changing the filters and chemicals frequently. Finally, locate the tub in a well-ventilated area; the basement probably isn't the ideal spot.

As for his own hot tub habits, Dr. Rickman says, "I only use public hot tubs when they're out of doors." ■

ALSO in the NEWS

Common Kids' Treatment Is All Air

Most kids, whether their parents know it or not, have had a bout with bronchiolitis, an acute viral infection of the lower respiratory tract. It typically hits in winter, with wheezing, runny nose, cough, fever, and irritability. For years, doctors treated the infection with drugs commonly used to treat asthma and allergies, such as corticosteroids and epinephrine. One problem: These medications don't work for bronchiolitis, and some, like corticosteroids, have potentially serious side effects.

That's what the federal Agency for Healthcare Research and Quality (AHRQ) found when it evaluated 83 studies on the use of such drugs for treating bronchiolitis. The researchers also discovered that a carefully conducted medical history and physical examination are just as effective for diagnosing the disease as the more expensive lab tests and chest X-rays that are often used. The good news: Researchers did find that monthly injections of palivizumab (Synagis), an antiviral medication, does help prevent the infection in high-risk infants, children with an underlying lung condition called bronchopulmonary dysplasia, and children under six months of age who were born prematurely. ■

Key Discovery
Quiz Measures Lung Cancer Risk

It's common knowledge that smoking increases your risk of lung cancer. But how much smoking? How much increased risk? Until recently, doctors had no idea. Now they do. Using data from a large study conducted with 18,172 former smokers, researchers from Memorial Sloan-Kettering Cancer Center in New York City and the Fred Hutchinson Cancer Research Center in Seattle came up with a formula that accurately predicts a person's risk of developing lung cancer based on age, sex, smoking history, and any exposure to asbestos. The results were published in a March 2003 issue of the *Journal of the National Cancer Institute*.

The researchers calculated that a 51-year-old woman (one of the study subjects) who smoked a pack a day for 28 years and quit smoking 9 years earlier had less than a 1 percent risk of developing lung cancer in the next 10 years, assuming she didn't start smoking again. Someone of a similar age and gender who never smoked would have a 0.07 percent risk. Another study subject, a 68-year-old man who currently smoked and had smoked two packs a day for 50 years, was figured to have 15 to 20 times the risk of someone like the former woman smoker, with an 11 percent risk of lung cancer if he quit smoking immediately and a 15 percent risk if he continued to smoke at his current level.

Lead researcher Peter Bach, M.D., of Memorial Sloan-Kettering sees two main ways this information can be used by the public and by researchers. First, it will provide a better screening tool for clinical trials designed to test ways to prevent lung cancer in smokers. (See "Seeking the 'Tamoxifen' for Lung Cancer" on page 00.) "Researchers want to select study participants who are at very high risk of getting the disease," says Dr. Bach. Until now, they had no way of knowing who those people were, "so everyone was really flying blind." For instance, no one knew if it mattered if the person smoked for 20 years or for 30 years. "Now we're able to show it matters," he says.

The test will also be useful for helping people and their doctors decide if they should undergo a screening test called spiral CT, which can identify some lung cancers at a very early stage. The test is controversial, since there's no clear evidence that identifying the cancers early makes a difference in survival. Plus, the test often identifies shadows that look like cancer and require surgical biopsies, some of which are negative for cancer. Using this screening tool would let doctors identify the people with the highest risk of lung cancer—the best candidates for the test.

The lung cancer prediction quiz is available online at http://jncicancerspectrum.oupjournals.org/cgi/content/full/jnci;95/6/470/DC1. The quiz is designed for people who are 50 to 75 years old and have smoked for 25 to 55 years. ∎

What's Your Risk?

Below are sample quiz results, showing the lung cancer risk for five people with different smoking histories.

| PERSONAL PROFILE | LUNG CANCER RISK PERCENTILE | | | | |
	5th	25th	50th	75th	95th
Age	51	54	58	56	68
Avg. number of cigarettes smoked per day	20	20	25	40	40
Years smoked	28	35	40	44	50
Years since quitting	9	0	3	0	0
Asbestos exposure	NO	NO	NO	NO	NO
10-year risk if no further smoking (%)	0.08	1.50	4.10	5.60	10.80
10-year risk if continued smoking	NA	2.80	NA	8.40	14.90

Source: Journal of the National Cancer Institute.

SKIN
HAIR AND NAILS

WHEN IS A ROLL OF DUCT TAPE MORE THAN A ROLL OF DUCT TAPE?

When it's a remedy for warts. A new study at an army medical center in Washington state found that giving warts the sticky treatment usually gets rid of them within a month—and it's much easier than Huck Finn's cure: leaving a dead cat in the cemetery at midnight.

Once you've gotten rid of your wart, how about tackling that acne? Two newly approved phototherapy (light) treatments offer quick, painless, and lasting solutions to that pride-wounding plight. (Too bad these treatments weren't around when we were teenagers!) If you're an older adult battling the face-reddening disorder rosacea, a new gel derived from wheat can stop you from seeing red when you look in the mirror.

Finally, an injectable drug represents a brand-new, gentler treatment approach to the maddening skin condition known as psoriasis.

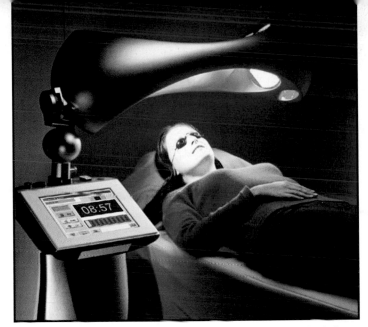

Seeing blue: ClearLight uses high-intensity light to kill *P. acnes*, the bacteria that cause acne, without harming the skin.

High-Tech Help
Let There Be Light Therapy for Acne

Acne creams are practically a rite of passage for most teens, and some adults need them, too. But there has to be a better way to tackle pimples. The answer may be light therapy, which some dermatologists are hailing as the beginning of a new era in acne control.

While currently available creams, ointments, oral antibiotics, and other drugs (such as Accutane), do some good for plenty of people, they're not without side effects and what doctors call compliance problems. Adolescents and young adults, it seems, aren't always good about rubbing on a cream or taking pills as consistently as they need to.

Enter two new light treatments approved by the FDA in late 2002. Both are virtually free of side effects, and they work fast. Patients usually notice improvement after the first session. The effects typically last for at least six months after eight 15-minute sessions over the course of a month (for blue light treatment) or four 20-minute sessions spread over four months (for laser treatment). Both procedures are entirely painless.

How it works. Acne is caused by bacteria. When tiny sebaceous glands near the skin's surface start overproducing an oily substance called sebum, skin pores become blocked, and the acne bacteria multiply in the accumulated sebum like trout propagating in a dam-created lake. One of the new devices, called ClearLight, aims high-intensity blue (rather

TOP Trends

JOIN THE (BOTOX) PARTY!

Ever since the FDA approved facial injections of botulinum toxin type A in the spring of 2002, the wrinkled set has gathered in homes and spas to share a little Bordeaux, Brie, and Botox to treat their frown lines and crow's-feet. In part, the parties offer a way to economize, since once a vial is opened, the Botox must be used within a matter of hours, and each pricey vial contains enough toxin for several treatments.

Although the American Society of Aesthetic Plastic Surgery (and plenty of other groups) has objected that parties are inappropriate venues for medical procedures, not everyone has heeded the warning. Many party on. Meanwhile, the potential uses for Botox are growing. For example, an article in the *Archives of Dermatology* reported in January 2003 that injecting Botox into the armpits reduces body odor. Other research points to even more potential targets, such as migraines, urinary incontinence, and pain following hemorrhoid surgery. ∎

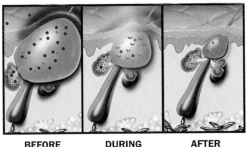

BEFORE **DURING** **AFTER**

With ClearLight, a narrow band of high-intensity light targets the bacteria that cause acne. The light triggers the proliferation of natural substances that attack and destroy the bacteria. Full-face treatments take about 15 minutes. In one study, 80 percent of patients showed significant improvement, with the number of pimples decreasing by 70 to 80 percent.

than skin-damaging ultraviolet) light at the problem area. The light penetrates the skin ever so slightly to excite organic compounds called porphyrins found inside the bacteria, causing them to kill the germs.

Smoothbeam, the other device, uses laser light to target the sebaceous glands themselves, disabling them just enough to stop the overproduction of sebum, which leaves the acne bacteria nowhere to collect. Smoothbeam was approved for treating acne only on the back.

Availability. Blue-light and laser equipment has been in many dermatologists' offices for several years and was used to treat other skin conditions. Some dermatologists had already begun using the devices to make patients blemish-fee before the FDA approval. ■

ALSO in the NEWS

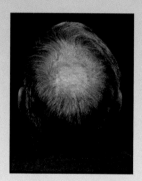

A "Cultured" Cure for Baldness?

When Israeli researchers tested a new wound-healing formula several years ago, they were surprised to find that it also appeared to help regrow hair in people who had sustained head injuries. Now, the same researchers are convinced that a rub-on gel made from cell culture medium—the substance in which skin cells are grown in the laboratory—is a promising path toward a better hair-growing treatment than the good (but not great) formulas now available. Study results published in April 2003 give their theory a boost.

The researchers tested a cell culture medium supplemented with three hormones (insulin, thyroxin, and growth hormone) on half of a group of 48 balding men, who applied the gel daily. After six months, their average hair count had increased by **17.1 percent.** The rate of hair loss also slowed, and existing hair grew faster. The study authors think the cell culture medium works by delivering a rich supply of nutrients (including amino acids) to the hair follicles. Stay tuned. ■

LIGHT THERAPIES TACKLE
SCARS & STRETCH MARKS

Acne scars and stretch marks are skin flaws that we simply have to live with—or do we? If you're determined to get rid of them, you can now look to light therapy for help.

The Smoothbeam system uses lasers to penetrate the skin and stimulate new growth of collagen (the fibrous protein that builds healthy new skin) in the scarred area. The result is a markedly improved appearance.

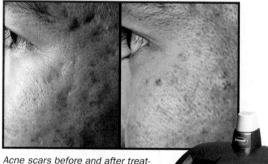

Acne scars before and after treatment with Smoothbeam. The laser device heats water and damages collagen in the upper dermis, triggering the formation of new collagen.

Another light-emitting device, ReLume, takes a different tack. A lot of long-term acne scarring and most stretch marks that are at least two years old are examples of what dermatologists call hypopigmented skin—areas that appear lighter against natural skin color because of decreased pigmentation. By aiming controlled doses of ultraviolet-B (UVB) light at the scarred area, ReLume stimulates production of melanin, the substance responsible for skin color. After such phototherapy, the scarred or marked area is more like the surrounding skin in color and texture.

The results are better than those seen with earlier techniques, and they come relatively quickly—often after the first few weeks of twice-weekly treatments. The full regimen typically lasts seven weeks. Since ReLume's "coloring-in" method isn't permanent, though, you should plan on committing to monthly maintenance sessions. Smoothbeam and ReLume are effective on all skin tones. ■

Drug Development
Smart Psoriasis Drug Targets Just the Troublemakers

Psoriasis itself is bad enough—an itchy, burning skin condition marked by red, scaly patches. Just as frustrating, though, are the various ointments, ultraviolet light therapies, and drugs that either don't do a lot of good or suppress the immune system. No wonder the 1.5 million people with moderate to severe psoriasis have been asking for a more aggressive treatment that's also safe.

Now they have it: a new injectable psoriasis drug called alefacept (Amevive), which hit the market in February 2003. It's more than just a new drug: It's the vanguard of a whole new treatment approach. Amevive is what's known as a "biologic" drug. Biologics are the result of a biotechnology company (in this case, Biogen of Massachusetts) working with proteins from living cells, rather than the usual scenario of a pharmaceutical company working with synthetic chemicals. Since biologics are more at home in the body, they're better able than traditional drugs to target the problem cells and leave the rest of the body alone.

That difference translates into two huge advantages for people with psoriasis. For one thing, Amevive is safer, since its immune-suppressing action is much more narrowly focused than that of existing drugs, which sometimes affect the entire immune system. What's most exciting, though, is how well its finely tuned action works.

In the studies leading up to FDA approval, between 40 and 56 percent of the volunteers who received Amevive instead of a placebo (dummy drug) saw their psoriasis symptoms cut in half within two to three months. Those who stayed on the medication longer, completing two 12-week courses of weekly injections instead of just one, did even better, with 75 percent of them experiencing at least a 50 percent improvement in symptoms. What's more, the benefits lasted seven months or longer after the last shot of the second course.

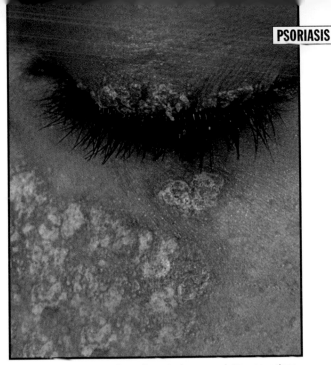

The itchy, scaly skin patches of psoriasis succumb to a new class of drugs that cut symptoms in half.

How it works. Psoriasis, like rheumatoid arthritis, is caused by a misguided immune system attack. In this case, specialized white blood cells called T cells become overactive. They travel to the skin and cause its cells to reproduce at 10 times the normal rate, causing itching, scaling, and other symptoms. Amevive's mission is to keep the T cells in line and "punish" any that do step out of line. Like a schoolteacher who knows that some kids are more likely to misbehave in the presence of certain others, Amevive works by blocking receptors on T cells to prevent contact with other "activating" cells that would start the skin-damaging process. At the same time, it helps other special cells identify and eliminate already overactivated T cells.

Availability. Any dermatologist in the United States can prescribe Amevive, which is recommended for people with moderate to severe psoriasis, not for the estimated 3 million Americans with mild cases. Because Amevive is a protein, it would be digested and rendered useless if taken orally, so 12 weekly injections into a vein or muscle are required. At this early stage in the use of the drug, that regimen can be pricey—an estimated $7,000 to $10,000. But keep in mind that Amevive is just the first shot in a major revolution in psoriasis care. A number of new biologics are performing well in clinical testing, and one that's not new, the rheumatoid arthritis drug infliximab (Remicade), is now being studied as a possible treatment for psoriasis as well. ■

237

Drug Development
An Antidote for the Celtic Curse

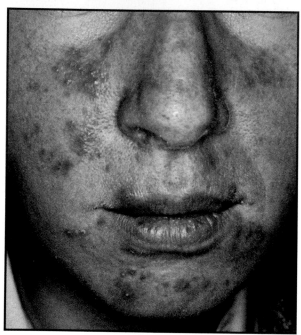

Rosacea occurs most often in people ages 30 to 50. The skin becomes red and may develop pimple-like pustules.

Move over, Celtic Curse—the Wheat Wonder is here. If you're one of the 14 million Americans who live with the face-reddening skin condition known as rosacea, you have a new ally in your struggle to keep your skin clear.

A gel known as azelaic acid (Finacea), a natural substance derived from wheat, was approved by the FDA as a rosacea treatment in March 2003. Water-based and fragrance- and alcohol-free, it works at least as well as (and perhaps better than) metronidazole, the existing topical medication.

That's great news for people with rosacea, most of whom are fair-skinned folks of northern and eastern European heritage (hence the nickname Celtic Curse). The disorder usually starts out as occasional blushing and flushing, and for the lucky ones, it stays that way. But the redness tends to become more persistent over time. Worse, papules and pustules (pimply facial protrusions) often appear. In its most serious form, rosacea can cause a W. C. Fields–like bulbous red nose, a condition known as rhinophyma.

How it works. Dermatologists aren't sure how Finacea reduces rosacea symptoms—which makes sense, since they're not sure what causes the skin condition in the first place. The problem could very well be inflammatory (the result of an over-blown immune response), infectious (caused by multiplying microorganisms), hormonal (the flushing episodes mimic those of menopausal women, who are at increased risk for rosacea), and/or vascular (that is, caused by a blood flow problem; people with rosacea are two to three times more likely to have migraine headaches, which are known to be vascular in nature).

In a slightly different formulation, azelaic acid is also used as an acne treatment (under the brand name Azelex) that's believed to kill acne-causing bacteria. Antibacterial properties, along with anti-inflammatory action, may help it fight rosacea. Whatever the mechanism, results from a study presented to the American Academy of Dermatology in March 2003 confirmed that twice-daily applications will get the red out. ■

ALSO in the NEWS

A Well-Rounded Answer to Ingrown Toenails

At any given time, all of us are only a millimeter away from a painful ingrown toenail. That's the distance between the edge of a healthy big toenail and the fold of skin alongside it. A bad trim, the wrong shoes, or a crushing mishap can embed the hard plate in the soft skin, where it will keep growing if it's not treated.

The only effective nonprescription treatment for ingrown toenails—a sodium sulfide gel—was nixed by the FDA back in 1993 because it often caused stinging and burning. Thanks to a new method of applying the medication, however, the FDA reversed its ruling in October 2002. The gel now comes with an application ring that you slip over your toe, positioning the small gel-dispensing opening right where the nail is ingrown. A specially formed bandage strip holds the ring in place. The nail-softening action of the gel relieves pain and causes the nail to lift out in about a week. Because of the FDA ruling, drug manufacturer Schering-Plough was expected to put a sodium sulfide ingrown toenail medication (complete with a ring applicator) on the market sometime in 2003. ■

Alternative Answers
Duct Tape Really Sticks It to Warts

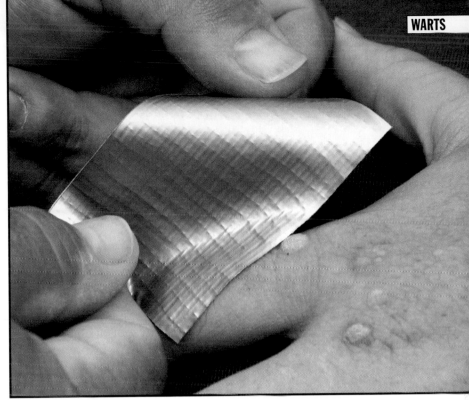

It's not just a garage staple anymore: Duct tape applied to warts seems to stimulate the body to fight the infection underneath. (And the tape isn't any uglier than the wart.)

They say that God made the world, but duct tape holds it together. So why shouldn't it cure warts as well?

Don't laugh. A serious study led by investigators at an army medical center found that sticking duct tape on the unsightly growths will usually get rid of them within a month or two. In fact, based on the research, duct tape looks like the treatment of choice for warts—faster, surer, safer, cheaper, and easier than traditional methods.

Are you laughing? Well, that's good, because the whimsical, nonthreatening nature of using a piece of sticky silver tape as medicine is another strong point in duct tape's favor. The most likely wart victims are children under 16, precisely the age group that tends to play hooky from treatment. And who can blame them? Cryotherapy, the most common method of wart removal, requires repeated applications of liquid nitrogen to freeze the warts. The treatment, which can cause an uncomfortable burning sensation, is an intimidating experience for many kids (and, let's be honest, for adults, too). Compared with cryotherapy, decorating parts of your body with little tape patches is loads of fun—which is why the researchers think compliance (that is, following through with the treatment) should be much better with duct tape.

What matters most, though, is that duct tape (also known to many as duck tape) is a far cry from quackery. It may actually work better than cryotherapy. The researchers found this out by gathering 51 young people (ages 3 to 22) with warts in Tacoma, Washington. While 25 of them underwent cryotherapy every two to three weeks, the rest were sent home with free duct tape and instructions for using it. After two months, the duct-tape team had scored a clear victory. According to results published in the October 2002 issue of *Archives of Pediatrics & Adolescent Medicine*, the warts completely disappeared in 23 of the 26 subjects who used tape, most of them within a month. Only 15 of the 25 who received cryotherapy saw their warts vanish.

How it works. To use duct tape as they did in the study, cut a piece that will just cover the wart. Stick it on and leave it there for six days. When you take the tape off, soak the area in water for a few minutes, then use an emery board or pumice stone to file away whatever dead skin has accumulated. Leave the wart uncovered overnight and apply a new patch in the morning. Repeat the procedure until you're wart-free.

What is it about duct tape that cures warts? Researchers suspect that the secret lies in covering the skin. Those hard, bumpy growths that we call warts are actually symptoms of a common viral infection, and it's likely that the skin irritation caused by the tape rallies your immune system to fight off the virus once and for all. No more infection, no more warts.

Before treating a child's warts, consult a pediatrician. And if a wart doesn't clear up within two months, try a different therapy. ■

URINARY TRACT

A WRINKLE CURE MAY BE THE ANSWER TO EMBARRASSING LEAKS.

Doctors have started injecting Botox into the muscles around the urethra to treat incontinence. If an overactive bladder is your problem, a new skin patch can help—without the dry mouth and constipation caused by oral drugs. That means no more frantic dashes to the bathroom. And speaking of the bathroom, men with their own urinary problems brought on by enlarged prostates may now find relief with an old friend: Viagra.

For the millions of people with kidney disease who are hoping to avoid complete kidney failure, there's tantalizing new evidence that the cholesterol-lowering drugs known as statins can slow the progress of the disease. Finally, find out what you should be eating and drinking to stave off dreaded urinary tract infections.

Drug Development
A Wrinkle Cure Moves South

While shots of botulinum toxin type A (Botox) to smooth facial wrinkles are still getting most of the media attention, some doctors have moved the action considerably southward. In the past year, injections of Botox into the urinary tract have become a promising, though still uncommon, treatment for urinary incontinence.

The new treatment got a boost March 2003 when Taiwanese researchers published the results of a successful test of Botox for the bladder. The study, described in the journal *Urology*, was small, involving just 20 subjects, but each had serious incontinence problems brought on by an underactive muscle in the bladder wall called the detrusor muscle. This muscle is supposed to contract to expel urine when the time is right. The researchers' strategy was to use Botox to paralyze another muscle group farther along the urinary route (the sphincter muscles in and around the urethra, the tube that carries urine from the bladder). That would equalize the pressure along the urinary tract and thus reestablish normal voiding.

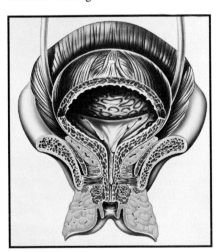

By using Botox to paralyze the sphincter muscles around the urethra (the tube through which urine exits the body), researchers improved bladder control in patients with serious incontinence.

The strategy worked. There was marked improvement in bladder control in 18 of the 20 patients within two weeks. Some were even able to remove catheters, or tubes, that had been inserted to control urine flow. The study complemented research by University of Pittsburgh researchers a year earlier that explored the use of Botox for incontinent patients with overactive detrusor muscles. The symptoms caused by either an overactive or underactive detrusor are often the same—leakage, the urgent need to urinate, and frequent nighttime visits to the bathroom. The Pittsburgh researchers injected Botox into the overactive detrusor muscle rather than the urethral sphincters.

Botox for urinary incontinence needs no new FDA approval. The extent of its availability may depend on the willingness of insurance companies to pay for the new treatment. ■

RESEARCH ROUNDUP

HRT May Lead to Leaks

Women still considering hormone replacement therapy (HRT) despite the apparent increased risk of breast cancer, heart attack, and stroke now have something else to think about—bladder control. Research results released in April 2003 show that older women who take the hormones estrogen and progestin to offset the effects of menopause have at least double the risk of developing urinary incontinence.

The findings were based on information gathered from 1,208 women (average age, 66) over a four-year period. The longer the women took hormones, the higher their odds of developing bladder problems. The study authors aren't sure why HRT would negatively affect bladder control, but something the women had in common may point to a possible path of inquiry: All of them, whether they were on HRT or not, had a history of cardiovascular disease. Ironically, estrogen was once thought to be a possible preventive treatment for urinary incontinence; now it's a possible cause. ■

Drug Development
A Patch Repairs Overactive Bladders— Without Side Effects

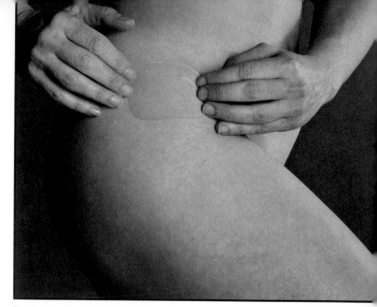

The Oxytrol patch offers the same bladder control as the oral drug oxybutynin, and it works at less than half the dose.

Put eight Americans in a room, and one of them, statistically speaking, will have an overactive bladder. For the other seven to understand what that unfortunate soul is going through, they'd have to remember what it was like to be riding in the back seat of a car at age four, desperate to tinkle. Or they'd need to recall early childhood episodes when they just couldn't quite make it to the bathroom in time. And then they'd have to imagine the frustration and embarrassment of feeling like that virtually all the time.

Fortunately, a drug called oxybutynin has been available for some 25 years to tame the various symptoms that fall under the umbrella term "overactive bladder." Those symptoms include a nearly constant urge to urinate, interrupted sleep from frequent nocturnal bathroom visits, and, for many, the involuntary release of urine (incontinence). Taken orally, oxybutynin does a good job of reducing urgency, frequency, and incontinence, but its users usually pay a price in side effects—most notably dry mouth and constipation. One way or another, they're uncomfortable.

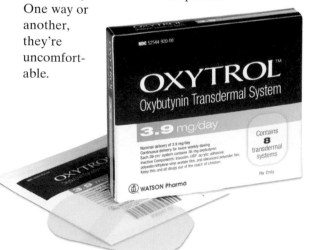

That changed for good in February 2003 when the FDA approved a new oxybutynin-releasing skin patch called Oxytrol that calms overactive bladders with no side effects. Simply by applying the small, thin, clear patch to their hip, abdomen, or buttock, the estimated 33 million Americans with overactive bladders can get relief for up to four days. What's more, a study released after the FDA approval showed that the new patch may clear the way for higher and more effective doses of the drug.

How it works. Transdermal systems—skin patches—release a steady, controlled dose of drug through the skin and directly into the bloodstream. That method has at least two distinct advantages over oral medications. One is that you can dispense with the bother of swallowing the medicine. Instead, just apply the adhesive patch and forget about it for four days (you can even shower or swim with it on), while a steady supply of oxybutynin calms the nerves responsible for urgency-producing bladder contractions.

The second advantage is even more important: The medication never has to work its way through your digestive system. Because your liver and gastrointestinal tract never process the oxybutynin, the digestive by-products that cause constipation and dry mouth are never produced, so there are no troublesome side effects.

Availability. Oxytrol is now available at pharmacies only by prescription. ■

Drug Development
Familiar Statins May Keep Kidney Disease at Bay

If you've been diagnosed with kidney disease, you know exactly what you want to do—stop your condition from reaching the ominously named "end stage." That's when kidney disease becomes kidney failure, and your kidneys are no longer able to eliminate waste from your bloodstream via the urine. At this point, the only thing that can keep you alive is regular dialysis, an hours-long procedure that filters your blood through a machine. Early detection, dietary restrictions, and medications to lower blood pressure and eliminate excess fluid from your body are still your best bets for keeping kidney disease from progressing.

But what if there were a class of powerful and readily available drugs that could do even more to stop kidney disease from worsening? According to new research, there already is. The so-called statins have been one of the great pharmaceutical success stories, helping millions of people worldwide reduce their risk of heart disease by controlling their cholesterol levels. Now, study results published in the March 2003 issue of the *American Journal of Kidney Disease* give hope that they can also help people with kidney disease.

After a year of giving daily doses of the statin drug atorvastatin (Lipitor) to half of 56 study volunteers with kidney disease, researchers from the University of Southern California made two encour-

aging discoveries. One was that the patients who took Lipitor were excreting significantly less protein into their urine than they did before taking the drug, while the others (who continued to receive standard care without statins) saw little or no change. Since too much protein in the urine is a marker for kidney disease, this is a good indication that the Lipitor was helping the kidneys. The other promising result had to do with a natural waste product called creatinine. Levels of creatinine in the blood rise as kidney function weakens. A standard kidney disease test measures creatinine "clearance" through the urine—the more creatinine that's expelled, the less accumulates in the blood. Over the course of the study, creatinine clearance dropped significantly in the kidney patients who didn't take Lipitor, while those who did maintained about the same clearance levels as when they started.

How It works. While the study results suggest that Lipitor (and probably other statins) can slow the progress of kidney disease, the process is still a mystery. The study authors believe that the drugs' well-documented ability to inhibit liver enzymes involved in the production of cholesterol is not a factor and that some other mechanism is responsible.

Availability. Statins won't be adopted as an early-stage kidney disease treatment based on this relatively small study and the even smaller studies and animal experiments that preceded it. But the encouraging findings by the USC researchers clear the way for a larger study to confirm the results. Such a study will take several years. ■

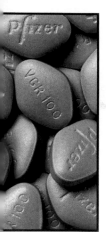

Key Discovery

Viagra May Help in the Bathroom as Well as the Bedroom

For years, Viagra has helped men overcome erectile dysfunction, revitalizing intimacy for countless couples. Now, British researchers have discovered that those little blue pills can solve another common problem as well.

For older men, urinary difficulties, often caused by an enlarged prostate gland, can turn the usually simple act of urinating into a bothersome and sometimes painful challenge. As if that weren't enough, many men with urinary problems also experience erectile dysfunction. The new finding may mean that a two-in-one drug is already available to help with both issues.

British urologists asked 100 men who complained of erectile dysfunction to fill out questionnaires about their sexual and urinary problems. Researchers used the questionnaires to measure the severity of the subjects' symptoms, then the men got what they came for—a supply of Viagra (sildenafil).

After three months of observation and many more questionnaires, the researchers could see a clear connection between Viagra use and better urinary function. Before the men began using Viagra, there was no correlation between the scores for the severity of erectile dysfunction and those for the severity of urinary discomfort, but as the study progressed, a link became apparent. Consistently, as the first score improved, so did the second. Just as important, the researchers were able to determine that it was the Viagra use itself—not the resulting improvement in the men's ability to achieve erections—that was clearing up the urinary symptoms.

How it works. In an article about the study published in the December 2002 issue of the *British Journal of Urology*, the authors proposed an explanation for Viagra's twin powers. The drug produces erections not by directly stiffening the penis but by relaxing key genital tissue so blood can flow into it more easily. While Viagra's in the neighborhood, so to speak, it may just as effectively improve urine flow by relaxing similar tissue lining the urethra.

Availability. Viagra, of course, has been on the market and widely prescribed for several years. The researchers don't recommend that men with urinary symptoms but no erectile problems start using it. They do suggest, though, that taking Viagra makes perfect sense for men who have both. ■

Alternative Answers

Say "Cheese!" — Plus Yogurt and Berry Juice

Many women who have recurrent bladder infections take advantage of the well-known benefits of cranberry juice, a popular folk cure. But new research indicates that the infection-preventing menu includes more than just cranberries. It turns out that regular consumption of any kind of fresh juice, along with a steady diet of cheese and yogurt, offers protection from urinary tract infections (UTIs), of which bladder infections (cystitis) are the most common.

Researchers in Finland discovered this by comparing the food and beverage habits of 139 women with bladder infections with those of 185 UTI-free women in the same age range (average age, 30). Those who ate fermented milk products—yogurt and cheese—at least three times a week were more than 75 percent less likely to have had recent UTIs, and regular juice drinkers were more than 33 percent less likely to have had them. The best juice choice? Any berry juice (not just cranberry) that's freshly squeezed or made from a concentrate with no added sugar. (Blackberry, blueberry, raspberry, and strawberry juices are available at health food stores.)

The researchers, whose results were published in the March 2003 issue of the *American Journal of Clinical Nutrition*, suspect that the "friendly" bacteria in yogurt and cheese make it harder for UTI-causing bacteria (usually *E. coli*) to find their way from the rectum up the urethra, the tube that carries urine out of the bladder. The preventive power of juice may be due to concentrated forms of natural chemicals that evolved in plants to protect them from infections. ■

Beyond cranberry juice: yogurt, cheese, and fruit juices of all kinds may help protect against urinary tract infections. But before you load up on too much fruit juice, read about a downside of the drinks on page 160.

INDEX

CREDITS